THREE FRAMES OF REFERENCE FOR MENTAL HEALTH

Anne Cronin Mosey
O.T.R., Ph.D.

First printing, September 1970
Second Printing, May 1971
Third Printing, September 1971
Library of Congress Catalog Care Number 77-140200

Charles B. Slack, Inc.
Thorofare, New Jersey 08086

Acknowledgments

The process of putting ideas into words is an arduous one for many of us. In acknowledging those who have helped it is often difficult to say whether the person who offered a cup of coffee during a moment of despair or the person who sat for hours listening, reading and criticizing was more significant in getting the task finished. Or is it more meaningful to acknowledge those who have assisted with this particular task or those who have pointed out that the real work lies ahead?

Recognizing that there are so many who have helped, I extend my deepest appreciation to those who have given me love; to the activities therapy staff at Hillside Hospital and, in particular, to Philip Petrolino; and to the students at New York University with whom I have had the privilege to study and learn.

To Jerry and Charles Paul

Who have shown me the wonder
and joy of change

Preface

I know well enough that every word I utter carries with it something of myself—of my special and unique self with its particular history and its own particular world. Even when I deal with empirical data, I am necessarily speaking about myself. But it is only by accepting this as inevitable that I can serve...
C. G. Jung. *Modern Man in Search of a Soul**

One of the delightful characteristics of students is that they ask questions— the kind of questions which jerk you out of placid class discussions and set you to wondering when you should be concentrating on something else. They ask things such as: What is dysfunction? Do you deal with symptoms or pathology? How do theories relate to me as a treating therapist? Why can't you take what you like from a variety of frames of reference? What techniques are best; analyzing unconscious material, giving the patient love and affection, group therapy, treating the patient in his home environment, encounter groups? And what is my responsibility as a therapist as differentiated from all those other people who are also trying to help the patient?

This book is written in response to these questions and a few others that have not been asked. Response does not mean answers—I truly believe that we have no answers. I have made an attempt to sort out ideas, to follow those ideas to some sort of conclusion, to offer suggestions and, as with all books, to "say my thing." It is primarily addressed to students who are engaged in learning something about the treatment of psychosocial dysfunction. But because workers in this area are continually engaged in rethinking their ideas, it is also addressed to therapists far removed from their student days.

Very briefly, I have attempted to plead a case for the conscious use of theoretical frames of reference as the basis for the treatment of psychosocial dysfunction. Intuitive approaches trouble me—I strongly believe that they ultimately lead to inadequate treatment. Such approaches may help a limited number of patients but they cannot be taught except through apprenticeship nor

---

*C. G. Jung, *Modern Man in Search of a Soul* (New York: Harcourt, Brace and World, Inc., 1933). p 118

can they be studied in a scientific manner. This limits wide applicability. As for the eclectic approach to treatment, I have no objection to formulating a frame of reference which draws from many sources. The frames of reference outlined in this book are, as a matter of fact, eclectic. But in being eclectic the therapist must utilize postulates which are logically compatible. "Eclectic" is too often a euphemism for an intuitive approach. The therapist does what he feels is right at a given moment without reference to any particular theoretical system. It is to this usage that I object.

We shall attempt to look at people and dysfunction in a somewhat different way. The classical labels for the supposedly various types of psychosocial dysfunction are not used. They are archaic, unrelated to the patient's problems or treatment, and useless except as subject matter when one cannot think of anything else to say. In addition, patients presenting problems, be they drug addic-

minimal attention. These things are of course, important and always taken into consideration by the therapist. The purpose of this book, however, is to look at the treatment of dysfunction as primarily a change process which transcends diagnosis or the presentation of symptoms. It is also considered to be a higher order of concern than the particular treatment setting or the patient's sex, age, cultural background or socioeconomic level. I was asked recently if I would want to have a student receive his entire clinical experience in psychiatry through the treatment of lower-class male adolescents who had been diagnosed as having character disorders. My answer was that I would prefer that the student receive good supervision in learning to apply various theories regarding human change rather than to worry about a questionably limited patient group. If theories of change have any validity they should be broadly applicable.

This book attempts to show that the question of the definitions of pathology and symptoms is a theoretical issue and can be answered only in theoretical terms. The security-giving ideas that "somebody knows" and "if only he were here he could deal with it but in the meantime I have to muddle through" will receive no validation here. There are no high priests, omniscient people, nor even any magic. There are only you, the therapist, and someone who needs help—trying together.

These pages give no answers as to which techniques are best. Techniques are developed from one's frame of reference. The use of a particular technique because it seems to fit one's own personal style, because "someone I admire uses it", or because "everyone else is doing it and it seems like the chic thing to do" is unfortunate. Techniques are considered to be only tools for the implementation of a consciously selected and understood frame of reference.

What is my role as a therapist? This book answers that question by stating that all professionally trained therapists should learn in such a way that they are capable of and comfortable in taking full responsibility for a patient. Certainly, as people with different educational backgrounds, we are able to offer assistance and advice to each other. And that is important and helpful. But taking full responsibility means that one does literally that. There is no one else that one can turn to and say, "I was just helping" or "I can deal with this little bit of the patient's problem." The therapist evaluates a patient, determines whether or not given his knowledge and skill, he will be able to assist that patient, and if the answer is affirmative goes on and treats the patient. There isn't anyone to tell you how or whether you should treat a patient. That is the therapist's prerogative and reason for being.

The three frames of reference outlined in the text are in no sense new. The reader is unlikely to find anything startling or revolutionary. They are presented to provide a systematic point of departure for the beginning therapist. In studying them it is hoped that the reader will gain a greater understanding of theory and its use as a basis for practice. The three frames of reference suggest various orientations to the treatment process rather than describe the foundation for practice of a large group of therapists. They were formulated out of an often conflicting matrix of ideas, intuitive actions, and feelings which is indigenous to a great number of practicing therapists. This book, therefore, is an attempt to capture spirits pervasive among us. In so doing it is hoped that the spirits are not smothered in words—all too often the fate of captured spirits.

This book is not addressed to any particular type of therapist or therapy. I speak to those students and therapists who are concerned with the psychosocial problems of another human being. All therapists are cast in the similar role of agents of change. We are all concerned with learning—we are all teachers in the very essence of what that concept means.

September 1970 *Anne Mosey*

Contents

Introduction

...While I make these rather dry statements, according to the best scientific tradition. I trust the reader may bring to them the poetic side of his experience as well as his scientific skepticism.

E. Kasin, *"Interpretation as Active Nurture"* *

Treatment is a change-inducing endeavor in which environmental interactions are synthesized into a dynamic experience in such a manner that therapist and patient are enabled to arrive at their mutually shared goals. Treatment is perceived as the nucleus of the therapist's activities—and it is this nucleus which will be explored in the following text. Before focusing upon treatment it seems useful to identify the other activities of therapist, placing treatment in a perspective relative to the many responsibilities of the practicing therapist. All of those activities are concerned with supporting—making possible and giving life to—the treatment process, and are here identified as: (1) becoming a therapist, (2) meeting mental health needs, (3) administration, and (4) scientific pursuits.

Becoming A Therapist   To effectively engage in patient treatment, the therapist needs to acquire many skills. The trained therapist must be able to enter into an intimate relationship, to interpret nuances of behavior, to act on the basis of his convictions, and to integrate theoretical material. The development of these skills is a continuing process which may seem difficult for the beginning therapist, but it soon becomes pleasurable to see the impact of that development on the treatment process. Becoming a therapist is a never-ending learning and growing process.

Meeting Mental Health Needs   Response to one's commonality and uniqueness must be available for an individual to maintain his sense of identity with humanity. This process is referred to as *meeting mental health needs.*[1] The environment must be such that an individual is able to satisfy the needs which he shares in common with all men as well as the needs that are uniquely his because

---

*In Emanuel Hammer (ed.), *Use of Interpretations in Treatment* (New York: Grune and Stratton, 1968) p. 199.

[1]G. Fidler and J. Fidler, *Occupational Therapy: A Communication Process in Psychiatry* (New York: The MacMillan Company, 1963).

of past life experience, age, sex, physiological makeup, interests, abilities and current life situation. The therapist works with others to create and to help the patient make use of an environment in which basic physical and psychological requirements are satisfied. No specific change in the patient is planned in the process of meeting mental health needs; although change may and often does occur, it is not predetermined. To illustrate: one of the basic human needs which has been identified is the need to be a contributing member of a social system. The therapist attempts to structure the environment in such a way as to enable the patient, given his capacities and limitations, to be productive. Effecting change in the patient's limitations so he may be a *more* productive member of a social system is defined as treatment. Disordered conditions tend to be sustained or intensified in an environment which does not gratify mental health needs. It is unlikely the treatment will be successful in such an environment.

Administration   The function of administration is to ensure the use of all resources that will help the patient to function once again at the highest level of which he is capable. Optimum use of human and material resources is of prime concern. Organization, education, supervision and communication are key areas of administrative responsibility. Administration is not defined as a position in the formal structure of an institution. It is rather a process in which all personnel are actively engaged to a greater or lesser degree. Any action directed toward coordinating or enhancing the therapeutic potential of patients, staff members, as well as the community and the nonhuman environment, is part of the administrative process.

Scientific Pursuits   When engaged in scientific pursuits the therapist is concerned with the formulation of theories and frames of reference, the assessment of the effectiveness of a given frame of reference, testing hypotheses, and the development of evaluative techniques. These activities help to move the treatment process from an intuitive, experiential base to a sound, systematic foundation. Scientific pursuits facilitate communication about and the teaching of therapy and, more importantly, lead to greater effectiveness and economy in the treatment process.

These activities, which support treatment, by extension delineate that which is not treatment. Treatment or therapy is here defined as a planned, collaborative interaction between the therapist, the patient(s), and the nonhuman environment which is directed toward eliminating or minimizing dysfunction. The nature of the desired change and the process utilized to initiate change are predetermined, delineated prior to action. *Nonhuman environment* refers to all aspects of the external environment which are not human.[2] It includes natural objects such as animals, trees, and water, as well as man-made objects such as clothing, books, furniture and machinery. In the treatment process, nonhuman

---

[2] See H. Searles, *The Nonhuman Environment* (New York: International Universities Press, 1960) for a detailed discussion.

objects are utilized in a number of ways: to develop perceptual and motor skills, to help the patient feel more comfortable, as a focal point for problem solving or tentative interaction with others, as a means of expressing unacceptable ideas and feelings in a physical manner, to provide the ambiguous stimuli which promote unconscious responses, to facilitate the production of symbols, etc. It is a part of the treatment process that has only recently been labeled and which is, unfortunately, often overlooked. Another word in the above definition of treatment that may also need explanation is *dysfunction.* Dysfunction is here used as a synonym for disordered condition, pathology or the patient's primary problem. It refers to that which the therapist evaluates and treats.

The therapy process is differentiated from medical practice on the bases of dysfunction treated and techniques used for treatment. Medical practice is a process which is concerned with those aspects of a psychosocial dysfunction which are able to be ameliorated (or partially amelioriated) through the use of pharmacological or surgical techniques. A therapist engages in a process which is oriented toward eliminating or minimizing those aspects of psychosocial dysfunction which do not respond to the use of drugs or surgery.

No distinctions are made here between the various therapies (that is, recreational therapy, dance therapy, art therapy, occupational therapy, psychotherapy, counseling, group work, special education, etc.) These distinctions are not made because it is my opinion that the differences are only superficial. The techniques used are indeed dissimilar but the core ideas are very similar. It is these core ideas which are most important; they are our common heritage. It is for this reason that this book addresses itself to *all* types of therapists.

We are concerned here with the treatment of psychosocial dysfunction. Recognizing that the distinction between physical and psychosocial dysfunction is only arbitrary, psychosocial dysfunction, for the purpose of this text, is defined as difficulty in areas commonly referred to as self identity, interpersonal interactions, perceptual-motor skills and cognitive processes. This is not meant to be a listing of the total pathology of concern to the therapist working in the area of psychosocial dysfunction. It is presented, rather, to provide some parameters for the discussion which follows.

The phenomenon of concern is frequently behavior culturally defined as "illness." To differentiate between "illness" and other forms of deviance (such as criminal behavior or benign abnormality) the cultural group utilizes various criteria. The individual is considered to be ill if: (1) the incapacity is interpreted as beyond the individual's power to overcome by the process of decision making alone; (2) the individual realizes his deviancy is inherently undesirable; (3) the individual accepts his obligation to eliminate his deviancy and cooperates with others to that end; (4) and those responsible for the individual or the individual himself accept the obligation to seek competent help. The distinction between "mental illness" and "physical illness" varies from culture to culture. If illness is seen as existing on a continuum from that which is primarily physical to that which is primarily psychological, physical illness tends to be universally defined and mental illness tends to be defined by the cultural group. Whether a given illness is viewed as mental or physical often depends on the cultural group's knowledge about and attitude towards mental illness and its capacity to treat mental illness.[3]

The cultural group is concerned with behavior. If there is a decrease in or absence of behavior which the group has delineated as necessary for adequate function and/or an increase in behavior which the culture has defined as incompatible with adequate function, then the person is considered to be in a state of dysfunction. It may be that the individual himself will perceive that he is in a state of dysfunction. Such a perception, however, is ultimately based upon the cultural definition of dysfunction. Delineation of a person as being in a state of dysfunction is a relative matter, dependent upon where the behavior occurs and where it does not occur. It is usually the individual's total repertoire that is considered rather than isolated performances. Pragmatically, the therapist is concerned with those individuals who are brought to a mental health facility, referred by anyone of the several types of mental health workers, or those who seek help independently.

It is the purpose of this book to suggest various frames of reference which may be utilized by therapists in the treatment of psychosocial dysfunction. The goals of professional education and, by extension, the expertise of a therapist have traditionally been divided into knowledge, skills, and attitudes. Frames of reference are the knowledge component of the tripart repertoire of a change-inducing therapist. The parts are interdependent and each part is essential for competent patient care. The book is concerned only with the *knowledge* aspect of being a therapist. Use of this knowledge, (that is, the skill and attitude aspect) cannot be learned through reading. It can be acquired only through application of the knowledge in conjunction with competent supervision. It is the framework, the reader must form the structure. Without a framework the structure cannot stand; without the structure the framework has no meaning.

It is the purpose of this book to provide information which will give meaning to the definition of treatment. It is essentially an introduction to and brief summary of three frames of reference. The bibliography will identify some basic resources that the reader may turn to for more detailed information.

---

[3]Talcott Parsons, *The Social System* (New York: The Free Press of Glencoe, 1951).

Chapter 1
THEORETICAL
FRAMES OF REFERENCE

(Therapy has typically been founded upon)...a body of intuitive techniques which have been reenforced by a sense of inner certitude and quasi-success. Inner certitude is both a dubious criterion of validation and a deterrent to discovery why it was right and how it may be more generally formulated in the interest of greater clinical utility.

E. Shoben, *"Some Observations on Psychotherapy and the Learning Process"** *

A theoretical frame of reference is a set of interrelated internally consistent concepts, definitions, postulates and principles that provide a systematic description of and prescription for a practitioner's interaction within his domain of concern. It delineates the nature of the human and nonhuman objects with which the practitioner interacts and in turn serves as a guide for his actions relative to these objects.[1]

It is the recognition of and the deliberate selection and application of a theoretical frame of reference which distinguishes the professional person from the layman.[2] It is that which differentiates any *helping* relationship from a systematically planned *treatment* process. When a helping relationship is based

*In O. Hobart Mowrer, *Psychotherapy: Theory and Research* (New York: The Ronald Press Company 1953). p 122.

---

[1]Works used as major references for this chapter are: Fred Kerlinger, *Foundations of Behavioral Research* (New York: Holt, Rinehart and Winston, Inc., 1964). D. Ford and H. Urban, *Systems of Psychotherapy* (New York: John Wiley and Sons, Inc., 1963); M. Marx and W. Hillix, *Systems and Theories in Psychology* (New York: McGraw-Hill Company, 1963); Ernest Nagel, *The Structure of Science* (New York: Harcourt, Brace and World, Inc., 1961); Carroll Pratt, *The Logic of Modern Psychology* (New York: The Macmillan Company, 1948); and Sigmund Koch, *Psychology: A Study of Science, Volume II* (New York: McGraw-Hill Company, 1959).

[2]Carroll Pratt, *The Logic of Modern Psychology* (New York: The Macmillan Company, 1948).

upon a frame of reference it is able to be controlled, studied, and altered. Any such relationship may or may not be effective in meeting the need of a troubled individual. But when the relationship is not based upon a frame of reference we are unable to assess the specific factors which lead to the positive results and to assist others in applying these factors in other situations.

A theoretical frame of reference is not a theory.[3] It is similar to theory in that it makes use of concepts, definitions, and postulates; the structures of theory. It is founded upon or deduced from a theory or the postulates of several compatible theories. A frame of reference is different from theory in that it contains principles for guiding action, which are deduced from scientific postulates regarding change. A theory is descriptive and does not imply action. For example, theories of personality describe the development process of the mature individual and deviations which may occur in that process. Principles of child rearing are deduced from theories of personality and provide a guide for action relative to the child. In this sense we may then speak of a frame of reference for child rearing. A theoretical frame of reference is, therefore, founded upon theories and is similar in some respects to theory.

THEORY

A theory is an abstract description of a circumscribed set of observable events. It is concerned with *how* and *under what circumstances* these events happen and how they are related one to the other. The purpose of a theory is to make *predictions* about events.

The parameters of the phenomena with which a given theory is concerned are delineated. Theories of small group interaction, for instance, deal with a set of phenomena that is different from theories regarding the development of cognition. Theories are concerned only with observable events simply because man is not capable of dealing with any other phenomena. Concepts such as hunger, group cohesion, and ego function may be used in a theory to facilitate descriptions or predictions. However, they are ultimately tied to and defined in terms of observable events. The predictive component of a theory rises from description of the relationship between events and assumes knowledge and control of all factors impinging upon a given event.

Theories are comprised of *concepts* (and their definitions) and *postulates*. *Concepts* are words or phrases which label some similarity between seemingly varied phenomena. They are systems of classification. The names of colors, geometrical shapes, and animals are familiar concepts. Concepts of this nature are directly observable. They are referred to as simple because of their visible and/or tangible properties. More complex concepts are called *constructs* or *intervening variables* because they must be defined in terms of both a stimulus and a response event. Fear, need, and justice are examples of this type of concept.

---

[3]Ford and Urban, *Systems of Psychotherapy* (New York: John Wiley and Sons, 1963).

Variables are concepts which are measurable and utilized in research to test hypotheses.

It is important to understand that concepts are only abstractions and not concrete entities. An ashtray is not an ashtray; it may be a blue object or a container. What it is called depends on the system of classification being used. There is a particular tendency to concretize constructs contained in personality theories. Thus one occasionally hears statements such as, "This theory of personality is not adequate because it does not deal with the unconscious." Freud used the construct of the unconscious to classify and describe certain observed behaviors. Other theorists have used other concepts to classify similar behavior.

A given set of phenomena may be classified in a number of ways. The system used is good or bad only in relation to its comprehensiveness. If the phenomena of concern is classified in such a manner as to allow for accurate prediction, the system is adequate. The number of concepts used must be sufficient to deal with the phenomena. Excessive, overlapping, and redundant concepts are avoided. Both simple concepts and constructs are defined. Ideally, they are defined in two ways: *abstractly*, through the use of word and phrases which are not used to label other concepts in the theory; and *operationally*, by pointing to some observable manipulation, event, or object.

Postulates state the relationship between concepts. The usual types of relationships outlined are *cause and effect* and *correlation*. In a cause and effect relationship, one event is described as leading to a second or third event. In a correlation relationship, causality is not inferred; it is a statement that events occur together. A postulate that fear of loss of self control is often accompanied by negative affect toward the self is an example of correlation.

The three major types of postulates are *assumptions, propositions,* and *hypotheses. Assumptions* are relational statements which cannot be or are not intended to be studied or tested directly. They are often of a philosophical or metatheoretical nature, but need not be. Two examples are "Man is a rational being" and "Behavior is influenced by the given biological substratum of the organism." Assumptions provide both a base for other postulates of the theory and a delineation of that which the theory is and is not intended to explain. Some students of science suggest that assumptions are superfluous and pretentious. Others attest to their importance. This is an unresolved issue. At times, assumptions are either definitions or deal with methodological issues; there is general agreement that such assumptions are to be avoided.

Propositions are directly concerned with stating the relationship between concepts. They may be on different levels. Higher level propositions give rise to lower level propositions or, in actuality, the reverse may occur. The deduced inference of a proposition generates other propositions. For example, a higher level proposition, "The type of group leadership effects the actions of a group leads to a lower level proposition, "Authoritarian leadership increases group productivity."

At some level, propositions are concerned with observable events. When formulated at this level, propositions are referred to as *hypotheses*. It is possible to test a hypothesis in order to determine whether or not it is a relatively accurate statement of the relationship between observable events. The word *relatively* is used to indicate that hypotheses are never proven or disproven. Conventionally, if statistical analysis of the data indicates that 95 times out of 100 the relationship between the concepts is as stated in the hypothesis, the hypothesis is accepted. The validity of a theory is assessed through testing all of the lower level propositions which are, in turn, an indirect test of the higher level proposition.

A *scientific* law is a well-established high-level proposition which has been frequently subjected to empirical testing. The hypotheses deduced from the proposition are repeatedly accepted when pertinent data is statistically analyzed.

Theories may be located on a continuum from the *particular* to the *universal*. For example, a proposition in a theory located at the particularistic end of the continuum might be, "Caring for plants and animals increases the ability of the post-partum depressed mother to care for her newborn infant." A theory at the universal end of that continuum might state the proposition that, "Experimentation in the nonhuman environment leads to a greater comfort and effectiveness in the human environment." As may be evident, the concepts and thus the propositions are limited in a particularistic theory and more inclusive in a universal theory. In a comprehensive theory, propositions tend to be universal but continue to have the potential for being stated in particularistic terms. A theory in the process of being formulated may be made up of either universal or particularistic propositions—but rarely both.

Theories are not concerned with the metaphysical question of why. Theories describe the relationship between objects and events but they do not specify the reason for the relationship. Causality in the scientific sense is not synonymous with *why*. Postulates which indicate cause and effect relationships state that given A, B, and C, event D will occur. The reason for this causal relationship is not provided in a theoretical system. For example, the postulate that lack of adequate oxygen ultimately leads to neurological damage indicates an oxygen-to-nerve cell relationship. It does not deal with the ultimate unknown of why there is a relationship between oxygen and viable nerve cells.

The process of theory building begins with tentative delineation of the phenomenon to be considered. For example, one might want to theorize about the nature of prejudice, the reaction of lower middle class persons to verbal psychotherapy or the impact of retirement on family interaction. The theorist often begins looking at a limited number of cases and attempts to identify similarities. These similarities may be classified by using a concept borrowed from another theory, or a new concept may be developed. The relationship between concepts is also observed and tentative propositions are stated. The theorist may observe several additional cases in order to assess whether his propositions continue to appear to be correct. Eventually, hypotheses are formulated and subjected to rigorous empirical testing. At other times the process may begin through testing isolated hypotheses. The theory is then formulated through interrelating and integrating several propositions. Theory building is usually not linear but rather moves back and forth between observation, concept and proposition formulation, and testing.

Pure science is the process of formulating theories and assessing their validity through testing hypotheses derived from the theory. What a scientist theorizes about depends upon his field of inquiry and his personal interests. Regardless of the field of inquiry, the scientist works in the direction of formulating universal theories whenever this is possible. For example, the psychologist ideally directs his attention to factors which lead to deviant behavior as opposed to studying factors which lead to neurotic behavior. Theories about neurotic behavior are particularistic, because neurotic behavior is a subclass of deviant behavior. Pure science is not concerned with the use or application of theory. Events and objects are studied for their own value; for the purpose of gaining knowledge. There is no attempt to make value judgments regarding theory or to imply or state how the theory ought to be applied. The pure scientist is often involved in studying phenomena for which neither he nor anyone else sees any practical use.

Applied science is the process of formulating or assessing theories for the purpose of dealing with objects and events in the here and now. Thus, the applied scientist might be concerned with studying the relationship between objects so as to develop a more efficient soap powder, or he may be concerned with evaluating the effectiveness of various techniques derived from different theories. In the latter case he may or may not be assessing the validity of propositions. The methods of testing used by the applied scientist are similar to the methods used by the pure scientist when he is involved in testing hypotheses.

Practice is the process of using science, of applying theories. The practitioner is involved in manipulating objects and events. His actions may be guided by one or more theories or by some propositions which are not a part of any formal theory. The professional practitioner may be differentiated from the layman or technician by his knowledge of the particular propositions which guide his actions and his conscious selection of these propositions.

A given individual may be engaged in pure science, applied science and/or practice. However, for clarity in functioning it is better to differentiate between these areas of activity. The particular skills required are somewhat different. An individual educated to function in one area may need to acquire additional knowledge and skill to function effectively in another area.

FRAMES OF REFERENCE FOR THERAPY

Ideally frames of reference for therapy are stated in an organized and logical manner. They are comprehensive and internally consistent. Again ideally, they deal with the following areas:

1. A statement of the theoretical base
2. delineation of function-dysfunction continuums
3. evaluation
4. postulates regarding change[4]

---

[4] Ford and Urban, *Systems of Psychotherapy.*

1. A Statement of the Theoretical Base

This aspect of a frame of reference delineates the assumptions, concepts and postulates which are necessary for an adequate description of man-in-environment. It specifies the nature of man and environment. It states the relationship between the environment, normal development and developmental deviations. Only one theoretical system may be utilized—or assumptions, concepts and postulates may be drawn from several different theories. Common sources used in the formulation of a theoretical base are: neurology, sociology, psychology (principally theories of perception, learning, and personality), and theories regarding the nature and function of the nonhuman environment. This is referred to as the *base*; it is this part of a frame of reference which identifies the parameters of the frame of reference and serves as the matrix from which all other parts of the frame of reference are deduced. (It is sometimes assumed that frames of reference deal with the factors which causes dysfunction. This is an inaccurate assumption and arises from a misunderstanding regarding the nature of dysfunction. Dysfunction may arise from and be maintained by any number of known and unknown factors which have influenced the individual. If these are organic in nature and still amenable to alteration, surgical and pharmacological techniques are used. However, this is not the business of the therapist and thus not a part of a frame of reference. If these causal factors are located in the individual's past history they are not amenable to change. We are unable to alter past events. If these factors are currently operating in the individual's usual environment, pathology is located in the environment. This environmental pathology is identified and dealt with as a separate area in the frame of reference. The *process* which leads to a state of function or dysfunction may be of concern in a frame of reference; this may form the foundation for postulates regarding change. If such is the case, the process is described in the theoretical base.)

2. Delineation of Function and Dysfunction Continuum

This aspect of a frame of reference describes the nature of the dysfunctions which are to be treated by application of the frame of reference. By extension, it describes what the therapist assesses during the evaluation process. One or several continuums may be identified. There is usually a somewhat arbitrary division on each continuum to delineate that which is considered functional and that which is considered dysfunctional. The continuums or specific areas with which the frame of reference is concerned should be relatively mutually exclusive and stated on the same conceptual level. For example, it is better to identify dimensions such as work habits, interpersonal skills and coordination than to identify ego strength, reality testing and impulse control. Reality testing and impulse control are considered to be ego functions. The evaluation process is greatly simplified when there is a clear distinction between the various continuums.

A frame of reference provides an operational definition of function and dysfunction relative to the various continuums and is stated in terms of verbal and nonverbal behavior. For example, dysfunction on the continuum of "impulse control" may be operationally defined as the inability to attend to a task, verbal and nonverbal demand for immediate need satisfaction, action prior to considering the consequences of that action, and marked distraction by extraneous stimuli. Behaviors which are used to identify dysfunction in a given area are referred to as *symptoms.*

The distinction between symptoms and pathology (a dysfunction) is sometimes unclear. *Pathology* is that which the frame of reference states is dysfunction, that which application of the frame of reference is designed to alter.[5] *Symptoms* are those behaviors which point to or indicate pathology. Whether a given behavior is considered to be pathology or a symptom depends only upon the frame of reference being used. Thus, in one frame of reference a slovenly appearance may be considered symptomatic of negative feelings toward the self; in another, it may be indicative of unconscious conflict between acceptance and rejection of parental standards, and in another it may be pathology.

In most frames of reference one given behavior is not symptomatic of a given pathology; rather, it is a gestalt of behaviors that indicate dysfunction. For example, a person may be considered to be "mistrustful of others" if he gives as little as possible information about himself, questions people's motivations and their interest in him, does not like to sit with his back to the door, and avoids situations where he must cooperate with others. Any of these specific behaviors, seen in combination with other behaviors may be indicative of pathology in another area.

It is assumed that symptoms will cease to be a part of the individual's behavioral repertoire when pathology is altered. Symptoms as such are not directly subjected to alteration. Thus, if through the treatment process, the individual comes to perceive himself as a positive object, his tendency to dress in a slovenly manner will no longer be evident.

3. Evaluation

Evaluation is the process of identifying whether or not an individual is in a state of dysfunction or function in the various areas of concern. A theoretical frame of reference describes the tools and techniques the therapist uses to observe behavior indicative of function and dysfunction as outlined in the above section.

---

[5]All frames of reference start with behavior to determine whether an individual is in a state of dysfunction. The effect of therapy is likewise determined through assessment of behavior. The goal of treatment is to diminish or eliminate dysfunction. Whether the goal has been reached is assessed from the individual's verbal and nonverbal behavior, what he says and how he acts. The criterion for making judgments regarding goal attainment is change in symptomatic behavior. For example, if anxiety was regarded as symptomatic of some dysfunction, the alteration of the dysfunction might be indicated by the patient's report that he no longer felt anxious and was able to relax and sleep well and by the therapist's observation that the patient no longer sat rigidly in his chair or fidgeted with his necktie and watchband.

Evaluation tools and techniques are essentially stimuli events that have been found to elicit responses which differentiate between function and dysfunction. They are described in such a way that they may be used by others to arrive at the same conclusion. Criteria for interpretation of the data are given if this is not evident from the outline of behavior indicative of function and dysfunction. Often, a frame of reference uses (in whole or in part) behavior observed in formalized evaluation procedures as the behavioral definition of function and dysfunction. This can be seen in some of the operational definitions of perceptual-motor skills.

If at all possible, a theoretical frame of reference states as well the extent of which the evaluative tools and procedures are reliable and valid. *Reliability* refers to the dependability, stability, and accuracy of an evaluative procedure. It is essentially concerned with the question of whether similar and consistent behavior would be observed if the patient were involved in the evaluative procedure several different times. Although small changes in behavior might be evident, evaluative procedures are designed to identify basic difficulties interfering with satisfactory interaction in the community. The behavior elicited in an evaluative procedure must be a currently fundamental part of the individual's repertoire. If an evaluative procedure is unreliable the therapist cannot make dependable statements about the patient's dysfunction. *Validity* refers to whether the evaluative procedure is assessing what it is supposed to assess. To clarify, if a particular evaluative procedure is designed to assess whether the individual has the capacity to form abstract concepts, the behavior exhibited during the test procedure must lead to an accurate interpretation of the individual's capacity to abstract.

4. Postulates Regarding Change

Postulates regarding change are descriptive or prescriptive statements deduced from the postulates of the theoretical base. They are descriptive for the therapist utilizing a frame of reference and prescriptive for the therapist contemplating utilization. Taken together they state what the therapist is ·doing or what to do. Postulates regarding change state the underlying principles by which an individual is assisted in moving from a state of dysfunction to a state of function. They delineate the interaction between man and environment which alters dysfunction. They are a guide for the therapist's arrangement of the nonhuman environment and his personal interaction with the patient.

The change postulates stated, ideally, are ones which have been subjected to empirical testing, but in reality this is not always possible. They may be specific to the treatment of one identified area of dysfunction or basic to the treatment of all function-dysfunction continuums with which the frame of reference deals. Some examples of change postulates are: purposeful motor activity enhances the integration of sensory stimuli; awareness of the historical origin of ambivalent feeling facilitates consciously planned interaction; establishment of a primary object relationship is dependent upon consistent need fulfillment by an accepting person; the frequency of a given performance is increased by providing a positively reinforcing stimulus subsequent to the performance; and reality testing is facilitated by consensual validation.

For the sake of clarity and greater specificity it is often necessary to define or give examples of the various techniques utilized in the treatment process. Techniques are formulated through reference to postulates regarding change and may or may not be particular to a specific frame of reference. Such techniques as task-oriented groups, role playing, dyadic interaction, work-oriented activities, and involvement in activities of living may be utilized in different types of frames of reference. However, the way in which a technique is used may vary to some extent. Other techniques such as interpretation, shaping, or providing activities which are symbolic of the mother-child nurturing relationship are usually considered specific to a given type of frame of reference.

Postulates regarding change also state relationships which guide the therapist's selection of sequentially immediate and long-term goals of treatment, the step-by-step progression of treatment in each area of dysfunction, and the specific techniques which are applied during each stage of treatment.

To summarize, a theoretical frame of reference for therapy deals with the following:

1. A statement of the theoretical base
   a. statement of the nature of man and environment
   b. statement of the relation between man and environment

2. Delineation of Function and Dysfunction Continuums
   a. identification and definition of the areas of concern
   b. listing of behavior indicative of function and dysfunction in these areas

3. Evaluation:
   a. identification and description of tools and techniques
   b. procedural information
   c. rules for interpreting evaluative data
   d. reliability and validity report

4. Postulates Regarding Change:
   a. deduced from the theoretical base
   b. statements regarding the alteration of dysfunction
   c. identification and description of techniques
   d. guidelines for selecting techniques
   e. step-by-step sequence of treatment process

The criteria for an adequate theoretical frame of reference as outlined above are stringent and, indeed, difficult to meet. It is a statement of the ideal rather than the actual. To the author's knowledge no frame of reference for the treatment of psychosocial dysfunction meets these standards. The three frames of reference presented in this text are by no means complete. They are merely an attempt to move in this direction. The above criterion has been suggested: (1) to stimulate thinking about what a frame of reference should or should not include; (2) to identify a goal for our work in this area and (3) to give an orientation for classification of the frames of reference currently available.

Frames of reference for treatment of physical dysfunction appear to be closer to the ideal than frames of reference for the treatment of psychosocial dysfunction. This is most likely due to the seemingly greater degree of comprehensiveness, specificity, and validity of theories used as the foundation for frames of reference for the treatment of physical dysfunction. Theoretical frames of reference for the treatment of psychosocial dysfunction are often founded upon embryonic theories which have been subjected to little or no empirical testing. They are utilized because without them all patient care would cease or the therapist would make no attempt to plan or control his interactions with patients. Neither course of action seems desirable. Thus the therapist, in addition to his role as a practitioner, engages in pure and applied scientific study. In this way he carries out his professional responsibilities in an ethical and logical manner while at the same time contributing to the creation of valid theories and concise frames of reference.

The process of formulating a theoretical frame of reference varies with each individual therapist. There appear to be four common methods which are either used singly or in combination. They are:

1. Exploration of Theory
   This method begins with a survey of various theories and postulates regarding change in human behavior. Study is guided by some flexible ideas about the areas of function-dysfunction and techniques that are traditionally a part of the therapy for which the theoretical frame of reference is to be formulated.

2. Exploration of Practice
   This method begins with observation of therapist-patient-nonhuman object interaction. The intuitive, nonsystematized ideas which appear to be the guide for practice are articulated and stated as principles of treatment. At this point the individual turns to theories and postulates regarding change and selects those which fit the observed interaction.

3. Exploration of Function-Dysfunction
   This method begins with an attempt to identify and describe areas of function-dysfunction which can or should be treated by the given therapy. This often involves construction of exploratory assessment procedures which ultimately serve as evaluative tools for identifying areas of function-dysfunction and the nature and extent of the patient's dysfunction.

4. Exploration of Theoretical Frames of Reference
This method begins with selecting a theoretical frame of reference which is utilized in another type of therapy. The areas of function-dysfunction and the postulates regarding change are usually taken over from the model frame of reference. Evaluative procedures and principles of treatment are altered to fit the techniques traditionally used by the therapy for which the frame of reference is being formulated.

Regardless of the method or methods used, the individual formulating a theoretical frame of reference eventually deals with all of the areas outlined above for an ideal frame of reference. Like theory building, this is a lengthy process. However, it is a rewarding process, for it will ultimately lead to more effective and efficient patient care.

CATEGORIZATION OF FRAMES OF REFERENCE

Therapists have many frames of reference available to them at this time. Such variety is stimulating and allows the therapist to select a frame of reference which is compatible with his value system and typical style of interaction. A suggested system of categorization is presented to bring some order out of the diversity to clarify similarities and differences, and to provide some orientation for the three frames of reference which will be discussed later. In outline form theoretical frames of reference may be classified as:

1. Analytic
2. Acquisitional
   a. Ego function
   b. Intermediate capacities
   c. Unlabeled behavior
3. Developmental

1. Analytic   The theoretical bases of analytic frames of reference usually describe man as striving for need fulfillment, expression of primitive impulses or control of inherent drives. Striving is regulated by external and internal norms, cognitive processes, and affectual responses and is both facilitated and inhibited by the environment. Given an optimal environment, the individual is able to deal with his needs, impulses, or drives in a satisfactory manner. However, the individual often finds that his needs, impulses or drives are in conflict with each other, with the realities of the environment, or with his judgments regarding what is acceptable or unacceptable. Because such conflictual experiences are anxiety-provoking, the individual represses or pushes out of consciousness experiences, affect, ideas, and desires which are related to the conflictual experience. Repressed material stored in the unconscious continues to influence the individual. The nature of the unconscious content is reflected in behavior in a lawful and thus identifiable manner. It is also reflected in dreams and waking fantasies. It is this unconscious content which is seen as the dysfunction in analytic frames of reference. Symptoms arise from and at least in part express unconscious content. The individual, however, is not always viewed as "sick" in an analytic frame of reference, but rather as someone who could reach a greater degree of health or self-actualization if he were more aware of his unconscious content. It is assumed that the individual is able to continue independently toward self-actualization when symptom-producing unconscious content is integrated with conscious content.

Identification of function-dysfunction is somewhat vague in analytic frames of reference. It is rather difficult to conceptualize this aspect of these frames of reference as continuums. The issues of concern to the analytically oriented therapist usually cluster around unconscious conflicts related to love, hate, aggression, sexuality, autonomy, feelings of inadequacy, and death. The specific nature of the symptom-producing unconscious content is inferred through psychodynamic interpretations of behavior. *Psychodynamics* is a concept used to identify a relatively formal system for describing the relationship between behavior, unconscious content, and past experiences. There is some variation in psychodynamic systems so that a given behavior may be interpreted in a number of different ways.

In analytic frames of reference evaluation is oriented toward the identification of the nature of the symptom-producing unconscious content. Initial evaluation is seen as providing clues or facilitating educated guesses. Evaluation continues throughout treatment and it is often only near the end of the process that the specific nature of the unconscious content is able to be identified. The initial evaluation process involves psychodynamic interpretations of historical information, verbal and nonverbal behavior and objects produced. Evaluative procedures identified as *projective techniques* are sometimes used. Behavior elicited through the use of projective techniques and objects produced are sometimes viewed as symbolic of unconscious content. A psychodynamic system is used to interpret the meaning of these symbols.

The major postulates regarding changes are: (1) Mature behavior is restored or enhanced by bringing symptom-producing unconscious content to consciousness and integrating this previously unconscious content with conscious content. (2) Unconscious content is brought to consciousness and integrated through facilitating non-ego-controlled behavior and interpretation of the patient's behavior to the patient.

Many of the techniques formulated through reference to the above postulates are related to facilitation of non-ego-controlled behavior. Some examples of these are: supportive and accepting attitude on the part of the therapist, the therapist remains a relatively unknown object to the patient so as to promote transference (transference is itself a facilitating technique), free association, presentation of dreams, working in unstructured media, and engaging in specially structured new experiences.

Interpretation is usually seen as being directed toward two processes: the development of insight and working through of conflicts. The development of insight is "...the process by which the meaning, significance, pattern or use of an object or situation becomes clear...."[6] Working through is "...the process of having the client face the same conflicts over and over again, under the analyst's supervision, until he can face and master the conflicts in ordinary life."[7] These processes are interdependent and their end results are believed to lead to the integration of previously unconscious content with conscious content.

2. Acquisitional The theoretical base for acquisitional frames of reference focuses upon the various skills or abilities which the individual needs for adequate and satisfying interaction in the environment. The abilities of concern are considered to be relatively *independent, quantitative, nonstage specific.* An example will perhaps clarify the last attributes. Piaget conceptualizes the developmental process of mature cognition as having clearly differentiated stages. Behavior in each stage is qualitatively different. Guilford, on the other hand, conceptualizes the development of cognition as quantitative increment of skills. No stages are identified. The theoretical base may describe the manner in which these skills are acquired in the normal developmental process or how they may be acquired if they are not a part of the individual's present repertoire. Inappropriate learning or lack of learning is considered to be the dysfunction and is assumed to be the casual factor in the development of symptoms. It is further assumed that corrective learning experiences will lead to acquisition of desirable abilities and thus allow the individual to continue the process of self-actualization.

Delineation of function-dysfunction continuums in acquisition frames of reference involves a categorization of human abilities: those abilities which are believed to be essential for creative adaptation to the environment. The manner in which these abilities are classified varies and is one of the distinguishing features of the three types of frames of reference in the acquisitional category. The function-dysfunction continuums of *ego function* frames of reference are what the literature on the subject describes as the basic functions of the ego and may be identified as: balanced use of defense mechanisms; differentiation, synthesis and organization of perceptions; reality testing; and control, investment, expression and use of libidinal and aggressive drives.

Intermediate capacities frames of reference classify human abilities in a somewhat different manner. The label for this type of frame of reference was selected to indicate that the function-dysfunction continuums are less basic than those of ego function frames of reference. No value judgment is implied here. The point to be made is that the various function-dysfunction continuums include a number of different ego functions. For this reason, the two frames of reference are mutually exclusive. They are on different levels just as are the concepts of chair and furniture. Some examples of common continuums are concept of self, concept of others, communication and control of impulses. The

---

[6]A. and H. English, *A Comprehensive Dictionary of Psychological and Psychoanalytic Terms* (New York: David McKay Company, Inc., 1958).

[7]English and English, *A Comprehensive Dictionary. . . .*

advantage of the intermediate capacities delineation of function-dysfunction is greater ease in comprehension and evaluation.

Unlabeled behavior frames of reference usually delineate function-dysfunction continuums relative to the specific responsibilities that the individual has in his social system. The presence of any behavior which interferes with adaptive functioning and/or the absence of any behavior which is required for adequate function is defined as dysfunction. For example, the inability to engage in house cleaning and shopping would be considered dysfunctional for most homemakers.

Symptoms or behavior indicative of function-dysfunction in ego functions and intermediate behavior frames of reference are usually specified or can be gleaned from the literature. They are so numerous that it would be impossible to list them here. In unlabeled behavior frames of reference, the medical model of "symptom indicative of pathology" is not utilized. Behavior or the lack of behavior is assessed relative to current life tasks. Maladaptive behavior is considered to be the dysfunction and is not indicative of anything.

Evaluation in acquisitional frames of reference tends to be focused more upon the individual's present interaction with his environment than upon past history. The therapist is primarily interested in assessing the patient's place on the various function-dysfunction continuums in the here and now. Evaluation may involve verbal discussion regarding current environmental interactions and/ or observation of the individual interacting with the environment. Interview content and observational situations are designed to focus upon environmental interaction which requires use of the various human capacities identified by the function-dysfunction continuums of the particular frame of reference being utilized. Or, in the case of unlabeled behavior frames of reference, evaluation focuses upon the way in which the individual is engaging in his current life tasks. As will be discussed below, in those acquisitional frames of reference which utilize postulates regarding change drawn from learning theories, evaluation also includes assessment of environmental factors which may be currently responsible for maintenance of particular behaviors.

Postulates regarding change in acquisitional frames of reference are of two major types: *general* or *continuum specific*. General postulates regarding change are usually drawn from learning theories. They are labeled *general* because they are applied to all of the continuums identified in a particular frame of reference. To illustrate, frames of reference which contain general postulates state that the crucial factors which promote change are similar whether one is concerned with dysfunction in the areas of problem solving, communication, sexual identity, etc. Postulates regarding change may be drawn from many different learning theories, but postulates from classical conditioning and operant conditions seem to be the most common. As these two theories are compatible, a given frame of re.erence may utilize postulates from both. Unlabeled behavior frames of reference usually utilize general postulates; ego function and intermediate capacities frames of reference may also make use of general postulates.

Continuum specific postulates regarding change are, as the label indicates, particular to each function-dysfunction continuum in a given frame of reference. Thus, for example, postulates regarding the learning or development of adequate communication skills would be different from postulates regarding acquisition of problem-solving skills. Continuum specific postulates usually specify a particular type of interaction that is necessary for learning. Examples of continuum specific postulates are: reality testing is learned through an opportunity for consensual validation, investment of libidinal energy in an external object occurs through experiencing the object as need fulfilling, and a more positive self-identity is acquired through success in mastering the nonhuman environment.

It is sometimes argued that continuum specific postulates may be replaced by general postulates without altering the substance of a particular acquisitional frame of reference. This is a fine theoretical point and we have little data to support this position. It seems more appropriate to maintain a distinction between the two types of postulates. There is an emotional issue involved here in that some practitioners reject postulates drawn from learning theories. They are more comfortable using continuum specific postulates. Until we have more supporting data it is impossible to say which type of postulate is a more effective guide for action.

Techniques deduced from general postulates are usually concerned with such therapist-patient-nonhuman environment interactions as: positive, negative, differential and lack of reinforcement; shaping, building chains of performances; extinction; stimuli discrimination; social imitation; modeling; schedules of reinforcement; and desensitization. These techniques are utilized singly or in combination. Generally all techniques are directed to decreasing the frequency of maladaptive behavior and increasing the frequency of adaptive behavior.

Techniques deduced from continuum specific postulates are multiple and varied. Description of techniques usually involves delineation of how particular characteristics of the human and nonhuman environment are arranged so as to allow change-producing elements to have an impact upon the patient. These descriptions, are, in essence, operational definitions of concepts utilized in the postulates regarding change. For example, techniques used in developing more adequate reality testing (deduced from the postulate previously mentioned) may be such as the following: the therapist responds to the patient regarding the degree to which the patient's observations are in agreement with those of his cultural group; and the patient is engaged in tasks which have clearly established standards, prescribed modes of action, and predictable results. These two techniques are believed to be only two in the constellation of elements which are referred to as *consensual validation*. These are, of course, only a sample of the techniques one may draw upon in order to develop more accurate reality testing.

3. Developmental   The theoretical base for developmental frames of reference is similar to acquisitional frames of reference in that it specifies the various skills or abilities which the individual needs for adequate and satisfactory interaction in the community. However, the abilities of concern are considered to be interdependent, qualitative, and stage specific. The theoretical base describes how these skills are acquired in the normal developmental process and the sequential, interdependence of the various stages of each skill. Lack of learning of age appropriate subskills is considered to be the dysfunction and the causal factor in symptom formation. It is further assumed that participation in situations which simulate those interactions between individual and environment stated or being responsible for the sequential development of a given human ability will allow the individual to learn all of the subskills fundamental to the mature skill.

In developmental frames of reference, function-dysfunction continuums are delineated through a categorical, sequential structuring of human abilities. Each continuum is one identified area which is subdivided into stages. If an individual has learned all of the behaviors which are an inherent part of each stage of development in a particular area (given his age) he is considered to be in a state of function in that area. If he has not acquired such behavior he is said to be in a state of dysfunction. These areas of human ability are considered to be interdependent. Inadequate development in one area usually impedes development in all of the others. (See Chapter Six for further discussion of this phenomenon.)

Some developmental frames of reference utilize only one function-dysfunction continuum in that they deal with only one area of human abilities. Others utilize several continuums and thus are concerned with various human abilities. An illustration may be useful: frames of reference based on Erikson's "eight stages of man" or Freud's outline of psychosexual stages are unidimensional, whereas frames of reference which include continuums labeled as cognition, perceptual-motor skills and interpersonal relations are multidimensional.

Behavior indicative of function and dysfunction has been more or less outlined through observation and formal testing of normal persons who have and have not passed through a given state of development (determined by age). Some psychodynamic principles have been used to describe the relationship between symptoms and dysfunction in the areas of interpersonal relations, self identity, and psychosexual development. The difficulty in the delineational behavior indicative of function and dysfunction in developmental frames of reference is related to the apparent difference between an adult who has not completed a relatively primitive stage of development and a child just prior to acquisition of the stage specific behavior. This problem remains under study.

Evaluation procedures for developmental frames of reference are ill-defined except in the areas of perceptual-motor skills, cognition, and interpersonal relations. Much work has been done in designing procedures for evaluating these areas. Some norms are available for limited populations (primarily children). Projective techniques have been used to gain information in those areas where psychodynamic principles have been defined for relating symptoms to retarded or inadequate development. Typical evaluative procedures are interviews regarding past and current behavior and the observation of individuals in situations which demand the use of stage specific behavior of various function-dysfunction continuums. (The former procedure is more difficult to interpret for the uninitiated therapist, while the latter is, in any case, somewhat more accurate.) There is a tendency to equate a supposedly growth-inhibiting environment at the usual time of development of a given stage with unsuccessful completion of that stage. The individual, however, may have completed the stage in such a growth inhibiting environment or he may have completed the stage later in a different environment. The therapist is concerned only with the stage specific behaviors the individual has available to him at the present time. The attainment of maturity on a given function-dysfunction continuum may have been retarded or difficult to acquire, but this information is not, however, essential for assessment of function and dysfunction.

One factor which makes evaluation more difficult in developmental frames of reference (and to a lesser extent in acquisitional frames of reference) is the tendency for the human organism to compensate for deficient learning; to acquire splinter skills or learn by rote. This is the learning of behavior which makes it appear that the individual is at the functional end of a function-dysfunction continuum. For example, an individual may have learned how to read yet with sophisticated testing show marked deficit in perception of form and space.

Postulates regarding change in developmental frames of reference may be described as *stage specific* or *general*. The theoretical base for frames of reference containing stage specific postulates are usually drawn from theories of human development which delineate the stage sequential development of a particular human ability and the interaction between individual and environment which allows the individual to successfully complete the various stages. Change postulates from several compatible personality theories may be used to delineate the individual-environment interaction necessary for mature development of one human ability. At times these postulates are more educated guesses than thoroughly tested hypotheses. General postulates regarding change in developmental frames of reference are usually drawn from learning theories. Their selection is based upon the assumption that although the behaviors learned at each stage of development of various human abilities vary, the crucial factors which allow for the learning of the behavior are similar.

Techniques deduced from stage specific postulates are concerned with the ways in which the therapist simulates individual-environment interactions which are described as being responsible for the necessary learning at each development stage of the human abilities delineated in the frame of reference. Examples of such techniques are: "stimulate tactile receptors", "provide activities in which cause and effect are apparent", "allow opportunities for parallel play", "permit negativeness," etc. Techniques deduced from general postulates are similar to those outlined in the discussion of acquisitional frames of reference. They differ only to the extent that they are applied to the learning of stage specific behaviors.

Whether stage specific or general postulates are utilized, the change postualtes in developmental frames of reference stipulate the sequence of treatment. On the basis of these postulates: (1) treatment is initiated in that area in which stage specific learning is most primitive; (2) treatment continues in that area through each sequentially more advanced stage until learning in that area is equal to learning in the area in which stage specific learning is next most primitive; (3) treatment in this second area is then initiated; and (4) this sequence continues until all necessary learning has occurred. Such a detailed outline is, of course, not needed in unidimensional frames of reference. Treatment begins at whatever stage the individual has not successfully completed.

SIMILARITIES AND DIFFERENCES

From this brief description of the categories of theoretical frames of reference it is possible to identify some of the similarities and differences. *The difference between acquisitional-developmental and analytic frames of reference is that in acquisitional-developmental frames of reference dysfunction is assumed to be faulty learning. In analytic frames of reference dysfunction is symptom-producing unconscious content.* To further clarify, an analytic orientation assumes that the individual "has a repertoire of previously learned positive habits available to him" which will emerge with the integration of unconscious and conscious content; acquisitional-developmental approaches assume that the individual has not learned these adaptive patterns. These two orientations are incompatible — although some persons in the ego analytic school have attempted to integrate them. The reason they are incompatible can best be seen in an attempt to delineate what it is that the therapist treats. Some ego analysts speak of unconscious conflict leading to defective ego function, then recommend treatment of the defective ego. This recommendation, however, deals only with symptoms and, by definition, one does not treat symptoms. Such a position is often explained by saying that alteration of ego deficit enhances the ability of the individual to deal with unconscious content; thus "justifying" alteration as treatment. The whole area has not been sufficiently clarified and is probably responsible for much of the confusion regarding dysfunction and symptoms. It seems more logically consistent and expedient in the long run to place frames of reference which focus upon the development of adequate ego functions under the major heading of acquisitional. This placement provides a more sound theoretical base and clarifies the treatment process.

It is not to be inferred from the above paragraph that the concept of the unconscious is or is not a part of acquisitional or developmental frames of reference. Acquisitional and developmental frames of reference vary; some make use of this concept and others do not. However, the concept of the conscious and unconscious conflict is entirely compatible with these frames of reference. When included, it is to be assumed that the individual has unconscious conflicts because he has not learned behavioral patterns which allow him to adapt to his environment. Unconscious conflict is, then, considered to be a symptom rather than the dysfunction which the therapist treats. It is assumed that once the individual has developed the abilities he needs for meaningful and satisfying environmental interaction he will be able to deal with unconscious material.

The differences between acquisitional and developmental frames of reference are in the assumptions regarding the developmental process of human abilities. In the former they are viewed as quantitative and non-stage specific; in the latter they are seen as qualitative and stage specific. Developmental frames of reference assume that the individual must go through these various incompleted stages before he will be able to function in a mature manner.

Differences between developmental and analytic frames of reference become more apparent in discussions of postulates regarding change. Some of the postulates regarding normal and abnormal development and the psychodynamics of symptom formation found in analytic theories of personality are utilized in developmental frames of reference. But there is considerable difference between personality theory and frames of reference for therapy. A frame of reference is not necessarily analytic if it utilizes change postulates drawn from analytically oriented personality theories. The theoretical base, delineation of function-dysfunction continuum, and techniques of therapy must also be taken into consideration in categorizing a particular frame of reference.

Developmental frames of reference do not make use of transference. If this phenomenon becomes evident in the treatment process, it is discouraged. Interaction is structured so that the patient (hopefully) comes to preceive the therapist as a new object, different from past significant persons. This is accomplished through affectual involvement with the patient; the therapist acting as a total, reacting, feeling person.

Interaction with human and nonhuman objects which have symbolic potential is utilized in some developmental and analytic frames of reference, but they are used in a different manner. In analytic frames of reference such interaction is used to help the patient to become aware of and to integrate unconscious content. In developmental frames of reference it is used to allow the patient to gratify infantile needs and to reexperience primitive stages of development. The patient need not be or become aware of the symbolic nature of objects and interactions for therapy to be effective.

Developmental frames of reference prescribe movement through various stages of development however these may be defined. In treatment based upon analytic frames of reference, various stages of development may be discussed. What occurred during these stages may be explored and brought to consciousness. However, there is no attempt to assist the patient in developing skills which are usually learned in these stages or concern about such learning. A therapist using an analytic frame of reference would never consciously and deliberately gratify an infantile need.

PUTTING FRAMES OF REFERENCE IN CATEGORIES

Placing ideas into a categorical system is a risky endeavor. Individuals who formulated an idea or champions of the idea usually disapprove, both of being categorized and of the category in which they are placed. But a system is useless if it does not organize phenomena. Judgment regarding placement is based upon statements relative to a particular frame of reference and descriptions of evaluation and treatment based upon the frame of reference. Some of the frames of reference which will be mentioned are embryonic in nature and some are more often thought of as movements than as formal statements regarding change.

A qualifying remark is necessary: no attempt has been made to cover all persons who have been engaged in formulating frames of reference. However, an effort was made to select a representative sample.[8]

---

[8]As an aside to my colleagues in occupational therapy, I would like to categorize some of the frames of reference which have developed and been articulated within our profession. Watanabe mentions four function-dysfunction continuums; life space, mastery, responsibility and life tasks. This manner of delineating human abilities and her description of one treatment case seems to indicate that here frame of reference would fit into the acquisitional-intermediate capacities category using continuum specific postulates regarding change. Diasio appears to conceptualize function-dysfunction as behavior relative to current developmental tasks and required social roles. Alteration of behavior through feedback from the environment is emphasized. Her frame of reference would seem then to fall in the acquisitional-unlabeled behavior category using general postulates. Smith and Tempone are placed in the acquisitional-unlabeled behavior category using general postulates. Ayres and the Azimas, fit easily into the development category using stage specific postulates. The Azima's frame of reference contains only one function-dysfunction continuum: S. Freud's outline of psychosexual development. Ayres is concerned with several continuums although they are all related to perceptual-motor abilities.

Placing the Fidlers' frame of reference in a category is difficult for several reasons: They share with other ego analysts the problem of distinguishing between dysfunction as symptom-producing unconscious content or defective ego function. In delineating function-dysfunction continuums relative to human abilities there is a blurring of ego functions and intermediate capacities. Function-dysfunction continuums tend to contain subcontinuums (e.g., "self identity" includes differentiation of self from others, body image, accurate perception of capacities and limitations, affect regarding the self, etc.). However, all subcontinuums are not clearly specified. Some continuums and their subcontinuums are defined as quantitative, nonstage specific and others are qualitative, stage specific. Three treatment approaches are outlined: psychoanalytic, supportive, and directive. This is confusing because it appears that in using the supportive and directive approach one is dealing with symptoms. The distinction between treatment and rehabilitation seems to divide the change process into two different entities. This statement appears to refer to the sequence of treatment more than a delineation of two different processes. Rehabilitation as defined is oriented toward bringing about some predetermined change in the patient. Thus rehabilitation appears to be part of treatment as this concept has been previously defined. Categorization of the Fidlers' frame of reference is only possible if one breaks it down into some of its component parts. Those aspects of their frame of reference which refers to the psychoanalytic orientation; evaluation of unconscious conflict relative to self concept, sexual identity, gratification of infantile needs, dependency, and concept of others; assessment of unconscious conflicts which are leading to difficulty in controlling and/or expressing hostility, distorted communication and the adequate organization of the ego; and treatment techniques which are identified as exploring and working through are placed in the analytic category. That part of their frame of reference which deals with the supportive orientation is placed in the acquisitional category. It can be subdivided by placing concern with ego organization in the acquisitional-ego function category, using continuum specific postulates regarding change and concern with self-concept, sexual identity, hostility, communication and concept of others in the acquisitional-intermediate capacities category under continuum specific postulates. Aspects of patient care which are identified as rehabilitation also fit into this category. The type of treatment which is referred to as directive seems to fit into the acquisitional-unlabeled behavior category using general postulates. The Fidlers' discussion of treatment of function-dysfunction continuums that are labeled infantile needs and dependency appears to fit into the developmental category using stage specific postulates. Treatment of some dimensions of their self concept continuum may also fall into the developmental category.

Classical psychoanalysis (S. Freud) is placed in the analytic category. Anna Freud, though labeled an ego-analyst, is also placed in this category. Much of her writing is devoted to delineating and describing ego functions and human development; reports of her treatment process, however, indicate more concern with unconscious conflict than developing ego functions. Erickson falls into this category for the same reason. Frames of reference based upon analytical psychology (Jung) and client-centered therapy (Rogers) and the use of "encounter or sensitivity groups" (Lipton, Mazer, Bradford) are also placed in the analytic category.

Sullivan, although concerned with the unconscious, appears in the treatment process to be more involved in enhancing the patient's ego function than dealing with unconscious conflict. However, at times his therapy also has a developmental orientation. He is placed in the acquisitional-ego function category using continuum specific postulates because this appears to be most typical of his treatment process. Reality therapy (Glasser) seems to fit into the acquisition-intermediate capacities category using general postulates. Mileu therapy (Commings, Edelson, Hyde and Kramer) and existential therapy (Boss, May, Burswanger) are placed in acquisition-intermediate capacities category using continuum specific postulates. The acquisition-unlabeled behavior category using general postulates contains such people as Dollard and Miller, Wolpe, Eysenck, Bandura, Ullmann and Krasner, and Shoben.

The major representative of the developmental category is Sechehaye. Her work is on a unidimensional continuum (S. Freud's *psychosocial stages*) and involves the application of stage specific postulates regarding change.

Llorens and Rubin identify function-dysfunction continuums as: capacity to relate to others, self control, sexual identification, expression of feelings, independence, expression of impulses, self-worth, self-concept and cognitive-perceptual-motor skill. Specific techniques for dealing with dysfunction in these areas are given. Their frame of reference does not deal with ego functions (as these functions have been defined here) but with intermediate capacities. Except for treatment in the area of cognitive-perceptual-motor skill, their frame of reference seems to fit best into the acquisitional-intermediate capacities category using continuum specific postulates. Their description of cognitive-perceptual-motor treatment indicates that this aspect of their frame of reference should be placed in the developmental category using stage specific postulates.

Reilly's frame of reference is concerned with both physical and psychosocial dysfunction. The major function-dysfunction continuum identified is occupational behavior which is subdivided into work and play. In regard to what has here been identified as the psychosocial aspects, her frame of reference appears to be concerned with human abilities which are necessary for satisfactory occupational behavior. The two cases presented by her colleagues seem to indicate that treatment is concerned with developing these abilities (Takata and Moorhead). Reilly calls for study of the ontogenesis of work and play but does not state whether this development is to be perceived as quantitative nonstage specific or qualitative stage specific. At this point in the articulation of this frame of reference it would seem to fit either into the acquisitional-intermediate capacities category or the developmental category. Intrinsic motivation is emphasized as important in the treatment process. (Whether this will be developed into a general postulate regarding change is unknown. It is impossible, therefore, to state whether the frame of reference would be categorized as containing a general postulate or continuum-stage specific postulates.)

"Crisis intervention" and "community psychiatry" are currently popular movements within the mental health field; crisis intervention often being regarded as one aspect of community psychiatry (Parad, Dunham, Caplon). Persons in these areas use a variety of frames of reference which makes classification difficult. One of their unique features is application of postulates regarding change to both the individual in a state of dysfunction and to his surrounding environment. Most typically, frames of reference utilized by persons working in these areas would be placed in acquisitional-intermediate capacities category using continuum specific postulates.

In summary, this chapter has been an attempt to delineate the nature and relationship between theory and theoretical frame of reference and to categorize the various theoretical frames of reference used by therapists for the treatment of psychosocial dysfunction. The purposes of suggesting a system of classification has been to provide some guidelines for studying various frames of reference and to clarify similarities and differences. As with any classification system, the nuances and richness of the phenomena categorized are often lost. Although probably necessary, it is unfortunate. Each frame of reference has a special beauty that is uniquely its own.

Chapter 2
SOME THOUGHTS ON EVALUATION AND TREATMENT

. . . the "scariness" involved in identifying oneself as an agent of change. The assumption of such a role is frightening, of course, because intervention, treatment planning, requires not only evaluative statements but also a statement of expectation. You are called upon to say this is what I know, this is what I think, this is where I feel another individual is, this is where I feel to the best of my knowledge he should go, and this is how such movement can best be accomplished.

G. S. Fidler, *Exploring How a Think Feels**

This chapter is written for a twofold purpose: (1) to add dimensionality to the discussion of the three theoretical frames of reference which follow; and (2) to clearly state my biases about the therapy process. It is essentially a series of more or less related ideas regarding evaluation and treatment—something about "what," "how," and "why." The ideas are at times descriptive and at other times prescriptive. I shall discuss the therapy process irrespective of the theoretical frame of reference used as the basis for treatment.

EVALUATION

Evaluative procedures are those methods which are used to gain knowledge regarding an individual's state of function and dysfunction relative to the various areas of concern. *Initial evaluation* is assessment of the patient prior to initiation of the treatment process. *Continued evaluation* occurs throughout the treatment process and involves assessment of the extent to which the patient has moved toward a state of function. (This last aspect of evaluation will be discussed later.)

The initial evaluative process is similar regardless of the frame of reference being utilized. The content—that which is to be evaluated and the tools to be used—is variable. In order to determine what evaluative technique to use, the

*In J. Mazer, G. Fidler, L. Kovalenko, and K. Overly, *Exploring How a Think Feels* (New York: American Occupational Therapy Association, 1969), p. 58.

therapist refers to his frame of reference—the section on evaluation may specify definite procedures. When this is the case the therapist duplicates the outlined procedures as closely as possible or administers the suggested standardized tests.

On the other hand a frame of reference may provide only conceptual labels and descriptions of stimuli events which are believed to be useful for evaluation. These concepts and definitions are here referred to as *evaluation concepts*. Such concepts serve as a guide to assessing various human-nonhuman interactions in terms of their suitability for evaluation. To illustrate: in an analytic frame of reference "projective techniques" might be suggested as an appropriate evaluative procedure. Using this concept, the therapist analyzes activities to determine whether and to what extent the activities are compatible with the operational definition of projective techniques. In some developmental frames of reference which are concerned with perceptual-motor skills *nonstereotyped motor activity* is suggested as an evaluative procedure. The therapist, then, analyzes various activities to assess whether they fall into this conceptual category.

Some frames of reference offer little information about evaluative procedures. If this is the case, the therapist refers to or identifies the statements regarding behavior which is indicative of function and dysfunction in the various continuums. Stimuli situations which are likely to elicit this behavior are either selected from available procedures or designed. These may be structured situations in which the therapist is able to directly elicit and/or observe behavior, or they may be reports about the patient's behavior from some other person. Efficiency and accuracy are of prime importance.

If the therapist feels that available evaluative procedures and reports about the patient's past and current behavior from other clinical personnel do not provide the needed information, the therapist designs an original evaluative procedure. Such a procedure may take the form of an outline for an interview, a questionnaire, individual involvement of the patient in a task, involvement with others in a task, or any combination of these. In designing the procedure the therapist must always take into account the behavior he wishes to observe. Procedures which provide extraneous information are avoided in the interest of efficiency. For example, it might be interesting to see what a patient would make out of a lump of clay. If, however, making a given object or manipulating the clay in a certain manner is not described as being indicative of function or dysfunction in a specific area of concern, then the procedure is not pertinent.

An evaluative procedure which involves direct observation of a patient's behavior is usually considered to have three steps: *observation, interpretation,* and *validation. Observation* is "... the act of noting and recording facts and events..."[1] The facts and events of interest to the therapist are the behavior of the patient; behavior in relationship to the self, other people and the nonhuman environment. Both verbal and nonverbal behavior are taken into consideration. As it is impossible to observe everything in a given situation, the therapist focuses attention on those particular behaviors which have previously been identified as indicative of function and dysfunction. It is often helpful for the

---

[1]H. and A. English, *A Comprehensive Dictionary...*

therapist to make notes during the evaluative process; and a guide or check sheet is useful, as it minimizes the amount of writing which is necessary. The patient is not usually opposed to the therapist making notes during the evaluative procedure if he is helped to understand that this will ultimately facilitate the treatment process. If for some reason the therapist does not make notes during the evaluative process, he will find it necessary to record the observations as soon after completion of the procedure as possible. The longer the time that elapses between observation and recording, the more likely some observations will be forgotten.

The next step in the evaluative process is *interpretation*. Interpretation is the ordering of observed behavior so as to be able to arrive at a statement regarding the individual's areas of function and dysfunction. Interpretation is based on the gestalt of behaviors which were previously defined as indicating function or dysfunction in a given area. Interpretation can be made only on the basis of available information. When a considerable amount of information is lacking, the therapist either makes no statement regarding function or dysfunction in a given area or makes a tentative statement with the understanding that this will be investigated further during treatment.

The third step in the evaluative process is *validation*. Validation involves seeking confirmation from another source regarding the accuracy of one's interpretation. Confirmation may be sought from the patient, fellow therapists, other staff members, or from the patient's family. Observation of the patient in a situation different from the evaluative procedure is also useful. Validation is not "finding out if my interpretations were right or wrong"—it is rather a shared learning process with no "final expert." The therapist may observe behavior indicative of function or dysfunction which is not observed by other staff members. The behavior of any individual will often vary from situation to situation; what is observed, therefore, may also differ.

Using a specially designed questionnaire or interview schedule as part of an evaluative procedure involves the same process as the one described above. Observation, interpretation, and validation are necessary. In interpreting the response to a questionnaire one is concerned with what is written, including the content and manner of presentation. The lack of response to some questions and/or seemingly inappropriate responses are noted. During an interview, both verbal and nonverbal behavior is taken into consideration.

In using information gathered by other staff members as part of the evaluative procedure, the therapist must be clear about what information is relevant to him. Just as some of the information gathered by the therapist may not be directly used by other staff members, so too all the information gathered by other staff members may not be used directly by the therapist. The therapist, ideally, reads the reports of other staff members or attends a staff meeting with specific questions pertaining to the information he wishes to gather. The type of information sought will depend upon the frame of reference being used for treatment.

A therapist will sometimes question whether or not to read reports from other staff members before or after his evaluation of the patient. There are advantages and disadvantages to each approach. Reading reports before evaluation allows the therapist to have some knowledge about the patient and the major difficulties he has experienced in functioning in the community. The disadvantage of reading reports prior to evaluation is the bias this may leave—the therapist may inadvertently make interpretations which are compatible with the interpretations made in the reports rather than on the basis of the specific behavior which he observed during his evaluative procedure. When this occurs, the therapist adds no new information about the patient; he may even give misleading information. It is my opinion that the therapist should evaluate the patient prior to reading reports. Arriving at an independent judgment about the patient's areas of function and dysfunction enables the therapist to present unbiased information to the staff concomitant with having an opportunity to assess the completeness of his evaluative procedures. The interpretations of the therapist and other staff members may then be validated without contamination. Alterations can be made where necessary.

The total evaluative process in which each patient is involved should be as efficient as possible—for several staff members to evaluate the same area is redundant and a waste of the patient's and staff members' time. If, for example, the social worker investigates a patient's past work history it is not necessary for the occupational therapist to evaluate this area also. The specific information that the therapist attempts to gather will, of course, be dependent to some extent upon the information that is available from other staff members; and some staff members are better prepared to evaluate certain areas or use certain evaluative procedures than others.

The therapist's evaluation usually takes place as soon as possible after the patient is admitted to the hospital or mental health clinic. The only exception to this recommendation is when the newly-admitted patient's repertoire consists almost entirely of those behaviors which have been found to be amenable to alterations through the judicious use of drugs. It is suggested that the therapist wait until medication has had at least some effect upon the patient's behavior. By waiting, the therapist is likely to gain more information about the patient and observe behavior which is more characteristic of the patient's usual repertoire. If, however, after receiving appropriate medication, the patient's repertoire continues to be made up predominantly of severe maladaptive behavior, the therapist evaluates the patient to the extent that he is able to do so and then initiates treatment.

Evaluation takes place as soon as possible so that the treatment process, too, may begin without undue delay. Waiting a month or six weeks to initiate treatment is justified only in those situations where there is no one available to treat the patient. Lengthy periods between admission and the initiation of treatment are often explained by the statement that it takes a long period of time to gain sufficient information for accurate determination of the patient's pathology.[2]

---

[2]Could it be that we are more comfortable in gathering information from the patient and talking about him then we are in treating him? One gets the impression at times that the therapist is in the business of writing biographies.

Although a short initial evaluation may not be as accurate as one that takes a long period of time, the continued evaluation which occurs during the treatment process will serve to identify any inaccuracies in the initial evaluation. The initial evaluation is always tentative regardless of the length of time taken to complete it.

The patient's contribution to and place in the evaluative process is sometimes overlooked—what he says about the nature of his own difficulties is often ignored or considered to be the statement of an individual who is sick or who lacks the psychological sophistication of the therapist. This is unfortunate because the patient is usually able to give valuable information. And, too, unless the patient sees some relationship between what he experiences as his difficulty in functioning and the treatment process, he is unlikely to be motivated to participate in the process.

Another question, rarely asked but of considerable importance, has to do with reporting evaluative findings to the patient.[3] I believe that the conclusions drawn from the evaluative procedures—and the reasons for these conclusions—should be shared with the patient. This sharing should take place in a language and manner that is understandable to the patient. Lack of such communication may easily be interpreted by the patient as, "The therapist doesn't know what is the matter with me." "My problem is so evil or severe that the therapist is afraid to tell me"; "Something is going to be done by another person to get rid of this thing that is the matter with me." These interpretations generally interfere with the collaboration between therapist and patient.

Evaluative findings are recorded in writing even when a summary report is given orally. It is made available to other staff members and serves as the therapist's point of departure for writing treatment plans and evaluating change. The report includes statements pertaining to whether the patient is in a state of function or dysfunction relative to the areas which are of concern to the therapist; and the nature of the dysfunction is specified. The therapist also gives some information regarding the behavior of the patient which was used as the basis for these interpretations.

TREATMENT

Regardless of the frame of reference used for therapy, the treatment process occurs in the following sequence: (1) Setting immediate and long-term goals; (2) writing a treatment plan; (3) implementation of the treatment plan; (4) continued evaluation; (5) alteration in goals and the treatment process; and (6) decision making regarding the patient's readiness for discontinuation of therapy.

A goal is a conscious end result toward which behavior is directed. Treatment's immediate goal is alteration of a portion of the patient's dysfunction—the

---

[3]Contrary to popular opinion, patients are truly human beings and not some ill-defined subspecies. They don't break. The hurt which they experience is much better relieved by a confident, direct approach. The "need" to speak indirectly is more related to the therapist's insecurity and lack of confidence than to the patient's objective state.

long-term goal of treatment is to eliminate or minimize the patient's dysfunction. The criterion for selecting the immediate goal varies according to the
frame of reference. However immediate goals should be limited both in terms of
number and the amount of change expected. The immediate and long-term goals
are usually set in conjunction with the patient. When the therapist and patient
discuss the evaluative findings, the patient is helped to perceive his major areas
of difficulty—if he is not already aware of them. At times, patients have difficulty in recognizing some problem areas. The issue must not be forced at this
point. At other times the patient identifies areas of difficulty which were not
recognized by the therapist during the evaluation. During discussion of the goals
of treatment, the therapist and patient may have the same goal in mind but use
different concepts to define that goal. Such difficulties in communication can be
corrected through discussion and through careful attention to the words of the
patient. Some at least of the goals selected must be meaningful to the patient at
the beginning of the treatment process—if they are not it is unlikely that the
patient will engage in treatment. Everyone will be wasting his time. Goals are
also set in collaboration with fellow staff members if they are to be involved in
treating the patient.[4] Through discussion by staff members, general common
goals for the patient are agreed upon. Each member of the team is then able to
more clearly state his specific goals for the patient's treatment. Sharing in this
manner insures that staff goals are in harmony with and complementary to each
other; incompatible goals will lead to confusion on the part of the staff and
patient and inhibits the patient's movement toward function.

It is only by stating goals in behavioral terms that movement toward or away
from the goal and goal attainment can be assessed. Measurement is possible only
through observation of behavior.[5] A behavioral definition of a goal may be
stated in terms of adding some behavior to or eliminating some behavior from
the patient's repertoire. For example, if dysfunction was identified on the basis
of the patient's sloppy appearance and subservient manner, the behavioral
definition of the goal might be stated as "the patient wears clothes which are
appropriate for his weight and height and compatible with the norms of his
cultural group" and "the absence of subservient behavior in interaction with
others." The therapist is then able to assess whether the delineated dysfunction

---

[4]It is my opinion that only one therapist should evaluate and treat a patient. The present
practice of several therapists involved in the care of one patient seems a shameful waste of time
and manpower. The "team approach" is used in the text only for the sake of a convention
which I hope will soon no longer be with us. If a particular therapist is not capable of taking
full responsibility, one wonders if that therapist should be involved in treatment at all. Any
person who has been professionally trained and who calls himself a therapist should be able
to take on this full responsibility. The therapist, of course, is concerned with ensuring that
the mental health needs of patients are met. He may spend a considerable amount of time
engaging in this process, but treatment and meeting mental health needs are two different
subjects. Let us call them by their proper labels and act accordingly.

[5]R. Mazer, *Preparing Instructional Objectives* (Palo Alto: Fearon Publishers, 1962).

is in the process of being minimized by observing an increase or decrease in the wearing of appropriate clothes or subservient interaction.

A *treatment plan* is a written report which states the immediate and long-term goals of treatment and defines what the therapist and patient are going to do relative to each other and the nonhuman environment. It is a statement of *anticipated interaction*. The interactions selected and the manner in which they will be structured, are determined by the goals which have been set and the frame of reference being utilized.

Selecting appropriate patient-therapist-nonhuman environment interactions for treatment involves two processes: *analysis* and *synthesis*. Using concepts from the postulates regarding change and concepts used to identify techniques, the therapist analyzes various available activities and interactions in order to determine if they contain characteristics labeled by the concepts. The concepts used for analysis are referred to as *treatment concepts*. Elements from various previously analyzed activities and interactions are synthesized in such a way that the patient-therapist-nonhuman environment interactions outlined in the treatment plan, are made up of those elements which are stated as being essential for treatment of the particular dysfunction.

The treatment plan is discussed with the patient. He is helped to understand the relationship between the agreed-upon goals and the interactions in which he will participate. If possible, he should be able to say, "I am involved in this interaction because it will help me with my difficulties in a specific manner." Through discussion with the patient and his own observation the therapist is able to assess whether or not the interaction is acceptable to the patient. If it is unacceptable, adjustments can usually be made without interfering with those aspects of the interaction which are believed to be change-producing. The treatment plan is also shared with other staff members to determine whether or not it is compatible with their treatment plans. Appropriate changes may be made in the plan through these consultations; and, in addition, the therapist is able to validate the plan at this time. The cooperation of staff members is solicited— they may play a crucial role in the effectiveness of the planned interactions.

The plan is implemented after discussion with the patient regarding the nature and purpose of the interactions outlined in the treatment plan. The integrity of the treatment plan is carefully maintained until such a time as there is evidence of a need for change. The therapist observes the treatment process to ensure that the interaction is compatible with the frame of reference and the treatment plan. Patient and therapist are participating in mutual interaction; they are partners in a joint venture—their roles are different but their responsibility is mutual. It is helpful if the therapist always remembers man's inherent capacity to judge what is harmful or beneficial to the self. This capacity may be stunted by dysfunction but remains viable in the individual. Attention is given to the patient's expressed opinion regarding the treatment process, for the information he provides is tremendously important. Disregard of this information all too often interferes with movement toward function.

Continued evaluation is the process of determining the status of the patient relative to the immediate goals of treatment. It involves assessment of change.

Although this is a continuous process it is usually formalized periodically and reported in a progress note. There are three kinds of change: *progressive, regressive* and *no change. Progressive change* is attainment of the stated goal or greater movement toward the goal than was evident at the time of a previous evaluation, and may include the elimination of some dysfunction which was not being dealt with directly in the treatment process. Alteration of dysfunction which is currently extraneous to the treatment process is fairly common. Because of the complex interrelationships between all elements which constitute the individual, change in one area often leads to change in other areas.

The second kind of change is *regressive change*. Regressive change is greater movement away from a goal than was evident at the time of the previous evaluation and/or evidence of additional dysfunction. Regression is not uncommon in the treatment process. The attainment of a goal rarely occurs in a continually progressive line. An individual may need to regress to a certain extent prior to ultimate elimination of dysfunction. Severe or extended regressive change is cause for concern and is considered undesirable.

The third type of change is *no change*. There is no change in the patient's behavior in comparison with the previous evaluation. As pointed out above, change is often not a continuous process and therefore there may be occasions when there is no change. On the other hand, change may be taking place but not yet be observable to the patient or therapist. Extended periods of no change are not desirable.

If the patient has attained the immediate goal, a more advanced goal is to be selected. The goal selected should be compatible with the criteria for goal selection outlined in the frame of reference. If there is undesirable change, the therapist and patient together explore three major factors: the *treatment goals, the interactions* being utilized, and *elements outside of the treatment situation*. The immediate goal may, for instance, be set too high. In other words, more basic dysfunction may need to be altered prior to treatment directed toward the stated goal. The patient is unable to attain the goal because he does not yet possess the capacity to attain that goal. When such a problem is recognized, the immediate goal of treatment is altered so that it is more compatible with the patient's current abilities.

The patient-therapist-nonhuman environment interactions being utilized may not be an appropriate method for attaining the stated goal. They may not be compatible with the patient's age, sex, cultural group, current adaptive and maladaptive behavior or interests. The interactions may not contain those elements considered necessary for change to occur. The therapist's behavior may differ markedly from the behavior outlined in the treatment plan. For example, the therapist may be required to be "warm and supportive," but feel uncomfortable in this type of interaction—he may say the right words, but his nonverbal behavior may indicate disinterest in the patient. Discrepancies between intended and actual behavior are often not evident to the therapist. This points to the need for collaboration with the patient, other staff members, and one's supervisor. The nature of the group being utilized in the treatment process may have changed. The changed condition may not be conducive to alteration of the patient's dysfunction. Finally, the therapist may not have made adequate provision for all of the factors which the frame of reference states are required for change to occur. The therapist makes the necessary adjustment in the treatment process if any of the above elements are interfering with goal attainment.

There are three major elements outside of the patient-therapist interaction which may interfere with treatment: (1) the goals and treatment plan of the therapist may be incompatible with other treatment the patient is receiving; (2) the environment of the mental health facility or factors in that environment may interfere with the gratification of human needs or in other ways fail to provide a milieu which is conducive to treatment; or (3) specific individuals significant to the patient (in the mental health facility, the community, or both) may communicate to the patient that they do not desire change in his behavior. The therapist attempts to eliminate these elements in whatever way is possible. The therapist, however, must also be aware that there may be interfering elements outside of the therapy situation which cannot be sufficiently altered to allow for treatment to continue. It is unethical to continue treatment when the therapist is quite certain that no change is going to occur.

During the treatment process, the patient and therapist are in an excellent position to make a more accurate assessment of the environment to which the patient will return (*expected environment*) and behavior required for adequate function in that environment. Through discussion, trial and error exploration and further evaluation, the patient and therapist may come to the conclusion that the expected environment should be redefined. It may have been found to be too demanding, not sufficiently demanding, or incompatible with the patient's present interests. If the expected environment is going to be different than the one used as the basis for initial evaluation, the patient's current behavior must be assessed relative to the new environment; this may lead to a restatement of the patient's areas of function and dysfunction. The goals and treatment process would then be directed toward helping the patient to acquire behavior that would be considered adaptive in the new environment.

Decision making regarding the patient's readiness for termination of treatment is a collaborative process between the patient, the therapist, and other members of the treatment team. The criteria used to determine readiness for termination are: whether the patient's pathology has been sufficiently altered so that he is able to function adequately in his expected environment and/or the patient's remaining areas of dysfunction can be altered outside of a treatment situation. Termination is often graded in that the hospitalized patient spends an increasingly greater portion of his time in the community. There may be a decrease in the time spent in the treatment situation as well as a decrease in the number of staff members with whom the patient interacts. The patient may need additional support at this time, and some degree of temporary regressive change may be evident because of uncertainty regarding his capacity to take fuller responsibility for himself. The therapist is able to assist the patient at this time through continued validation of the extent to which the patient has moved from a state of dysfunction to a state of function.

Chapter 3
OBJECT RELATION ANALYSIS

Knowing one's self meant to Socrates a continuous, rigorous and relentless, tho joyful and immensely gratifying endeavor to penetrate to the deeper levels within oneself and then to act on the basis of a unity of these levels with the conscious self.

R. May, *"Historical and Philosophical Pre-Suppositions for Understanding Therapy"* *

Object relation is a term used to identify the process wherein the individual becomes attached to or invests in objects—people and things—which satisfy his needs. Through exploration of the satisfaction of needs and factors interfering with that satisfaction the individual comes to know himself more completely and is therefore better able to satisfy his own needs and those of others. These ideas are understood to be germaine to the continued development of all persons. Thus, as a frame of reference, *object relation analysis* speaks not only of the treatment process but also of one means of enhancing the function of any individual.

The theoretical base for object relations analysis is eclectic in that it has been synthesized out of the work of many persons. Those borrowed from most heavily are Maslow, Sigmund Freud, Jung, Fidler, Azima, Arieti, and Naumburg. However, no attempt has been made to incorporate the total theoretical system of any of these persons. Only certain concepts and postulates were selected and, in truth, not always utilized as their originators intended.

There are several major concepts and postulates which must be outlined before discussion of the theory as a whole.

1. The behavior of man is described in terms of a dynamic balance between needs, drives, affect, cognitive processes and the will.

---

*In O. Mowrer, (ed.), *Psychotherapy: Theory and Practice* (New York: Ronald Press Co., 1953), p. 18.

2. Through the interrelationship of these inherent elements, man relates to objects in such a way as to realize his unique potential.

3. This interrelationship, however, is rarely perfectly tuned, and imbalance leads to inattention to aspects of the self and the environment. Some of these aspects or complexes are actively relegated to the unconscious; other complexes are not allowed to emerge from the unconscious. It is these unconscious complexes which interfere with self-actualization.

4. Man has also acquired the capacity to make contact with these split-off, unknown parts of the self and to integrate them with the conscious self. *Phylogenesis* has endowed man with the cognitive processes of symbol formation and conceptual thinking. Through the use of these processes in conjunction with his other inherent elements, man is able to correct the imbalance between that which is conscious and that which is unconscious and thus continue toward self-actualization. In so doing man manifests his *human-ness*, ". . . this affirmation of life, battle and all, this gritted determination to live and experience, to take on the struggle with the contradictions of one's own nature."[1]

THEORETICAL BASE

Needs, Drives and Objects   One of the organizing concepts used to describe human behavior is needs. Needs are inherent predispositions. Their presence motivates the individual to sustain life and interact as a social being. The individual learns patterns of behavior which satisfy or, at least, partially satisfy most of his needs. Some needs, however, can never be totally gratified. They provide motivational forces for continued growth and development of the individual. Needs are here viewed as positive predispositions which are not only concerned with the survival of the organism but with ". . . a state of being that is more than equilibrium or surcease from external pressures."[2] They are concerned with being as well as the continual process of becoming.

There appear to be a number of human needs which usually influence behavior at different periods of the life cycle. This is perhaps best described by Abraham Maslow's *hierarchy of needs.*[3] He has proposed five categories of needs which emerge sequentially. As lower level needs are essentially satisfied, higher level needs become manifest and influence behavior. The five basic needs, in sequential order are:

1. The physiological needs. These are basic to the adequate maintenance of life. They include the need for food, oxygen, shelter from extreme temperatures, an optimal amount of sensory stimuli, motor activity,

[1] E. Hammer, *Use of Interpretations in Treatment*, p. 8.

[2] T. Clayton, *Teaching and Learning* (Englewood Cliffs, N. J.: Prentice-Hall, Inc., 1965), p. 72.

[3] A. Maslow, *Toward a Psychology of Being* (Princeton, N.J.: D. Van Nostrand, 1962).

maturation of the organism, and release of sexually induced tensions. When there is deprivation of physiological needs, the individual's attention is focused almost exclusively upon their satisfaction.

2. The safety needs. These are satisfied through interaction in an environment which is experienced as relatively free of harm-inducing elements. Such an environment is characterized by: (a) a shared reality in which the majority of persons in the environment are in agreement regarding the nature of objects and the appropriate response to objects; (b) predictable responses from others; (c) known expectations regarding appropriate behavior; (d) relatively consistent ordering of events; (e) recognition of the individual's right to need satisfaction; (f) some degree of change as a consequence of the individual's actions; and (g) a limited number of unknowns. Safety needs, at least in part, motivate attempts to understand the world which surrounds us.

3. Love and belonging needs. In order for these needs to be satisfied the individual must feel that he is loved and accepted because he is a unique person. It is his *being* as opposed to his *doing* that must generate positive response from others. Satisfaction of these needs requires consistent unconditional acceptance. It is through gratification of these needs that the individual comes to perceive himself as an acceptable, concrete, unique person who is worthy of love.

4. The esteem needs. These are concerned with receiving respect from others for doing; for acting in relationship to the environment in a meaningful and productive manner. These needs motivate the individual to engage in activities which will lead to a positive response from others. To satisfy them the individual must have an opportunity to do something that is perceived as having particular worth by others. His actions must be acknowledged and validated by others.

5. The self-actualization need. This is the need to be oneself. It motivates discovery of one's assets, limitations, and potentials. It leads to the development of self knowledge, acceptance of the total self, and an understanding of one's place in time and space. Activities motivated by this need are self-oriented in the sense that validation from others is not required for satisfaction. There is an alone-ness element in self-actualization motivated behavior even when the activities involve intimate interaction with others.

As previously mentioned, these needs are conceived as being hierarchical. Thus, for example, the need for esteem will not motivate a person's behavior until his need for love has been at least partially satisfied. However, there may be evidence of a higher level need while the individual is primarily concerned with satisfying a lower level need. Thus the need for self-actualization may influence some of the behavior of an individual who is still concerned with gaining respect from others. All of the needs are present in a mature individual. However, such an individual has acquired behavior patterns which readily lead to satisfaction of lower level needs. Satisfaction is automatic and attention may be turned to higher level needs.

Another organizing concept used to describe human behavior is *objects*.[4] Objects are any human being (including the self), nonhuman thing or abstract concept which has the potential for satisfying needs or interfering with need satisfaction. The individual seeks need-satisfying objects and attempts to eliminate objects which interfere with satisfaction. The word "elimination" is used here to describe the act of dealing with or manipulating interfering objects so that they no longer impede need satisfaction.

The ways in which human objects satisfy needs or interfere with satisfaction are probably evident to the reader; they may not, however, be as evident in the case of abstract and nonhuman objects. Abstract objects are values or ideas. They are referred to as abstract because they are intangible and are typically given form through the use of language. Examples of need-satisfying abstract objects are value judgments regarding people, events, or particular actions; concepts such as democracy and peace; religious beliefs; ideas we have about what kinds of persons we are; and particular explanations regarding human behavior. These objects may satisfy different needs. For example, an individual adheres to a particular value system in order to satisfy his need for love, or for esteem, or for self-actualization. Love motivation is typical for the child, esteem for the adolescent and self-actualization for the mature adult. Abstract objects may also interfere with need satisfaction. For example, particular ideas which we hold regarding ourselves are able to interfere with acting in such a way that we are unable to gain esteem from others.

Nonhuman objects may be animate such as dogs, trees or flowers; or inanimate such as water, a favored doll, or a set of crystal goblets. They may be a part of nature or manmade. Examples of nonhuman objects which satisfy the various needs are: food, oxygen, toys, pets, books, a home, tools used in one's work, clothes, materials and tools used in the creative process, mementos of pleasant experiences, and gifts which one has received. Examples of nonhuman objects which may interfere with need satisfaction are dirty dishes, a broken appliance, a book which is difficult to comprehend, an unassembled hi-fi set which does not have adequate directions for construction, or a noisy cement mixer across the street which impedes concentration.

Drive[5] is a concept utilized to explain the organism's active efforts to seek need satisfaction and to deal with factors which interfere with satisfaction. Drives are conceptualized as being quantities of psychic energy which arise from the biological functioning of the organism. This energy is considered to be limited. Thus it must be utilized in an economical manner if one is to satisfy all of his needs. If excessive energy is utilized in satisfying one need, the individual is unable to satisfy other needs. Thus he is less effective in adapting to the environment.

---

[4]S. Freud, *Basic Writings of Sigmund Freud* (New York: Random House, 1938); W. Fairbain *Psychoanalytic Studies of the Personality* (London: Tavistock, 1952).

[5]S. Freud, *The Basic Writings of Sigmund Freud*; M.Schur, *The Id and the Regulatory Principles of Mental Functions* (New York: International Universities Press, 1966).

Two drives have been identified: *libidinal* and *aggressive*. *Libidinal* drive, plus an experienced need, activates the individual to seek objects which will satisfy that need. Objects which are need satisfying are said to be invested with libidinal energy; such an investment helps to ensure continual satisfaction of the need. There is, therefore, a dynamic relationship between an experienced need, libidinal drive and the need-satisfying object. *Aggressive* drive is invested in objects which interfere with need satisfaction. It serves to focus the individual's attention upon the need-inhibiting object and to mobilize and sustain various behaviors which will be effective in eliminating the interfering object. Aggressive drive is here viewed as positive energy which is utilized for creative adaptation to the environment. The investment of libidinal or aggressive drives in an object is referred to as the *formation of an object-relationship*. An object invested with libidinal drive is referred to as a libidinal object whereas an aggressive object is a person, nonhuman thing or abstract concept which has been invested with aggressive energy.

Aggressive objects do not necessarily have belligerent or antagonistic characteristics. That is, the objects in and of themselves are not destructive or injury producing. They are referred to as aggressive objects only because they are invested with an individual's aggressive energy. Elimination of aggressive objects does not mean destruction of or injury to the object. It refers, rather, to removal of the object as an obstacle to need satisfaction. The individual s manipulation of aggressive objects is regulated by abstract libidinal objects (personal value system and/or the norms of his cultural group). Libidinal and aggressive energy may be invested in the same object. For example, to a teenager, a mother may be said to be invested with libidinal energy because of her capacity to gratify the need for love. At the same time, however, she may also act as an obstacle to gaining esteem from his peers. Similarly, different aspects of one's work may gratify one's need for esteem and present obstacles to one's need for self-actualization. This dual investment gives rise to ambivalence or incompatible affects towards a particular object.

When libidinal and aggressive energy is invested in objects we speak of *attached energy*. However, energy may also be *free-floating*; unattached to objects, which in itself creates a need: the need for investment in objects. It is normally utilized to satisfy more mature needs, or it may be expended in action. Energy usually comes to be free-floating through need satisfaction. It appears that a considerable amount of energy is utilized in the process of seeking satisfaction; and during the initial period of forming an object relationship. Once a relationship has been established and does indeed lead to need satisfaction it can be maintained with less energy expansion. Free-floating energy may also be present when no objects are identified as appropriate for need satisfaction or the objects interfering with need satisfaction cannot be identified. This is usually only a temporary situation for the normal individual.

The objects utilized for satisfaction of a particular need often change over a period of time. This seems to be a function of initial satisfaction, idiosyncratic elaboration of needs, normal development and the demands of the social system. Thus the need for love may initially be satisfied by the parents. This need may be gratified later in the developmental process by friends and one's spouse. Objects which satisfy the need for esteem are different during the adolescent period than during the period of initial vocational stabilization. Although bread and butter may satisfy a need for food, steak may well be preferred.

An *appropriate libidinal object* is an object which satisfies a need and is considered acceptable according to the norms of one's cultural group. An *inappropriate libidinal object* is an object invested with libidinal energy but not experienced as need satisfying and/or not considered acceptable by one's cultural group. An example of the former would be the attempt to satisfy the need for love by libidinal investment in a teacher who gives approval only for completion of class assignments. Investment in the concept of race inequality might be an example of the latter. *Appropriate aggressive objects* are the true obstacles to a libidinal object. Objects not causally related to difficulty in obtaining libidinal objects are *inappropriate aggressive objects*.

Substitute libidinal objects are less-preferred objects which nevertheless lead to partial need satisfaction. *Substitute aggressive objects* are not the true obstacles to need satisfaction but their manipulation leads one closer to the libidinal object. For example, an individual may attempt to gratify his need for self-actualization by working for world peace. Because he is not able to identify or manipulate the true obstacles to peace, he may select the war in Vietnam as a substitute aggressive object.

An individual who has mature object relations has selected appropriate and substitute objects which satisfy his needs in such a manner that he is able to attend to his need for self-actualization. His object relations are diffuse; a particular need is satisfied through investment in a number of different objects. Investment in libidinal objects is relatively continual and involves the total as opposed to a part of the object. An individual who has immature object relations (this is typical of a child) has difficulty selecting appropriate and substitute objects. He is primarily concerned with needs other than the need for self-actualization. His libidinal object relations may be discontinuous; he invests in objects only when they are in the process of gratifying a particular need. He may have limited object relations in that one or only a few objects are perceived as need gratifying, or he may invest in only a part of an object rather than in the total object. An example of the latter (part object relations) may be seen in hero worship. Particular qualities of the hero figure are invested with libidinal energy, other more human qualities are ignored and even perhaps unknown.[6]

A moderate amount of need deprivation has a positive function in the development of the individual. Rather than the passive acceptance of satisfaction (which is normal for the infant) the individual is moved to take a more active role in seeking need satisfaction. Moderate deprivation directs the individual's attention toward the identification of the frustrated need, appropriate or substitute libidinal objects, and obstacles to the need-satisfying object. Severe need deprivation, however, is dysfunctional because it inhibits development.

---

[6]R. Spitz, *The First Year of Life* (New York: International Universities Press, 1965).

Deprivation of this type gives rise to negative affect *(see following section)* which is experienced as anger, fear, hostility or frustration. Massive amounts of aggressive energy tend to be mobilized and are often difficult for the individual to control. This mobilized energy interferes with identification of the deprived need, appropriate or substitute libidinal objects, and obstacles to the libidinal object. Inappropriate libidinal and aggressive objects may be selected and lead to inhibited effectiveness in the elimination of appropriate aggressive objects. Object destruction may be a distinct possibility.

Affect[7]   Affect is an inner, subjective experience which may or may not be expressed in motoric or verbal response. It is the feeling tone or emotions one experiences relative to objects. Affect is inherent to the human organism and may be conscious or unconscious. *Positive affect* tends to be associated with libidinal energy and objects whereas *negative affect* tends to be associated with aggressive energy and objects.

Some common types of positive affect are: satisfaction, a feeling of well-being; liking, a pleasant attraction toward objects; and love, an intense, pleasant experience relative to an object. When love is experienced the need-fulfilling aspect of the object becomes secondary. The object comes to be needed because it is loved rather than loved because it is needed. Some common types of negative affect are: fear, which leads to a flight response; rage, which leads to a fight response; anger, rage predominantly expressed in verbal form; and hate, which leads to calculated action.

Depression is experienced as negative affect although it is associated with a libidinal object, usually a loved object, and is the natural and typical response to object loss. Considerable aggressive energy invested in the self often gives rise to behavior which resembles a depressive response. This is in reality a disguised form of rage, anger and/or hate—a pathological condition arising from difficulty in locating the appropriate aggressive objects or the inability to invest aggressive energy in an object because of its association with fear. Fear leads to a flight response, therefore investment of energy and manipulation of the object are impeded.

The affects of guilt and shame are experienced when an individual acts (or thinks) in a manner which is contrary to his libidinal objects. Guilt is experienced in relation to abstract libidinal objects which describe acceptable acts. Shame is experienced in relation to human libidinal objects when an individual acts in a manner which is unacceptable to those objects. The same act may arouse both guilt and shame.

Anxiety is the affectual response which occurs when the individual feels helpless in a situation which he perceives as dangerous. These situations are originally actual events but anxiety is also associated with memory of these events. Mild anxiety is functional in that it motivates an individual to learn to deal with the dangerous event. Severe anxiety is dysfunctional in that it leads to physical avoidance, inattention, and the formation of complexes.

---

[7]S. Arieti, *The Interpsychic Self* (New York: Basic Books, 1967).

The Will[8]   *Will* is the concept used to identify man's capacity to select a specific course of action. Man therefore is not understood as driven by internal forces but as an organism which has the capacity to make choices. The need system of man provides motivation for constructive activity. The will accounts for the selection and investment of libidinal and aggressive energy in appropriate or substitute objects by the individual.

The will has both conscious and unconscious aspects. The unconscious part of the will is manifest only after a choice has been made; the individual recognizes its influence subsequent to the act of willing. Many of our actions are directed by the unconscious will and it is usually only when we are confronted with an unusual problem that the conscious will takes over. Conscious willing involves knowledgeable consideration of the various alternatives and deliberate selection of the preferred course of action. The entire process is attended to by the individual; it is a part of his immediate awareness. The conscious and unconscious aspects of the will are interdependent and influence each other. One cannot always be substituted for the other, however. For example, if one cannot concentrate while reading an interesting book, conscious willing does not increase concentration. The unconscious will is directing the individual's attention to other matters.

The extent to which behavior is willed (as opposed to being predominantly influenced by complexes, drives, or needs) varies from individual to individual. A person dominated by complexes or uncontrolled drives is limited in his capacity to will. Mature conscious willing is characterized by: (1) the ability to evaluate several alternatives, (2) the choice of one alternative, (3) the planning of the chosen alternative, (4) the determination to carry out the chosen and planned alternative, (5) the motor execution of the chosen alternative, and (6) inhibition of nonwilled forms of behavior. The characteristics of unconscious willing are unknown in that we are unable to attend to or observe this type of willing.

Attending and the Formation of Complexes[9]   The concepts *conscious* and *unconscious* have been formulated to classify attention to immediate external and internal stimuli and memory traces. For our purposes these concepts will be subdivided into the following terms: *conscious, preconscious, personal unconscious* and *collective unconscious.* Stimuli or memory traces with which the individual is presently concerned are defined as *conscious content.* Preconscious content is stimuli or memory traces which can be called up or focused upon by the individual without undue effort. Personal unconscious content consists of stimuli or memory traces of the individual's own experiences which are not readily available to the individual. The collective unconscious, identified by Jung, contains archaic memory traces. These memory traces are common to all mankind and are not part of the personal experience of the individual; they

---

[8]L. Farber, *The Ways of the Will* (New York: Basic Books, 1966).

[9]C. Jung, *Modern Man In Search of a Soul.*

are acquired through phylogenetic heredity and are considered to be an expression of brain structure. Collective memory traces are concerned with the questions, experiences, anxieties and suffering of mankind; birth, role transitions, need satisfaction, old age, death, afterlife, hunger, war, disease and cosmic forces, to name just a few. Archaic memory traces are usually referred to as *archetypic patterns.* They emerge into consciousness in symbolic form.

The unconscious is neutral. Like all parts of nature, it can be used to further adaptation or misused to impede that adaptation. The unconscious becomes a destructive force only when complexes are repressed or when the individual does not listen to the guiding information of the collective unconscious. "The unconscious is only overwhelming when it is excluded from life."[10]

Repression is the active process of forgetting, of pushing out of consciousness that which was previously conscious, and occurs when objects or events lead to an intolerable amount of anxiety. This extreme anxiety is usually caused by some type of conflict. The individual's wishes, desires, needs or actions are incompatible with his abstract libidinal objects. If the individual is unable to resolve this conflict, the gestalt of affect, energy, and mental content associated with the conflict-producing situation is repressed. This repressed gestalt is referred to as a *complex.* Aggressive energy is utilized both in the initial process of repression and in keeping the repressed conflict out of consciousness. Complexes become a part of the individual's personal unconscious and, although repressed, continue to interfere with adaptation. They are disruptive and at times even harmful to the individual.

Almost any experience can form the nucleus of a complex. However, there are universal human experiences which often lead to their formation: difficulty in the perception of the self as non-inferior, the differentiation from the non-human environment, the development of trust in one's fellow men, the control of sexual impulses, the emotional separation from one's parents, the establishment of mature love relations, the search for one's place as a contributing member of a social system, the choice of a guiding system of values, the acceptance of physiological and psychological changes which occur as the result of the aging process and the inevitability of death.

There are other experiences, less universal but still common, which also give rise to complexes. In order to differentiate this group from those listed above, they may be described as arising more from a faulty environment than from the necessity of dealing with human existence. Perception of the self as an unacceptable object; lack of gratification of safety, love, and esteem needs; investment of aggressive energy in the self; free-floating psychic energy; and threatened emergence of unconscious content are examples of such complexes.

Complexes express themselves in a number of ways. The overt expression of complexes is often referred to as *symptoms.* Symptoms bear some relation to that which is contained in the complex and the abstract libidinal objects which led to repression of the complex. Careful study of the individual's behavior,

---

[10]Carl Jung, *Modern Man in Search of a Soul*, p. 17.

therefore, allows one to identify the nature of the complex. Symptoms also assist in keeping the complex out of consciousness and, to some degree, to gratify repressed needs. There appear to be certain inherent human responses which occur when complexes are repressed and it is this phenomenon which allows us to interpret the meaning of an individual's symptoms. The following discussion speaks to the process of these inherent responses, not to the content. To clarify, by an example, repression is an inherent response to severe anxiety (process), that which is repressed is the content. The content is specific to the complex. Some common responses are:

1. Denial: statement that the anxiety-provoking situation never took place.

2. Reaction formation: thoughts and actions which are the direct opposite of thoughts and desired actions contained in the complex.

3. Transference: response to objects in a manner similar to the way in which the individual responded to complex-related objects in the past.

4. Projection: attributing feelings and responses which are part of the complex to others.

5. Rationalization: an illogical explanation for behavior which is related to the complex.

6. Undoing: repetitive thoughts or actions which are quasi-symbolic of the complex and an attempt to cancel out the complex.

7. Displacement: a response which is part of the complex emitted toward an object other than the appropriate object.

8. Regression: responses which are characteristic of the developmental period during which the complex was originally repressed.

These various responses may be identified by their exaggerated, persistent, time-consuming, "unreal" qualities.[11]

The unconscious is phylogenetically and ontogentically older than the conscious. Consciousness develops out of unconsciousness, and is, to some extent, dependent upon maturation of the nervous system. It is important for the individual to learn to attend to stimuli, to use language as the primary vehicle for thought and communication, and to solve problems through conscious willing. The maturing individual must develop his consciousness; in so doing he acquires the ability to gratify his own needs and in turn, the needs of others. The development of consciousness, however, takes place at the expense of the unconscious. The unconscious, therefore, atrophies to a certain extent and

---

[11]D. Ford and H. Urban, *Systems of Psychotherapy.*

the individual loses contact with the guiding archetypes of his collective unconscious. This imbalance between the unconscious and conscious is not conducive to the satisfaction of the need for self-actualization. Once the adult has found objects which will satisfy his need for esteem it is necessary for him to become reacquainted with his unconscious if need satisfaction is to continue.

The individual can engage in satisfying his need for self-actualization only if he understands or is aware of his total self, for the total self is made up of all the responses and affect of which man is capable. The inherent responses and affect of mankind are neutral. The time and place of their manifestation is the only determinate of their worth. Thus hate or the capacity to kill another person are not inherently evil — at times they serve a very useful function. The individual is typically unaware of several of the aspects of the self: the "shadow side," one's *animus* or *anima*, one's relation to the nonhuman environment; less well developed psychological functions are also often unrecognized.[12]

The *shadow side* refers to all those human responses and affects which the individual judges as base or unworthy of himself. Through accepting and understanding this aspect of the self the individual frees aggressive energy which has been utilized to suppress these responses and feelings. With recognition of aspects of his shadow side the individual is able to control them — acceptance of his shadow side gives the individual substance and mass.

Animus refers to the masculine element in the female; *anima* to the feminine element in the male. Opposite-sex characteristics are often concealed from the conscious self, particularly during childhood, adolescence, and young adulthood when the individual is striving for sexual identity. However, once this identity is relatively self-established, the animus and anima seek recognition and expression. Such expression allows the individual to be a total sexual object. False attitudes toward the opposite sex, concerns about homosexuality or loss of sexual identity, and fears of castration or of being castrating are finally laid to rest.

Relation to the nonhuman environment is inhibited during the development of consciousness. In order for consciousness to emerge, the individual must differentiate himself from the nonhuman environment — he must experience his human-ness. Once the individual has established human-ness, however, it can not be maintained unless it is reaffirmed through acceptance of the nonhuman aspect of the self. Mature relation to the nonhuman environment is characterized by an affectual understanding of the commonality of atomic structure and chemical compounds we share with our inanimate environment, the cell structures and processes we share with our plant environment, and the anatomical, physiological, and psychological processes we share with our animal environment. The recapitulation of phylogeny in ontogeny; the role of the nonhuman environment in sustaining physical life, promoting physical maturation, psychosocial development, and facilitating new learning; and the functions of the nonhuman environment in enhancing self-actualization, providing relief from the human environment and existential alone-ness and increasing one's awareness

---

[12]C. Jung, *Man and His Symbols.*

of the individual's place in the cosmos — all are relationships which will be recognized by the mature individual. Mature relatedness to the nonhuman environment is also characterized by the acceptance and tolerance of two human conflicts; the desire to be nonhuman versus fear of regression to the nonhuman level and the desire for one-ness with the universe versus the desire for human-ness and individuality.[13]

Psychological functions are the various ways in which man apprehends and adjusts to the world. Four different functions have been identified: *thinking* and *feeling* (the rational functions), *sensation* and *intuition* (the perceiving functions). *Thinking* consists of apprehension and adjustment through logical, conscious, cognitive processes directed towards reaching a specific conclusion. Emphasis is placed upon objectivity and ordering of perceived data. *Feeling* consists of apprehension and adjustment through evaluation of pleasant-unpleasant, like-dislike, acceptance-rejection, etc. — the individual may say, "I feel this is a good thing to do" without making any attempt to analyze why. There is a value judgment attached to events and objects. Abstract libidinal objects play a significant role in this function, but the individual finds it very difficult to state specific reasons for his value judgments. *Sensation* refers to apprehension and adjustment through the sensory processes — there is minimal concern with reaching a conclusion or assigning value judgments and exact details are super-ordinate to the general context. The individual is often acutely aware of physical needs and enjoyment of sensual experiences. *Intuition* consists of apprehension and adjustment through identification of the possibilities or inherent potential of objects and events. The perceiving function is focused less on detail than on the total gestalt. The individual often acts on the basis of premonitions and tends to be more in contact with his unconscious.

In the development of consciousness, one psychological function comes to be superior to the others. The rational or perceiving function, opposite to the superior function, is usually poorly developed and referred to as the *inferior function*. The other functions, although better developed than the inferior function, are less well developed than the superior function. In order to satisfy the need for self-actualization, the individual must discover, develop, and learn to tolerate his inferior functions. In so doing the parts and potentialities of the self move in the direction of wholeness.

The unknown aspects of the self form complexes similar to the repressed complexes discussed above. They differ from repressed complexes only in the sense that these unknown aspects of the self have never become a part of consciousness. They have not, therefore, been repressed. However, agressive energy is utilized to hold these complexes at the level of personal unconscious.

Complexes are in one sense predetermined — although they are personal and specific to the individual, they also have archetypic qualities. All men have been confronted with the various problems which give rise to complexes. The process of dealing with these problems is a part of our phylogenetic past and as such is

---

13Harold Searles, *The Nonhuman Environment.*

recorded in archaic memory traces. There is thus an intimate relationship between archetypic symbols and complexes. Many archetypes speak specifically to and are symbolic of the common events, objects and aspects of the self which have caused wonder, suffering and growth since the beginning of life.

The relationship between the conscious and the collective unconscious is compensatory. The symbols produced from the collective unconscious give us information about complexes and attempt to bring us to an awareness and acceptance of the total self. They give us information about self-regulation which can lead to self-expansion. Through exploration and understanding of the personal unconscious and respect for and attention to the collective unconscious we free ourselves from their domination. This is the process of *individuation*. The gravitational center of the self reaches a mid-point between the conscious and unconscious — the safest and really the only foundation for engaging in self-actualization need-fulfillment. The process of individuation does not, however, necessarily take a smooth, affectually comfortable course. Consciousness, phylogenetically and ontogenetically more recently developed than the unconscious, is liable and vulnerable to fragmentation — it is fragile and must be cared for like any fragile object. It is possible for the emergence of content from the unconscious to have a disintegrating effect on consciousness, leading to disorientation, excessive free-floating energy, outbursts of affect and thoroughly disagreeable moods. It is obvious,therefore, that the flow from the unconscious must be compatible with the capacity of consciousness to deal with and assimilate unconscious content. The unity of consciousness must be protected and supported.

Cognition[14]   The process of perceiving, representing and organizing stimuli is referred to as *cognition*. It may be conscious or unconscious — the individual need not be consciously aware of stimuli in order for it to be perceived. Archaic memory traces, for example, are not perceived; they are, according to Jung, considered to be an inherent part of the organism. Stimuli tend to be arranged in units (as opposed to isolated elements), the sizes of which appear to vary.

Representation is the manner in which perceptions are stored in memory. Perceptions are stored as *exocepts, images, endocepts* and *concepts. Exocept representation* is the term for memory of stimuli as action response to the stimuli or action directed toward the stimuli, and is reflected through motor behavior. Exocept representation can be illustrated by the definition of the length of an object through the use of gestures, memory of the weight of an object by taking the appropriate posture and exerting a specific amount of physical energy to move the object, and by memory of the movements necessary to hit a tennis ball accurately.

Image representation is the memory of stimuli in terms of an internal, pictorial, quasi-reproduction. The modifier *quasi* is used to indicate that the image is not usually an exact reproduction of the stimuli event or object.

---

[14]S. Arieti, *The Intrapsychic Self.*

Reproduction tends to be partial; some elements will not be included in the image. The expression, "I can see it in my mind's eye," describes perceptions remembered in the form of images. Whereas perceptions stored as exocepts are connected to specific stimuli experiences, images are able to be attended to without the presence of the corresponding stimuli.

Endocept representation is the memory of perceptions in terms of a felt experience. It is not affect (such as pleasure or guilt), though affect is associated with an endocept as it is with all representations. Many persons experience endocepts in terms of bodily sensations. The expressions, "I have a gut feeling", or "I feel it in my bones," are often used to describe endocepts. Perceptions stored as endocepts are extremely difficult to communicate to others. Often the individual attempts to translate endocepts into images or verbal concepts which can then be communicated by some art form or the spoken word. However, endocepts invariably lose something in translation. The communicator feels the loss and may even state, "It is something like this but I haven't said it (or drawn it) exactly right." (The ability to respond in an empathetic manner, for instance, is based upon endocept representations.)

Concept representation is the memory of perceptions in terms of words or some other notational system (numbers and musical notes, for instance). Although notational systems are important in studying some phenomena they do not play a significant role in the cognitive processes of most persons; our discussion, therefore, will focus only on concepts as words. Concept representation may be divided into two sub-types: *denotative* and *connotative*. Denotative concepts are words which are treated as if they only stand for or name objects. The word is perceived as part of the object or equivalent to it. Thinking based upon denotative concepts is described as being "concrete.' *Connotative concepts* are words which are treated as a classification of phenomena which have some common characteristics. Words are not seen as attached to particular objects but rather as a method of talking about objects and events. Thinking based upon connotative concepts is described as being "abstract" — The person who uses concepts in a denotative manner will interpret "A bird in the hand is worth two in the bush." as referring to the act of hunting birds; while the person who uses concepts in a connotative manner will interpret the analogy as making reference to the fact that available objects are more useful than potentially available ones.

The *organization* of represented stimuli is the process of associating, combining, or manipulating representations. When this process is conscious it is commonly referred to as thinking. The organizational aspect of cognition may, however, also be unconscious. Representations may be organized in three different ways, termed the *primary*, *secondary* and *tertiary* processes.[15]

Primary process is characterized by disregard for formal logic; temporal and spatial relationships are confused, one representation may fuse into others (condensation), affect usually associated with one representation may become

---

[15]S. Arieti, *The Intrapsychic Self*; D. Ford and H. Urban. *Systems of Psychotherapy*

associated with another and/or one representation may come to stand for another (displacement), confusion regarding what is external and internal relative to the self, all events may be perceived as determined by the will of man or anthropomorphized forces (teleologic causality); and thinking cannot be reflected upon after it has occurred. Primary process usually involves the organization of exocepts, images, endocepts and denotative concepts. One representation often comes to stand for a whole aggregate of representations which have been grouped in some sort of a loose assemblage. This process is sometimes referred to as *primary* or *paleologic aggregation.* Unconscious content, dreams and fantasies are usually organized by a method of primary process.

Secondary process is characterized by adherence to the rules of formal logic, attention to temporal and spatial relationships, lack of condensation and displacement, knowledge regarding what is internal and external relative to the self, reflectivity, and a search for the antecedent, physical cause of an effect (deterministic causality). Secondary process usually involves the organization of connotative concepts (although denotative concepts and images are occasionally organized in this manner as well). Secondary process is predominant in the organization of conscious and preconscious content. It is a less stable process and is liable to disruption by experiences which bring about strong affect, while primary process, ontogenetically more fundamental, emerges as a consequence of uncontrolled affect.

Tertiary process involves a combination of primary and secondary process organization. Mental content is subjected to primary process organization and becomes, in a sense, recombined or restructured. The newly-organized content is then subjected to validation by secondary process organization. This is believed to be the essence of the creative process, here defined as a process leading to an end product which transcends the common responses of the individual's cultural group and "brings about a desirable enlargement of human experience."[16] It involves a temporary freedom from usual and ordinary secondary process organization. The creative product must, however, be compatible with secondary process — if it is not, the product is bizarre, not creative. Creativity, as here defined, is therefore relatively rare. Exploration of symbols is in many ways similar to tertiary process; it is not, however, a creative process as creativity is defined above. It enlarges the individual's experiences as opposed to human experience and connects the individual to the human experience.

The function of cognition is to secure adequate need satisfaction within the normative limits of the cultural group. It serves to organize internal and external stimuli and memory traces; to give them form, meaning, and expression. Secondary process, conscious thought, guides the willing individual in such a way that he is able to control behavior and affect; to select appropriate or substitute libidinal and aggressive objects; to manipulate aggressive objects. He is able to invest free-floating energy; to delay need satisfaction; and to tolerate some degree of need deprivation. This type of thought is also used to filter

---

[16]S. Arieti, *The Intrapsychic Self*, p. 327.

circumstances and alternative kinds of behavior prior to the selection of a particular act. The performance selected is one which the individual believes will lead to a desired consequence. This reflection upon situation prior to action is often referred to as *reality testing.*

Less is known about the functions of primary process cognition. It is, as previously mentioned, important to the creative process and it also enables us to study and interpret symbols formed in the personal and collective unconscious. Such study ultimately enhances the individual's opportunity to engage in meeting the self-actualization need by providing information about the self. One is unable to be oneself until one knows what the self is.

Symbolism   A *symbol* is an action, object, image or word which has special complexities of meanings in addition to its conventional and obvious meaning. It implies something vague, unknown, or hidden and has aspects which can never be fully defined or explained. Human, nonhuman and abstract objects, events, affect, and personal and archaic memory traces, may give rise to symbols. The term *referent* identifies that which is symbolized.[17] Symbols may be differentiated from signs. A sign is an action, object, image or word which stands for another action, object, image or word. A sign can be easily explained and understood; it has no hidden or unknowable aspects and is directly attached or connected to that which it represents. Signs are usually shared by a cultural group, although an individual within that group may have personal signs which are not shared with others and which remain private to that individual. Such signs are referred to as *paleosymbols*, and are not useful for shared communication.

Because symbols are affective in nature, response to symbols is typically emotional as well as cognitive. Libidinal as well as aggressive energy may be in-
                        /mbol. Affect is rarely associated with signs, nor are they usually invested with psychic energy.

Symbols are perhaps best understood by considering three interrelated aspects; *representation*, *form*, and *content*. The *representational* aspect of a symbol is the way in which a symbol is experienced or produced. Symbols may be represented as exocepts, images, endocepts, concepts or concrete objects. Exocept symbols are expressed through the actions of the symbol producer; they are seen in their purest form in the dance. Exocept representation is the most primitive type of representation ontogenetically and, perhaps by extension, phylogenetically. It has been suggested that exocept symbols present the deepest layers of the unconscious and that they are the least disguised of all symbols. Exocept symbols are sometimes combined with and thus confused with image symbols. For example, there is sometimes a tendency to overlook the exoceptual aspect of dreams. The movement in a dream may not be explored. More attention is given to the referent of the dream figure itself than to the referent of what the dream figure is doing. Similarly, in doodling, it is often the movement itself which is significant, not what is produced. Both aspects, however, usually

---

[17]Carl Jung, *Man and His Symbols.*

complement each other. Both aspects must be explored in order to gather valuable information.

Image symbols are also phylogenetically and ontogenetically primitive. Archetypes usually appear as image symbols, though they do have many exocept elements as well. Dreams, a universal and constant source of information from the unconscious, contain numerous image symbols. Image symbols also occur in the production of visual arts and in fantasies.

Endocept symbols are internal experiences which must be translated into another type of representation to be communicated. Images and concepts are often used as vehicles for the communication of endocept symbols, although there is always something lost in the process. Denotative and connotative concept symbols are the least primitive type of symbol and are probably fairly rare. Words are often used to label image symbols and, by association, the word itself may become a symbol. However, words tend to be signs of symbols more often than symbols in and of themselves.

Concrete object symbols are people or things which take on or are invested with symbolic meaning. This type of representation differs from the above-mentioned types of representation in a subtle way. It can be differentiated from an image symbol which comes to consciousness in some specific form (for example, a dream image of a bird in flight). Observation of a bird in flight may, in turn, be perceived as a symbol by a given individual. This is concrete object representation. In observing the bird the individual may experience a vague but powerful affective response and a stirring of undefined unconscious content. It is this experience which would indicate that observation of the bird in flight had special symbolic meaning to the individual. In order to explain this phenomena we may say that unconscious content of a specific type is "ripe for emergence." It becomes manifest through its attachment to a concrete object.

The two other elements of a symbol are *form* and *content*. *Form* refers to the manifest structure of symbolic representation. For example, a symbol might be represented as an image. The form of the image might be a wheel, a ferocious animal, a color, or water. The form of a symbol often has many parts. The *content* of a symbol is concerned with the referent or referents.

Form and content may be archetypic, cultural and/or idiosyncratic.[18] An archetype consists of represented archaic memory traces. The content of an archetypic symbol concerns the universal questions, anxieties, experiences, and suffering of mankind. The representation of an archetypic symbol tends to be exocept, images and concrete objects; common forms are natural nonhuman objects, human objects and geometric shapes. Both the content of the memory traces and the tendency to organize these memory traces in specific forms are inherited from our phylogenetic past. As in all symbolic processes, a particular content may be symbolized in a number of different forms and a given form may symbolize many different referents. The following examples are by no means exhaustive but are presented to give the reader some idea of what is

---

[18]J. Mazer et al., *Exploring How a Think Feels* .

meant by an archetypic symbol.[19] The first examples specify content followed by common forms utilized to symbolize this content:

1. that which is unusually potent, particularly in relation to healing and fertility: bull, ass, pomegranate, lightning, horses, hoofs, menstrual fluid, the dance, phallic-shaped objects and stones
2. guide to lead out of confusion: wise man, savior, redeemer
3. perfect being: an object rounded on all sides, unity of the two sexes, union of opposites
4. immortality: fruit, embryo, child, living body, stones, gems
5. birth-death-rebirth cycle: destruction of objects, dismemberment, cannibalism
6. feminine side of men (anima): anything which is characterized as having feminine qualities (mother, flower, butterfly, etc.), a beautiful young girl, an old woman, half-human object, snake, tail of fish
7. masculine side of woman (animus): anything which is characterized as having masculine qualities, a strong young man, a crippled man
8. evil or the devil: dragon, night raven, roots, body, black eagle, fire, darkness
9. birth: water, egg
10. the unconscious: forest, deep water, sea, trees and fish (content of the unconscious), plants, darkness, below, left, snake (the dual nature of the unconscious; blind instinctuality and wisdom)
11. life or soul: anything mobile, colored or iridescent, butterfly, mind, breath, moving air, fire, flame, shadow, blood
12. consciousness: light, head, angle, death of snake (overcoming of the unconscious)
13. inferior functions: clown, fool, servant, member of minority group

The following examples specify forms followed by common content which is symbolized by those forms:

1. Mother: place of origin; that which passively creates, substance and matter; lower body; womb; vegetative functions; unconscious; that which carries, nurtures, embraces, protects; emotional being
2. Horse: subhuman animal side, drives, power, locomotion, mother (as beast of burden), sorcery, magic, that which heralds death (black horse)
3. Mandala forms (anything which has a circle-like form, often has a tendency toward quaternary division): oneness, unity, devotion to life (what is or that which is desired)
4. Dragon or serpent: initial state of unconscious (because it "dwells in caverns and dark places"), revelation

---

[19]More complete discussions of the subject can be found in C. Jung, *Modern Man in Search of a Soul, Man and His Symbols, Alchemical Studies*; E. Kris, *Psychoanalytic Exploration in Art* (New York: International Universities Press, 1952); and in J. Campbell, *The Mask of God: Primitive Mythology* (New York: Viking Press, 1959).

5. Metals: inner man, spiritual growth, highest illumination
6. Tree: historical view of the developing self; passive, vegetative principle; earthbound; the body; maternal (contact with earth); life (flowers and leaves on trees); arrested growth and fear of future (stunted tree); growth; protection and shelter; nourishment; solidarity and permanence; old age; death and rebirth.
7. Snake: active, animal principle; emotionality, possession of a soul; (in unison with tree) animation of the body and materialization of the soul
8. Birds: spirits, thoughts
9. Cross: wholeness, becoming whole, healing
10. Helpful persons: adequate ways of dealing with unconscious content or present life situation

Archetypical content remains the same but it may take endlessly different forms. The forms which an archetype takes are often influenced by the culture of the individual; one may find the content of potency symbolized in our culture in the form of a space module or a huge piece of machinery. Similarly, archetypical content may take a form which is idiosyncratic to the individual. The form of a symbol is archetypic if it can be shown to exist with the same meaning in the records of numerous cultural groups which have been distant in time and space. It need not have an archetypic form to be an archetypic symbol, however; the richness and vitality of archetypic symbols are expressed in their compounded meaning and changing form.

The examples of archetypic forms and contents listed above have been identified through a study of mythology, alchemy, fairy tales, art and language. Some relationships have recently been found between various aspects of the content, form, and process of art productions and psychological functions, unconscious content, affect, use of psychic energy, need states, etc. In studying these relationships it is difficult to determine whether we are seeing the result of a symbolic or sign process. It is also difficult to determine whether the symbols (if they are symbols) are archetypic or cultural. Much remains unknown about these relationships. Some examples of these findings are listed below.[20]

1. Symmetry
   a. lack of: overwhelmed by unconscious content, fear of being overwhelmed by unconscious content
   b. slight loss of: no major unconscious complexes
   c. well balanced: self-directed, adaptive
   d. bilaterality stressed: rigidity and compulsivity

---

[20]Complete discussions of the subject may be found in E. Hammer, *The Clinical Application of Projective Drawings* (Chicago: Charles C. Thomas, 1958); L. Abt and L. Bellak, *Projective Psychology* (New York: Grove Press, Inc., 1950); E. Kris, *Psychoanalytic Exploration in Art*; M. Naumburg, *Schizophrenic Art: Its Meaning in Psychotherapy* (New York: Grune and Stratton, Inc., 1950) and *Psychoneurotic Art: Its Function in Psychotherapy* (New York: Grune and Stratton, Inc., 1953).

2. Placement
   a. centered: preoccupied with self (if extreme), self directed (if not extreme)
   b. off center: unmet love and acceptance needs
   c. right of center: well-controlled drives
   d. left of center: uncontrolled drives
   e. below center: experiences the self as inadequate, preoccupied with object loss, aggressive energy turned toward the self, denotative concept representation
   f. above center: distant from people, striving for unattainable goals, seeks need satisfaction in fantasy
   g. clinging to edge of paper: seeking support, experiences the self as inadequate.

3. Size
   a. small in relation to whole: experiences the self as inadequate, experiences self as being overwhelmed by external environment, overly dependent on others for need satisfaction
   b. large in relation to whole: difficulty in controlling drives, compensation for experiencing the self as inadequate, overwhelmed by affect

4. Direction of Lines
   a. horizontal: femininity, over-involvement in fantasy, fear of external environment
   b. vertical: masculinity, self assertive
   c. continual change of direction: unfulfilled safety needs

5. Pressure
   a. heavy: psychic energy available for acting on the environment, self assertive
   b. light: little psychic energy available for acting upon the environment, energy tied up in unconscious complexes
   c. variation: flexible and adaptive, unstable

6. Shape of Strokes
   a. angular or jagged: free floating aggressive energy
   b. long: controlled use of drives
   c. short: difficulty in controlling drives
   d. straight: assertive, avoids close interpersonal relations, deals with environment realistically
   e. broken, sketchy: insecurity, high anxiety
   f. thin: fear of loss of control
   g. erasures: dissatisfaction with the self, experience of uncertainty
   h. free and rhythmic: unrestructured
   i. circular: femininity, tendency to withdraw, difficulty in satisfying need for love and acceptance

j. clear and sharp: decisive
k. squares, rectangular and verticals assertive, self-reliant
l. diagonals: difficulty in satisfying need for love and acceptance

7. Movement
   a. considerable: restless, seeking of need satisfaction; creativity, overwhelmed by complexes
   b. minimal: experience of object loss, aggression turned toward self
   c. ·rigidity: energy directed toward maintaining complexes at the unconscious level, attempting to control external environment
   d. mechanical: experience of the self as nonhuman, depersonalization
   e. even rhythm: masculine
   f. odd rhythm: feminine

8. Color
   a. warm: expression of satisfactory investment of libidinal drive; expression of difficulty in locating or manipulating aggressive objects, feeling function
   b. cool: effort to control drives, thinking function
   c. light, watery: fear of self revelation
   d. bright: self assurance
   e. dark: experience of object loss, aggressive energy turned toward self, regression to primitive levels of functioning
   f. black and brown: complex related to anal control, constricted personality
   g. red: self centered, feeling and intuitive functions
   h. blue: control, self-restrained
   i. yellow: difficulty in satisfying love and acceptance needs, feeling and intuitive functions
   j. red and yellow: spontaneous in environmental interactions
   k. orange: active adaptation to environment
   l. green: difficulty in controlling aggressive drives
   m. purple: projection of negative affect and aggressive drive
   n. unharmonious warm colors: difficulty in investment of libidinal energy
   o. too much: inadequate need satisfaction, difficulty in controlling drives
   p. too little: difficulty in forming meaningful relationship with others, self-constricted

9. Mode of Handling Materials
   a. smearing: complex related to anal control
   b. scribbling: fearful of unconscious content, complexes related to infantile period
   c. scrubbing, pushing, pulling, scratching, slapping, picking: difficulty in controlling aggressive drive or manipulating aggressive objects
   d. patting, stroking: complex related to oral period, investment of libidinal energy in object

10. Content
   a. inadequate: experience of object loss, aggressive drive turned toward self, fear of unconscious content
   b. excessive: attempting to keep complexes unconscious through rigid control of the self, difficulty in entering meaningful relationships with others
   c. organization chaotic: overwhelmed by unconscious content
   d. flowers and fruit: feminine
   e. boats: feminine, womb, journey
   f. manufactured objects: masculinity, over-reliance upon nonhuman environment
   g. diagrams, maps, plans: projection of negative affect or aggressive drive, inadequate fulfillment of safety needs
   h. water, egg, fish: fertility, birth, renewal
   i. personification of nonhuman objects: projection of anxiety provoking unconscious content
   j. objects in series: number of persons in family (arrangement indicative of relationships)

11. Person
   a. head: related to thinking function, intellectual aspirations, consciousness, fantasies
   b. hair: related to libidinal investment in the self
   c. teeth: related to aggressive drive
   d. mouth: related to satisfaction of love and acceptance needs
   e. eyes: related to projection of affect and aggressive drive, affect of shame and guilt
   f. chin: related to strength and determination
   g. neck: related to conscious control versus unconscious content, thinking versus feeling functions, sensation versus intuitive functions, intellectual endeavors versus sensuous pleasures
   h. arms and hands: related to mode of dealing with aggressive objects
   i. legs and feet: related to safety needs, aggressive energy turned toward self, discouragement
   j. internal anatomy shown: overwhelmed by unconscious content

12. House
   a. roof: related to conscious mental content, fantasy, intellectual operations
   b. walls: related to individual's perceived ability to satisfy needs and deal with unconscious content
   c. doors and windows: related to contact with environment
   d. chimney: related to potency
   e. smoke: conflict in home, threat of being overwhelmed by unconscious content

13. Trees
   a. trunk: related to perceived ability to cope with internal and external environment

b. branches: related to ability to derive satisfaction from the environment
c. organization of whole: related to intrapsychic balance, integration of aspects of the self
d. age: related to desired or perceived age of the self
e. roots: related to security needs, unconscious content
f. degree of life: related to hope, future anticipated

The content of cultural symbols is related to the values, norms, preoccupations, and concerns of a particular cultural group. Although content is not universal, it may not be unique to a given culture, either. Some examples of common content which is expressed in symbols in our culture are the ideal of democratic interaction, the value of work, integration of minority groups, the function of religion, drugs, and the sharing of power. The representation of cultural symbols tends to be exocept, image, concept, and concrete objects. Common forms are nonhuman objects which are relatively specific to the culture, gestures, words, and specific people. Examples of symbolic forms found in our culture are: the phrases "black power," "death of God" and "turn on"; people such as John Kennedy, the astronauts, McCarthy, and Goldwater; nonhuman objects such as the computer, automobiles, the American flag, draft cards, and the cross; and gestures such as the raised, clenched first and formation of a V with the index and third finger. Cultural symbols tend to be changeable in both form and content, especially in cultural groups which are experiencing rapid alteration. There is a learned quality to cultural symbols not found with archetypic and idiosyncratic symbols. The enculturation process itself, whether it be the enculturation of a child or an adult who is moving into a new cultural group, is characterized in part by gaining some understanding of cultural symbols. As with all symbols, however, the individual is never able to fully define or explain a cultural symbol.

The content of idiosyncratic symbols is concerned with the unique experience of the individual; his view of his own world, self identification and with the objects which he has invested with libidinal and aggressive energy; and with his mental content. For example, an individual's idiosyncratic symbols might deal with such content as lack of adequate nurture during infancy, the realization of an unknown ability, the conception of his first child, and the need to withdraw libidinal energy from a loved object. Idiosyncratic symbols may be represented in any of the identified ways. The form of an idiosyncratic symbol varies tremendously. It may be a recurring doodle, a gesture, a nonhuman object (often an object invested with considerable libidinal energy for a reason which is unknown to the individual), a vague somatic-cognitive experience, a particular phrase or a mental image. The form of a symbol is considered to be idiosyncratic if it expresses content in a manner different from known archetypical or cultural forms. An individual is often unaware of his idiosyncratic symbols both in relation to form and content. Thus they tend to be unshared.

There is a considerable interrelationship between the three different aspects of symbols. In most cases, a symbol produced by a given individual contains archetypical, cultural and idiosyncratic content; its form will also have archetypic, cultural and idiosyncratic elements. For example, a young woman had a sudden mental image of three rectangular, light reflective pillars of uneven height. This symbol was explored and interpreted in the following manner:

Archetypic content: potency, animus, life, consciousness
Cultural content: emphasis upon logical thinking
Idiosyncratic content: the ability to use connotative concepts
Archetypic form: metal, three
Cultural form: I-beams used in building construction
Idiosyncratic form: not a typical archetypic or cultural form, probably related to a childhood fantasy of "having a hard, metal core."

This is, of course, an incomplete interpretation—as are all interpretations of symbols. They can never be completely known. In addition, a descriptive interpretation such as this does not express the affect attached to or libidinal energy invested in the symbol.

The formulation of symbols is a process which takes place within the individual. It appears to be motivated by man's inherent tendency to classify or categorize mental content. Perceptions are combined and recombined in a number of ways and are rarely arranged in isolated units. Perceptions represented as exocepts, images, endocepts and denotative concepts are the raw data for symbol formation. Perceptions represented as connotative concepts may also be utilized in symbol formation; but it appears that this occurs only when the perceptions come to be represented in another manner. They must be translated into another form of representation. Formulation of symbols is an unconscious process. It can not be controlled by the individual nor can the individual deliberately formulate a symbol. Symbols appear to be formulated through primary process organization of represented perceptions and come into being through the process of primary aggregation. The symbol is one representation which stands for a number of representations which have been grouped in some sort of loose assemblage. The grouping process seems to be based upon some similarity of the represented perceptions. There may be similarity in time or place of perception, function, associated affect, type of energy invested, or physical property. This grouping, based upon similarity, accounts for the fact that a symbol has some common characteristic which it shares with its referents. This factor also accounts for the multiple meaning of a particular symbol form. The form itself has many elements, each of which can become grouped with perceptions, which have similar elements. It is unknown why a particular representation comes to stand for the whole aggregate.

As previously mentioned, the symbols formulated by an individual often are a combination of archetypic, cultural and idiosyncratic content and form. The combination resulting from the interrelationship of man as a unique object, a cultural being and a given moment in phylogenetic development. The individual's stored perceptions are a result of his uniqueness, his membership in a cultural group and inheritance. Perceptions specific to each of these aspects of the individual are not separated; they become intertwined and overlapping.

Symbol formation, then, is influenced by personal experiences; human, non-human and abstract objects and language relatively unique to one's cultural group; inherited memory traces, and the inherent tendency to represent these memory traces in particular forms.

Symbols are formulated by individuals and not by collective groups; cultural and archetypic symbols exist as definable entities because the experiences (and thus the perceptions) of mankind and the members of a cultural group have many common elements. When the individual or a collective group recognizes the referent, responds affectively, and invests energy in a symbol formulated by another individual, it appears that the overt form of the symbol communicates with a primary aggregate which already exists within the individual or the individuals of the collectivity. Emotional response to archetypic symbols occurs in a similar manner. Archetypic forms and content are an inherent part of the individual; response is to an existing but unconscious part of the self.

One of the major functions of symbols is to facilitate communication between the unconscious and the conscious. Unconscious content can be expressed only in symbolic forms. Conversely, the unconscious can be reached only through symbols.[21] Symbols communicate personal and archaic memories to the conscious mind so that such content can be translated into connotative and denotative concepts—the language of consciousness. Thus, this previously unconscious content can be assimilated with conscious content. There is a widening or expansion of the self and at the same time, an integration of the various aspects of the self. Because archetypic symbols bring about awareness of content and forms which are common to all men, the individual experiences his relation to past and future man. A lessening of the isolation which is an inherent part of consciousness takes place. Exploration of symbols produced by the self frees energy which was utilized to maintain content in the unconscious. Exploration also frees some energy invested in the symbol and its referents. There is, therefore, more libidinal and aggressive energy available for need satisfaction. The production of symbols is an attempt to bring a balance between the conscious and unconscious.

Another function of symbols is to guide the willing individual; they present a more objective view of the individual's current situation.[22] Many experiences are not stored in the conscious mind and thus consciousness tends to be less knowledgeable and subjective. Symbols provide information about the current deficiencies or one-sideness of the personality. They warn of danger if the individual does not take corrective action. Symbols may foreshadow future events. The historical precipitating factors which lead to these events may be stored only as unconscious content. A symbol which foreshadows an event is communicating information which the conscious mind has failed to perceive or grasp. It follows that symbols may forecast an event—often a transitional event, in that the event itself will cause a profound change in the individual's situation.

---

[21] J. Mazer, et al., *Exploring How a Think Feels.*
[22] C. Jung, *Modern Man in Search of a Soul.*

Symbols may suggest a specific cause of action which would be beneficial for the individual or give information about the consequences of a planned action.

Another function of symbols is to allow the individual to experience symbolically that which can not be experienced in reality, because of the absence of required objects or personal and cultural taboos. In this situation, a symbolic act or object may be utilized to allow for the need-fulfilling experience. Symbolic experiences are frequently related to fulfillment of sexual needs and the need for love.[23] Symptoms which arise from repressed complexes are often an attempt to experience, in a symbolic manner, that which was forbidden in reality. Substitute libidinal objects may be symbolic of the desired libidinal object. All substitute objects are not, however, symbolic.

Symbols are utilized by cultural groups in two ways; first, as a means of communication and, secondly, as a tool for dealing with the unknown. As a method of communication, symbols are a type of shorthand which facilitate the communication process. They also allow individuals to express, at least in part, that which is essentially inexpressible. As a tool for dealing with the unknown, symbols are used to control anxiety; affect that arises in man's contact with the unknown, since unknown is usually perceived as having a destructive force which must be bound and placated. Symbolic acts, objects and words are used for this purpose. Man perceives himself as having some control over the unknown through the use of symbols; they help to satisfy the need for safety and are usually invested with a considerable amount of libidinal energy. The symbols which a cultural group uses for communication and control of the unknown help to consolidate the identity of the group and contributes to maintaining its cohesiveness.

FUNCTION-DYSFUNCTION CONTINUUMS

An individual is said to be in a state of dysfunction when one or more complexes are interfering with his ability to seek and obtain need gratification. Some common complexes are listed below together with various behaviors and symbols which are indicative of the presence of the complexes.

1. Feelings of Inferiority
   a. many statements regarding personal inadequacy
   b. functions inadequately
   c. size of productions small relative to size of paper and amount of material available
   d. one aspect of picture very small and other aspects very large
   e. human images very vague and/or inadequate appearing
   f. arms and hands hidden or not well drawn relative to other body parts
   g. trees young and appear to be weak
   h. light, sketchy lines
   i. hesitant in performing test battery

---

[23]See H. and F. Azima, "Outline of a Dynamic Theory of Occupational Therapy" (*AJOT*, Vol. XIII, No. 5, 1959). Also see G. and J. Fidler, *Occupational Therapy: A Communication Process in Psychiatry* (New York: The Macmillan Company, 1963).

j. many statements regarding the inadequacy of others
k. many statements regarding the adequacy of the self which have a grandiose quality
l. large productions but with an uncontrolled aspect
m. glorification of parents or persons in authority
n. symbols of that which is weak and inferior or powerful and potent

2. Differentiation from the Nonhuman Environment
    a. speaks primarily of importance of nonhuman environment relative to the self
    b. never mentions nonhuman environment
    c. productions made up primarily of nonhuman objects
    d. human objects have nonhuman qualities (i e. mechanistic, animal or plant-like)
    e. nonhuman objects have human characteristics
    f. various parts of the production blend into each other
    g. delusions regarding parts of the self as nonhuman
    h. feels that the self is directed by nonhuman external forces
    i. evidence of primary process organization

3. Trust in One's Fellow Man
    a. expresses fear of others
    b. acts shy and fearful of the therapist
    c. makes derogatory comments about others
    d. has few friends
    e. difficulty in getting along with people
    f. suspicious of other's intentions
    g. fearful of investing libidinal or aggressive energy in others
    h. belief that manipulation of aggressive human objects will be destructive to the self
    i. productions show isolated objects
    j. lack of human objects in productions
    k. human figures vague, threatening or ugly
    l. symbols have destructive or controlling aspects
    m. cool colors

4. Control of Sexual Impulses
    a. does not mention sexual material or talks exclusively about sexual matters
    b. promiscuous or inhibited in sexual behavior
    c. dress, mannerisms, activities outside of the parameters considered normal for the individual's cultural group.
    d. excessively sexually provocative or acts as an asexual object
    e. warm or cool colors
    f. symbols express sexual intercourse to exclusion of other content
    g. sexual aspects of human figures emphasized or absent
    h. absent or highly disguised masculine or feminine symbols
    i. sees no sexual content in productions which have such content or sees only sexual content to the exclusion of all other content
    j. productions restrictive

5. Emotional Separation from One's Parents
    a. glorifies or condemns parents or one parent
    b. blind acceptance or total rejection of parents' value system
    c. spends considerable time with parents
    d. financially dependent upon parents beyond age at which this is appropriate
    e. speaks of friends or marital partners as if they were parents or expected to act like parents
    f. infantile in appearance
    g. productions contain many father and mother symbols and symbols of transition

h. the self is portrayed as infantile, inferior or in need of support
i. house is portrayed as idealistic, prisonlike, or tension ridden
j. doors and windows are small or absent
k. productions have a passive quality
l. productions contain symbols which have threatening, destructive qualities

6. Establishing Mature Love Relations
   a. no evidence of mature love relations relative to friends, spouse or children
   b. preoccupation with the self
   c. relationships with others are cold, mechanical and lacking in affect
   d. major libidinal investment is in nonhuman objects
   e. complaints that he has difficulty getting close to other people
   f. overprotective of others
   g. cool colors
   h. affect toward production is muted
   i. one primary object in productions
   j. great care in drawing one human figure
   k. warm colors which are in some way restricted
   l. lack of connectiveness between objects

7. Finding One's Place as a Contributing Member of A Social System
   a. frequent change in vocational pursuits
   b. dissatisfaction with vocational choice
   c. minimal or no involvement in any type of vocational pursuit
   d. minimal or no involvement in the public domain
   e. negative feelings expressed regarding work and people who work
   f. productions symbolize pleasure seeking attitude and desire for immediate gratification
   g. productions have a noninvolved aspect
   h. symbols express rootlessness, restless movement, lack of foundation or base
   i. somewhat chaotic organization of objects
   j. productions symbolize poor control of libidinal and aggressive drives

8. Selecting A Guiding System of Values
   a. libidinal investment in abstract objects which prohibit investment of aggressive energy in external objects, manipulation of these objects, pleasure seeking and any form of deviant behavior
   b. much expression of guilt and shame
   c. aggressive energy turned toward the self
   d. use of dark colors
   e. symbols of threat, distraction
   f. father symbols with ominous characteristics
   g. "all seeing" eyes
   h. hell and damnation
   i. small human figures overshadowed by environment
   j. lack of libidinal investment in any abstract objects which are judgmental in character
   k. preoccupation with philosophy or religion
   l. questions regarding the meaning of life
   m. symbol of soul or life
   n. mandala (symbol of what is desired rather than what is)
   o. geometric shapes
   p. symbols express reaching upward toward the spiritual or downward toward that which is basic and enclosing

9. Physiological and Psychological Changes
   a. attempts to act as if the aging process is not taking place

b. preoccupation with care of the self
c. many physical complaints
d. withdrawal from usual activities
e. perception of the self as an asexual being
f. young sapling, budding tree
g. human figures young, well formed
h. objects which have eternal quality
i. potency symbols
j. expression of object loss (external objects or the self)
k. symbols which express perfect being

10. Inevitability of Death
   a. loss through death or impending death of a highly significant human libidinal object
   b. fear of impending death of the self which may or may not be based on factual information
   c. belief that one has an incurable illness
   d. symbols expressing birth-death-rebirth cycle and/or immortality
   e. mandala forms
   f. fragile appearing human figures
   g. dark colors
   h. old or withered trees
   i. symbols which refer to the soul

11. Perception of the Self as an Unacceptable Object
   a. minimal attention to personal hygiene and dress
   b. uses negative terms to describe self
   c. speaks of others as unattractive, ugly
   d. unaware of personal assets
   e. human figures poorly formed or deformed
   f. stick figures
   g. preoccupation with drawing human figures and forming them as perfectly as possible
   h. animals which have characteristics which are considered socially unacceptable
   i. symbols which refer to rebirth
   j. symbols which refer to evil

12. Lack of Gratification of Safety Needs
   a. confusion
   b. vague fears regarding the environment
   c. restricted interaction in the environment
   d. statements regarding lack of knowledge of what other people think, how they will respond or what is expected of the self
   e. experience the self as unable to have an impact upon the environment
   f. many paleosymbols
   g. predominant use of highly idiosyncratic symbols
   h. constricted production
   i. emphasis upon that which provides a base or foundation
   j. border circumscribed around drawing or fingerpainting
   k. productions disorganized
   l. symbols refer to impending destruction
   m. inappropriate objects selected for need satisfaction

13. Lack of Gratification of Love and Acceptance Needs
   a. dependent or extreme independence
   b. excessive use of drugs, alcohol or cigarettes
   c. excessive overeating, severe limitation of food intake or preoccupation with food

    d. seeks love from others indiscriminately
    e. inability to satisfy esteem needs
    f. promiscuous sexual behavior
    g. preoccupation with stroking, patting
    h. large, open mouth on human figures
    i. symbols which refer to womb, nurture, protection
    j. infantile appearing human figures
    k. young, immature trees
    l. soft coloring
    m. inappropriate objects selected for need satisfaction

14. Lack of Gratification of Esteem Needs
    a. rejection of the standards set by others or over-concern with standards
    b. concern with order and cleanliness
    c. feeling that others do not recognize or appreciate work done by the self
    d. experience of isolation from others
    e. inappropriate objects selected for need satisfaction
    f. jealousy of other's success
    g. preoccupation with work and vocational achievement
    h. symbols which refer to anal control
    i. potency symbols
    j. preoccupation with producing attractive objects
    k. continual change in direction of line
    l. mechanical objects

15. Investment of Aggressive Energy in the Self
    a. perception of the self as the primary obstacle to need satisfaction
    b. feelings of hate or anger toward the self
    c. anxiety and guilt regarding identification, investment in or manipulating of aggressive objects
    d. self destructive behavior
    e. dark colors
    f. symbols which refer to destruction
    g. minimal movement
    h. symbols which refer to evil or the devil
    i. deformed or threatening appearing human figures
    j. production restricted
    k. ominous tone to productions
    l. predominant teeth

16. Free-floating Libidinal Energy
    a. restlessness
    b. urge toward continuity
    c. dissatisfaction with current libidinal objects
    d. vague desires to help others or act as a change agent relative to the social system
    e. desire to nurture and give love
    f. warm, intense colors
    g. circular flowing lines
    h. much movement
    i. symbols which refer to life
    j. large objects
    k. extended tree branches
    l. patting, stroking

17. Free-floating Aggressive Energy
    a. difficulty in locating appropriate or substitute aggressive objects or in manipulating aggressive objects
    b. antisocial acts
    c. verbally abusive for little or no apparent reason
    d. perceives others as harmful to the self
    e. preoccupation with power and control
    f. symbols which refer to evil, destruction
    g. scrubbing, pushing, pulling, scratching, slapping mode of handling materials
    h. intense warm colors
    i. too much color
    j. angular, jagged strokes
    k. heavy pressure

18. Threatened Emergence of Unconscious Content
    a. primary process organization
    b. denotative concept utilized in secondary process organization
    c. confusion, great anxiety
    d. feels threatened by unknown forces
    e. highly controlled in expression of affect and interactions with other people
    f. symbols which refer to conscious, unconscious and destruction
    g. mother symbols
    h. mandala
    i. light or variation in pressure
    j. considerable or restricted movement
    k. too much or too little content
    l. chaotic organization of content

19. Acceptance of the Shadow Side
    a. ascribing undesirable personal characteristics to others and condemnation of these characteristics
    b. preoccupation with judging the behavior of self and others
    c. rigid moral codes
    d. appears too good or too nice
    e. lack of empathy for those who transgress social norms
    f. dark colors
    g. symbols which refer to evil or the devil
    h. mechanical movements
    i. symbols which refer to the unconscious
    j. animals which have socially unacceptable characteristics
    k. instinctually directed animals
    l. symbols which refer to chaos

20. Animus and Anima
    a. overly masculine or feminine
    b. rejection of opposite sex characteristics in self and others
    c. difficulty in empathizing with persons of the opposite sex
    d. rejection of opposite sex parent
    e. rigid differentiation of sexual roles
    f. productions have only masculine or feminine characteristics
    g. human figures of the opposite sex are lacking, vaguely reproduced or distorted
    h. opposite sex symbols have unattractive characteristics

    i. considerable use of mother or father symbols
    j. productions have one-sided quality or there is over-emphasis upon symmetry or unity

21. Relatedness to the Nonhuman Environment
    a. emphasis upon human relations
    b. minimal awareness of the nonhuman environment
    c. lack of libidinal investment in nonhuman objects
    d. dislike of animals or involvement in the natural environment
    e. views nonhuman objects only in terms of their utility
    f. minimal or no nonhuman objects in productions
    g. nonhuman objects poorly formed or grotesque
    h. clear distinction between human and nonhuman objects
    i. no personification of nonhuman objects
    j. reproduces only utilitarian nonhuman objects
    k. glorifies human objects

22. Thinking Function Superior
    a. analyzes the situation and arrives at specific conclusions
    b. able to bring order out of confusion
    c. emphasis upon objectivity, logical thought processes
    d. comfortable with theoretical material, abstract ideas
    e. minimal evidence of other functions
    f. symbols which refer to consciousness
    g. difficulty in expressing feelings regarding productions
    h. cool colors
    i. emphasis on head of reproduced human figures

23. Feeling Function Superior
    a. feelings finally differentiated and given close attention
    b. able to evaluate objects relative to their positive and negative aspects and acceptance of both aspects
    c. avoids negative thoughts
    d. relates well to people
    e. sees the value or importance of what should be done and goes ahead and does it
    f. sets standards
    g. minimal evidence of other functions
    h. symbols which refer to emotionality
    i. verbalizes about productions primarily in terms of feelings
    j. warm colors (red, yellow)

24. Sensation Function Superior
    a. relates in a practical way to objects, concerned with facts
    b. acute observer
    c. handles money easily
    d. good esthetic sense
    e. persistent in carrying out tasks
    f. aware of physical needs, enjoys sensual pleasures
    g. minimal evidence of other functions
    h. symbols which refer to bodily functions
    i. enjoy manipulation of media used in test battery, handles media in a variety of way`

25. Intuitive Function Superior
    a. guided by premonitions, perceives potential or possibilities
    b. foresees future trends
    c. loses self in objects
    d. views sex as sacred or coarse
    e. artistic or poetic leanings
    f. has contact with archetypic symbols
    g. minimal evidence of other functions
    h. predominance of archetypic symbols
    i. difficulty in looking at parts of production
    j. red, yellow
    k. emphasis on head in reproduced human figures

EVALUATION

Initial evaluation is an attempt to make some assessment of the complexes which are inhibiting the capacity of the individual to function in a manner which is satisfying to himself and, perhaps, to others. This assessment is tentative—it may be subject to major alteration during the treatment process. The initial evaluation also provides the therapist with some information pertaining to the patient's fear of self revelation, capacity for concept representation and secondary process organization, and need for support.

The suggested initial evaluation has two parts: an *interview* and a *test battery*. The interview focuses upon the patient's past, current and future life experiences. It is useful to systematically explore infancy, childhood, preadolescence, adolescence, young adulthood, middle-age, etc.—as many aspects of the past as are feasible.[24] The patient's current situation is explored relative to interpersonal relations, work, recreation, familial relations and the difficulties which have brought him for treatment. The future plans of the patient and his desires for the future are also explored. Areas of success and competence are identified as well as problem areas. The content of the interview should be anecdotal as well as factual. The therapist tries to identify during the interview responses which are indicative of unconscious complexes as well as the nature of those complexes. The patient reports, for example, with great affect that his co-workers are wonderful, kind and considerate people. This, of course, may be true, but the therapist must determine whether or not the statement has a hollow ring, for the patient may be using reaction formation to express a complex which, in part, contains very negative affect relative to other persons.

The test battery, usually administered after the interview, is made up of three sub-tests and is designed to facilitate production of symbols.[25] Administration of the test involves (1) giving the patient a box of colored pencils and

---

[24] H. S. Sullivan, *The Interpersonal Theory of Psychiatry* (New York: W. W. Norton and Company, 1953).

[25] This test battery was originally developed by the Azimas and later modified by G. Fidler. The only work on the subject which is readily available is Catherine O'Kane, *The Development of a Prospective Technique for Use in Psychiatric Occupational Therapy* (monograph, Buffalo: State University of New York, 1968).

paper and directing him to draw what ever he wishes; (2) giving the patient a variety of different-colored fingerpaints, water, and paper, and directing him to use the paints in any way he wishes; and (3) giving the patient a ball of moist clay and directing him to make anything he wishes. After the patient has completed each sub-test the therapist asks him to talk about his method of procedure, organization, color, content, affect, ideas and associations that he has relative to his productions. It is suggested that the test battery be given in a quiet room where the patient and therapist are alone and undisturbed. The therapist sits at the work table with the patient in such a position that he is able to observe the patient's facial expressions and work. Directions are repeated if necessary but no suggestions are made. During discussion about each production the therapist attempts to gain as much information as possible but must not lead the patient or attempt to elicit material which the patient indicates he is not able or willing to express.

Using the interview information, the patient's own discussion of his productions, observation of the patient by the therapist during the test battery, the therapist's knowledge of symbols, and his understanding of common responses which occur when complexes are repressed, the therapist attempts to identify the various complexes which are disturbing the patient. (A patient may have only one complex, but it is more common for several complexes to be present.)

POSTULATES REGARDING CHANGE

Complexes are identified and brought to consciousness through affectual-cognitive exploration of symbols produced by the individual relative to his past, current, and future situation.

They are integrated into consciousness through conceptual representation and secondary process organization of the complex content.

With integration into consciousness, psychic energy previously invested in the complex is freed and available for use in need satisfaction.

The information gained through integration of unconscious content therefore becomes available to guide willful selection of appropriate or substitute objects for need satisfaction.

Exploration and integration of complexes is facilitated by reproduction of symbols originally produced in dreams and wakeful fantasy, the production of exocept and image symbols in the use of art media and the companionship of a knowledgeable and empathetic guide.

THE TREATMENT PROCESS

Symbols produced by an individual may have many meanings. Symbols are usually related both to complexes and to the individual's current life situation. There are, therefore, several factors to keep in mind in exploring symbols;

symbols produced by an individual cannot be separated from that individual.[26] The individual's past, current and future life situation; his philosophical, religious, and moral convictions; and his cultural background must be taken into consideration. Symbols must be explored with an attitude and orientation of innocence — that is, no fixed meaning is assumed regarding any symbol. They are explored with a sense of discovery. Many symbols have common referents which provide some landmarks in exploring the unconscious; yet, a symbol produced by an individual also has an idiosyncratic aspect. To assign a fixed meaning to a symbol is to inhibit discovery of how the symbol relates to that individual. The common referents of symbols are utilized in evaluation to assess a patient's problem areas. In the treatment process itself, however, no pre-determined meaning can be assigned to symbols.

Exploration of symbols is facilitated by formulating conscious chains of association relative to the symbol and various aspects of that symbols' form and content. This process is differentiated from the process of free association, which involves reporting all thoughts, memories or affect which are experienced by the individual. Conscious association is focused and directed by the individual—thoughts, memories and affect related to the symbol are articulated. Free association may be utilized on occasion, as, for instance, upon the event that no conscious associations are available. Jung, however, believed that free association tends to move the individual away from his symbol; it may lead him to discovering complexes, which is, of course, one of the purposes of exploring symbols. Jung states that a given symbol is produced at a given time for some specific purpose; it is expressing something very definite which the unconscious is trying to say. Ignoring this fact does a great disservice to the potential of the unconscious for providing guiding information.

The meaning of symbols is discovered through exploration of their various aspects. The whole becomes known through its parts. The meaning of a symbol also may be discovered through exploration of the context in which it occurs, other symbols which occur at the same time, other symbols which have been formulated in the past or symbols which will be produced in the future. The meaning of a symbol is often obscure until it is related to other symbols. Symbol content which takes the same or a different form repeatedly usually provides more guiding information than a symbol which occurs only once. This is not, however, a hard and fast rule. Looking for similarity in symbols is often a fruitful undertaking, for the relationship between two symbols which occur together may provide a clue to the meaning of both.

Since the unconscious reflects consciousness, it is useful to question the compensation by a symbol for conscious attitudes or current actions. Is one aspect of the self dominating and inhibiting expression of other aspects of the self? For what purpose was the symbol produced? This is not causality (what caused the symbol to be produced) — looking primarily for cause inhibits free exploration of symbols and the symbol loses dimensionality and life.

---

[26]For further discussion regarding the exploration of symbols, see C. Jung, *Modern Man in Search of a Soul* and *Man and His Symbols*.

Symbols are invested with energy and affect. Without this component the symbol is a lifeless, empty shell; such symbols cannot serve as a guide to the individual, for they are without dynamic force. Since the symbol is not consciously connected to the need-affect aspect of the self, it has no meaning to the person. Some symbols are produced without conscious awareness of their energy-affect components. The individual may feel neutral toward the symbol; or, at best, he may be somewhat curious. Such a symbol may come to life only through the exploration of the fashion in which it is meaningful to the individual. Awareness of affect may be miniscule and allusive at first. Affect which is foreign or disagreeable to the individual requires especially patient nurturing. At other times affect might come as a mighty rush, even to the point of overwhelming the individual. When this occurs it is the conscious, concept representation and secondary process aspect of the self which requires support. Just as affectless symbols are lifeless, symbols whose content remains unconscious are also without life. They cannot be a dynamic factor in the growth of the individual. An individual may produce a symbol and experience great affect toward the symbol; it remains, however, isolated, something which is only there, until its content or at least part of its content becomes known. The energy-affect-content components of a symbol must be brought together and integrated in order for symbols to have dynamic meaning, and it is for this reason that we speak of the *effectual-cognitive exploration* of symbols.

Symbols can never be completely understood. In exploring a symbol produced by the patient, one is, at best, able to comprehend only those aspects of the symbol which are currently relevant to the patient. Although one may intellectually explore all aspects of a symbol, it is usually only those aspects which are associated with affect or which come through exploration to be associated with affect which are of current significance. This process of abstracting out currently significant content helps the individual to focus upon and therefore make use of a symbol in the present. This orientation facilitates affectual-cognitive exploration rather than a one-sided cognitive approach. Other aspects of a symbol may become known only at some future time. A symbol, once produced, may remain in the individual's preconscious or personal unconscious. It may periodically become reactivated and re-explored by the individual and, in turn, yield new information. For example, an individual produced an image symbol of a very beautiful adolescent girl, originally identified by the therapist and patient as being an unconscious message of the childishness of the symbol-producer. The symbol remained in the individual's preconscious for some period of time and became reactivated later in response to the individual's struggle to find a balance between the masculine and feminine aspects of the self. Even later, it was reactivated a second time and identified as a personification of the feeling function of the individual. All of this content was contained in the symbol at the time it was originally produced, but the various aspects had meaning only as the individual continued to develop.

The content of a symbol must be integrated with conscious content — more than just brought to consciousness. If only this first part of the process takes place, the content remains isolated and meaningless. It is difficult to explain how this content becomes integrated; we see the result of integration in the individual's actions but are able to learn little about the process. We do know that the process of conscious association facilitates integration. In this process the individual moves from the known to the unknown, never losing sight of the conscious self. The primary aggregate from which the symbol was derived is broken up, represented in concepts and subjected to secondary process organization. The past and the future can be reconsidered, now in the context of the present. The individual is able to attend to the unknown aspects of the self, make conscious judgments about these aspects and utilize this knowledge in conscious willing.

Integration of unconscious content usually occurs only when the content is translated into connotative and perhaps denotative concept representation and secondary process organization: the individual must put into words that which has been nameless. This process in turn allows the individual to organize mental content in a logical manner. This is necessary not only for unconscious content which has been repressed or never allowed to become conscious but also for current experiences which are not being recognized. The individual's current situation may be as unknown to him as his past situations and his future potentials.

Secondary process thinking allows the individual to recognize relationships between events in a manner which is similar to his cultural group, to make judgments about events, control thought sequences, postpone or delay motor responses, control antecedent thoughts so that events may be perceived objectively, and to be aware of affect associated with thoughts, which in turn enables him to control affect. On the basis of secondary process thinking, the conscious will directs motor activity. It is thus assumed that all behavior is influenced by attention and cognitive processes. The more the individual is able to attend to his external and internal environment, represent perceptions in terms of denotative and connotative concepts, and utilize secondary process organization, the more able he is to make conscious, willed choices regarding his behavior.[27]

Exploration of symbols and integration of their currently significant content leads to alteration of the self. This change may or may not be reflected in overt actions—the individual, for instance, may not do anything differently, yet may experience affect toward the self, others, and his actions in the environment far differently. There is a mistaken belief that symbols dictate a specific course of action which must be followed. Yet the unconscious is neutral and objective — it tells us only what the situation is; and it is the conscious will which must choose the desired course of action. The idea that one must act in a certain way because his symbols tell him, for example, that he has not developed a particular aspect of the self, is false. When action is dictated by symbolic content, the individual is experiencing the unconscious as an alien master, not a part of the self. The change which comes about through the exploration of symbols is slow, experienced as growth and desired by the conscious self. Change may occur outside of

---

[27]D. Ford and H. Urban, *Systems of Psychotherapy*.

awareness; if so it is experienced as something which has happened or is happening. The change may be planned, on the other hand, by the individual in a very deliberate manner, investing much time and energy in the process. It may at times be experienced as frightening, foreign, and extremely difficult; still it is desired and willed by the individual — motivated and produced from the self.[28]

Once the currently significant content of a symbol has been integrated into consciousness, energy is freed from the symbol. It loses its power or dynamic force   at least for the present. The energy invested in the symbol and used to maintain the referent of the symbol in the unconscious becomes available to the individual. There is more energy available to be used in fulfilling needs, though the symbol itself may continue to be of some importance to the individual— often remembered fondly as one thinks of a past friendship or a pleasant experience. A symbol which was particularly meaningful for an individual may be given some concrete form; for example, one individual who had gained valuable information from a dream image later bought a painting which reminded him of this symbol. A common situation occurs when the currently significant content of a symbol is unknown or only partially integrated with conscious mental content; and energy continues to be invested in the symbol. Its potency is maintained. Highly disguised symbols are often produced by the unconscious to protect consciousness. These symbols periodically pull at the individual's awareness, seeking but not demanding understanding. The individual in his own time and fashion slowly extracts meaning from the symbol. This process may take a period of years and, indeed, it cannot be rushed — attempts to do so always seem to fail. A symbol will become known and integrated only when the conscious self is ready. Symbols which foreshadow events are often of this type; they may not become known until after the event has occurred. An example of this phenomena occurred with a patient who attempted to decipher the meaning of a particular dream. Many facets of the dream were explored and several interpretations were attempted, both by the patient and his therapist, without success. It was only much later, when the patient had become aware of a marked change in his relationship with his mother, that he was able to interpret the dream. The dream had foreshadowed this change.

Exploration of a symbol is a very personal matter because only the symbol producer can judge whether the content of a given symbol is applicable to himself. There is a feeling of fit or rightness when the individual comes upon the pertinent content of a symbol. The therapist may discover the meaning of a symbol and, indeed, he may have much data to support his discovery; but if this does not feel right to the patient, the identified content is not currently applicable. The patient may not yet be ready to accept the content on a conscious level and acceptance may occur only much later. On the other hand, the therapist's interpretation of the symbol may not have been accurate. The information is meaningless and useless to the symbol producer. One does not have to be overly concerned with accuracy of interpretation. A patient may feel correct about the content of a particular symbol only to discover later that another

---

[28] J. Mazer, *Exploring How a Think Feels.*

interpretation is more accurate. "Sooner or later the psyche rejects the mistake, much as an organism does a foreign body." [29]

Discussion of dreams and wakeful fantasy has been a typical way in which to explore an individual's symbols and therefore the nature of his unconscious content. In so doing there has been a tendency to overlook manipulation of the nonhuman environment as a potential source of useful information. The individual's actions often express exocept symbols, and the end product which might be produced is frequently highly symbolic in nature. Various tools and materials which are used often become concrete object symbols for the individual, for they reflect unconscious content. This is evident when an individual invests considerable libidinal or aggressive energy in various tools or materials and strong affect comes to be associated with these objects [30] A young girl who was assigned to the hospital woodworking shop decided to make a spoon and fork salad-mixing set from walnut. She discovered that gouging out the bowl of the utensils was very difficult for her. Rather than carving the handles, which was suggested in the directions, the patient used an electric sander to form the handle into soft curves. Much additional time was spent rubbing oil into the wood. In exploring this process with the patient it became evident that a chisel and the act of gouging symbolized the penis and sexual intercourse. This was an aspect of life experience which was terrifying to the patient yet at the same time a source of great curiosity. This ambivalence was symbolized in the patient's selection of the particular project, difficulty in forming the bowl of the utensils, and in her decision not to carve the handle. The spoon and fork and the gentle rubbing of the wood were found to be symbolic of continued yearning for a satisfying nurturing experience. Finally, the patient's selection of walnut wood and the curved handles symbolized a budding desire to nurture and give love.

Any manipulation of the nonhuman environment, especially when the patient selects his own project, is very useful for evaluative purposes and can be used in treatment as well. However, it is suggested that painting, drawing, sculpting and collage work are particularly useful in the treatment process. [31] One reason for this suggestion is efficiency for art productions allow for a much higher frequency of symbols than do other activities which make use of the nonhuman environment. There are several other reasons for this suggestion. Dreams and wakeful fantasies are the most common sources of symbols, but such symbols are allusive and vague to the individual, and, as such, they are difficult to study. By reproducing the dream or fantasy symbols, they are given concrete forms, which facilitate study. Reproduction endows symbols with reality — with something which actually exists. The deliberate act of giving a symbol concrete form encourages identification, clarification and elaboration of the various aspects of that symbol. A symbol reproduced in graphic form remains available for future

---

[29] Carl Jung, *Modern Man in Search of a Soul* p. 65.

[30] Fidler, *Occupational Therapy.* . . .

[31] C. Jung, *Modern Man in Search of a Soul*; Margaret Naumburg, *Schizophrenic Art: Its Meaning in Psychotherapy* and *Psychoneurotic Art: Its Function in Psychotherapy*.

study with less distortion than one which is only held in consciousness and is therefore less likely to be forgotten or ignored. The act of reproduction often releases energy from a symbol and the complex with which it is associated so that the symbol producer is able to study the symbol more objectively. Art production itself promotes the creation of symbols. The ideas which spontaneously come to mind when one is asked to produce a work of art (or while production is in progress) are often symbols which can then be given concrete form and studied. Art productions facilitate the manifestation of exocept symbols; one is not only able to observe action, but the impact of the action is usually recorded in the production. Although endocept symbols can be translated into verbal concepts, it appears that there is less distortion when they are translated into images and exocept symbols. The exocept aspect may first manifest itself as the individual plays with the art materials — the image aspect grows out of the playful experiment. The form that it takes may vary from highly abstract to realistically produced identifiable objects. Art production is probably least useful in the case of concept symbols. However, if these symbols cannot be adequately explored or their meaning remains stubbornly unclear, art production may be a useful device. Concept symbols would be translated in the same way as endocept symbols.

The reproduction of symbols is only a device to facilitate exploration of the unconscious. Reproduction without exploration does not help the individual to become acquainted with his unconscious self; at best, it may facilitate the release of some energy leading to a temporary experience of well being. But energy is quickly reinvested in the repressed content, since the complex has not been identified nor integrated into consciousness.

If the patient is unfamiliar with art production, easily manipulated materials are offered first. However, a variety of materials are always available, as the patient may find one mode of expression more meaningful and useful at a given time in the treatment process than at another time. Brief instruction may be necessary but should be kept to a minimum. Patients who are hesitant in beginning work are often helped by suggesting that they draw simple free-form, scribble-like pictures. They are then encouraged to look at their production to see whether they can identify the suggestion of any objects. This allows for the projection of unconscious content in that contemplation of unknown objects " . . . acts as an irresistible bait for the unconscious to project itself into the unknown nature of the object. . . ."[32] The patient is then encouraged to expand and further amplify the identified object. Although this method is often used at the beginning of treatment, it can be utilized at any time during the treatment process. It is particularly helpful when the patient is having difficulty in manipulating media.

It makes no difference whether the patient works in art media during the treatment sessions or at other times. Nor does it make any difference if he reproduces dream images, fantasy images, something remembered from his past

---

[32] C. Jung, *Alchemical Studies*, p. 205.

life or something which occurs to him as he is beginning to work or while he is working. Drawing, painting or sculpting whatever he wants, whenever he wishes, helps the patient to feel that he is more of a partner in this discovery adventure and is therefore able to experience a sense of control.

The patient is told at the beginning of treatment that the purpose of using art media is to help him discover unknown aspects of the self, not to develop his skill as an artist — nor are highly artistic productions desired or expected. Thus the amount of time spent on one production may be indicative of the great significance of the symbols being produced or of anxiety regarding the production of new symbols.

Each production is explored in a detailed manner. It is often best to start with an attempt to identify what the patient was experiencing and the associated affect at the time he began to work and during the production. The conscious circumstances which evoked the production are also identified. This, in a sense, sets the stage for detailed exploration. A preliminary context is established. Exploration involves conscious association relative to symmetry, placement, size, direction of line, pressure, shape of strokes, movement in production, color, mode of handling materials and all aspects of that which is contained in the production. It is suggested that the patient begin conscious association relative to any of the forementioned aspects of the production. His attention may need to be directed to other aspects during the course of exploration. Cognitive and affectual associations are encouraged in order to determine what conscious mental content is related to aspects of the production, and what affect is aroused by these various aspects. Each part is explored in isolation, relative to the whole, other symbols previously produced, and the context in which the production was made. The therapist at times may also offer conscious association to the production. This tends to widen the patient's perspective and offer another dimension for his consideration.

Symbols can be explored by an individual in isolation, but exploration shared with a sympathetic participant facilitates the process. The other, in essence, accompanies the individual on the journey of self-discovery. This is the role of the therapist. As previously stated, the consciousness of the individual is one-sided. Thus there may be many aspects of a symbol which he does not perceive, and the therapist will be able to point out these aspects for the individual's consideration. The therapist's conscious association to the symbol may open up areas that are unknown to the patient. Shared verbalization about a symbol requires concept representation and secondary process organization. This, in turn, facilitates integration of unconscious content with conscious content. The individual tends to view himself in a relatively stereotyped manner, but the therapist may suggest a new view or a wider perspective. Similarly, the therapist may see relationships between symbols, aspects of symbols, a given symbol and the current situation which are not perceived by the patient. The therapist is able to nurture affect and give support when affect is overwhelming. It is important to emphasize that the therapist must never impose himself on the patient; he empathetically leads, guides, supports, and provides companionship as the situation dictates.

Exploration of symbols occurs prior to or in conjunction with interpretation.[33] Interpretation is here defined as articulation of the personal meaning of a symbol in relation to an individual's past, present, or future life situation. It usually offers the patient an alternative way of perceiving experiences, behavior, and affect. The purpose of interpretation is to facilitate identification and integration of unconscious content. Initially, the therapist may be the most active partner in making interpretations. However, one of the sub-goals of treatment is to help the patient to learn how to interpret his own symbols. He is therefore able to consult his unconscious and to continue independently toward self-actualization. The patient's movement toward independence is always one of the primary considerations in therapy.

Symbols produced by the patient do not necessarily refer to the cause of his complexes. They may refer to the patient's present situation, compensate for the patient's present situation, foreshadow future events, point the way to more adequate need fulfillment, or reflect an element in the treatment process. All these possibilities must be kept in mind during the interpretation of symbols; the fixed meaning of symbols is held in abeyance during exploration and interpretation. The therapist is guided by the assumption that symbols contained in the patient's production have meaning — to discover that meaning is the essential purpose of the treatment process. Symbols are often difficult to understand, and there is no reason not to admit lack of understanding. This will come in time, but not necessarily during the period of treatment. At times the therapist comprehends the meaning of a symbol yet his interpretation does not reach the patient. It makes no sense, it is meaningless. Interpretations must touch the patient's being and response must be affectual, experiential and cognitive. The therapist never tries to convince the patient of the correctness of his interpretation. This limits the patient's independence and makes him a subordinate partner in the treatment process. Therefore, any interpretation which does not win the true assent of the patient is considered invalid for the present, and the therapist and patient must search for another interpretation, even if it is only temporary.

Adequate and meaningful interpretation must be learned from practice, in conjunction with skilled supervision. It has been said that each therapist must recapitulate the history of analytic therapy in the process of becoming a therapist.[34] There seems to be much truth in this statement. The therapist should remember that the guidelines developed for interpretation should not be regarded as rules, for it is often in their breaking that the most creative therapy occurs.

---

[33] For additional discussions of the subject of interpretation, see E. Hammer, *Use of Interpretation in Treatment*; R. Ekstein and R. Wallerstein, *The Teaching and Learning of Psychotherapy* (New York: Basic Books, Inc., 1958); R. Greenson, "The Problem of Working Through," in M. Schur, ed. *Drives, Affect, Behavior* (New York: International Universities Press, Inc., 1965); and F. Alexander, *Psychoanalysis and Psychotherapy* (New York: W. W. Norton and Company, 1956).

[34] Franz Alexander, *Psychoanalysis and Psychotherapy* (New York: W. W. Norton and Company, 1956).

Interpretations have been categorized as *horizontal* and *vertical*. *Horizontal interpretation* refers to the identification of common elements in the patient's present life situation. For example, a symbol may point to the underdeveloped nature of the patient's feeling function. This is causing difficulty with his co-workers and his wife, since he appears cold and aloof. It is also interfering with his work for he experiences primitive and uncontrollable feelings. Connecting these various aspects of the patient's situation is horizontal interpretation. *Vertical interpretation* refers to the identification of common elements in the patient's past, present, and at times, future life situation. For example, a symbol may refer to the patient's very negative feeling about her body. Through association it is discovered that this relates to past strenuous periods of dieting; her present affinity for dark, conservative clothes; and anxiety regarding her future chosen profession as a teacher. Identification of these relationships is vertical interpretation.

Interpretation is useless if the patient is not ready to hear or comprehend the relationships which are being suggested. Thus, the therapist must be truly with the patient in order that he might experience the patient's readiness. Interpretation is usually most successful when it is focused upon content which has emerged from the unconscious and is nearing concept representation and secondary process organization. The therapist is only a half of a step ahead of the patient, since he interprets that which the patient is almost ready to comprehend. Interpretation deals with the patient's concerns in the here and now of the treatment session. For example, the patient may report one of his relatively common experiences of *moving-away;* a widening of psychological space between self and others. It happened that the patient described this experience just after he had hesitantly mentioned that a poem he was writing was going well. An interpretation was made by the therapist that perhaps this experience was related to the patient's fear of criticism regarding his writing. This interpretation was more easily accepted by and useful to the patient because he was experiencing moving-away and had just mentioned his writing. Interpretations which are made when the patient is not experiencing anything relative to the interpretation tend to be meaningless and, if at all, registered on the cognitive level. The necessary affectual-experiencing aspects are missing.

During the treatment process, patients often engage in various behaviors which are directed toward maintaining content in the unconscious. This is referred to as *resistance*. When this occurs interpretations regarding unconscious content are not useful to the patient and it is necessary to help the patient to recognize his resistance, prior to engaging him in exploring that which his behavior is keeping out of consciousness. Resistance is not consciously willed; the patient is not deliberately attempting to interfere with the treatment process. His behavior is as unknown to him as the unconscious content which it is directed against.

Interpretations are used sparingly. Too many interpretations confuse the patient and often overwhelm him to the point of not listening. Even if he does attend, it is only on the cognitive level and the process becomes intellectualized and non-affectual. Excessive interpretation by the therapist places the patient in a passive position; spontaneity and self-direction are limited. The patient has no opportunity to formulate his own interpretations. Since one of the sub-goals of treatment is to develop the patient's capacity to consult his own unconscious independent of the therapist, he must also develop the ability to interpret. This can be done only by the patient's active engagement in interpretations. The process must be one of collaboration.

Collaboration is often facilitated by stating interpretations in a tentative or questioning manner. This helps both the therapist and patient to view the therapist's role as a guiding participant—as opposed to an all-knowing being. The patient is usually then more comfortable when he disagrees with the therapist and will also be free to alter a part of the interpretation or to accept only some aspects of the interpretation. The words the therapist uses also enhance collaboration and integration of unconscious content. The patient has his own unique manner of speaking, and it is often useful for the therapist to use the patient's expressions when he suggests an interpretation. This tends to establish contact with the patient's most intimate ideas and memories. This can also, however, be carried too far. The therapist's own vocabulary offers another dimension for the patient's consideration. It would be unreasonable to deny this additional dimension to the patient.

It has been suggested that the therapist use direct terms to discuss human experiences as opposed to euphemisms. This indicates to the patient that such experiences can be spoken about in a simple and matter-of-fact manner. The therapist must be cautious, for what is a euphemism to one person may be a specially meaningful word to another, and therefore the identifying labels a patient uses should be explored. For example, many persons use the expressions "intercourse" and "making love" to speak of very difficult kinds of sexual experiences. Substituting one for the other may be a form of denial, but it may also be a way of distinguishing between two experiences.

It is best for both the patient and therapist to stay away from technical terms or the concepts used in a particular theory. When patients use such terms it is often a way of covering up or speaking negatively about the self or others. When this occurs it is necessary for the therapist to suggest to the patient that he try to select other words to discuss experiences or affect. By so doing the true meaning of what the patient is saying is likely to become more evident both to the patient and the therapist. The therapist's use of technical terms may be misunderstood by the patient as a derogatory comment. Such words as "compulsive," "controlling," "infantile," etc. have a negative meaning to much of the lay population. It is true, too, that the use of technical terms often makes the patient experience the self as something out of a text book; a case rather than an affect-laden, unique person.

Gaining self-knowledge is a painful experience—in all growth there is some pain. Conversely, an optimal level of pain promotes growth. The therapist helps to regulate the pain of growth—not to eliminate it. The patient must be allowed to *experience*. Thus false reassurance and withholding of painful interpretations is not helpful to the patient; it interferes with his growth and demeans both his intelligence and courage. The destructive pain of therapy emanates more from interpretations which carry a derogatory, critical, evaluative theme than from an honest articulation of the therapist's perceptions. Interpretations which demonstrate a sincere interest in the patient, and a nonjudgmental understanding attitude toward behavior, affect and feeling go a long way in regulating the hurt of growth. It is also helpful to remember that interpretations are not always threatening to a patient. Often they are experienced as relief-giving. A bit of the darkness is rolled back and the light of consciousness shines a little brighter.

Gaining self-knowledge is a lonely experience even when accompanied by an intuitive guide. In discovering uniqueness one may lose the sense of commonality with one's human and nonhuman environment. Conversely, lack of self-knowledge also generates a feeling of aloneness. The self is perceived as so unique that relation to others can be severed. For these reasons it has been suggested that the therapist help the patient to view his complexes as the essence of the human condition. Interpretations which touch archetypes and are presented in the form of fables, proverbs or quotations are often useful for this purpose. The patient is helped to experience membership in the human group and oneness with his environment.

As mentioned previously, complexes often express themselves in the form of transference. This may occur during therapy. The nature of the transference relationship provides useful information for discovering the nature of complexes. Exploration and interpretation of the transference relationship is particularly useful in that it is dealing with what the patient is presently experiencing, and therefore has an immediacy which is rare in discussion of the past. The patient's transference experiences, positive, negative, or ambivalent, are encouraged to the point where they are relatively solidified; not, however, to the point where they are so intense that they blind the patient to the real therapist-patient relationship. At the opportune moment the patient may focus on the transference relationship, either overtly or through formulated symbols. If this does not occur, the therapist may introduce this significant aspect of the therapeutic process by inquiring what the patient thinks, experiences and feels about the therapist. The exploration which follows is often extremely fruitful in revealing the split-off aspect of the patient's self.

The therapist helps the patient to learn to make interpretations independently by enumerating several possible connections; by pointing out aspects of the patient's symbols, past life or current situation unnoticed by the patient, by articulating basic themes which appear to be evident; and by reminding the patient of past statements, omissions and apparent contradictions. There is in all of this an atmosphere of quiet sharing.

Interpretations bring order out of chaos. The conscious self is usually better able to deal with verbalized, concept-represented affect, experiences, objects and events better than those which are represented in an exocept, image or endocept fashion. Man in his inherent need for safety requires ordering of his internal and external environment. Chaos is the darkness which can be accepted only in its partial amelioration by the light of order—the naming of the nameless brings the security-giving light.

Chapter 4
ACTION-CONSEQUENCE I

Learning results from experience, the learner must in some way act upon or react to a situation that impinges upon him. Learning depends upon what the learner does. This involves how he perceives, how he thinks, how he feels, and how he acts . . . the end result of the learning process is some change in the learner . . . (and) tends to be fixed by consequences of his behavior . . .

T. E. Clayton, *Teaching and Learning**

Action-consequence, the label given to this theoretical frame of reference, is founded on the learning theory of operant conditioning. It may be briefly summarized as a description of, or a prescription for, the teaching of those skills which are necessary for adequate functioning in activities of daily living, avocational pursuits and work through the application of techniques deduced from the postulates of operant conditioning. As a frame of reference it would be placed in the "acquisitional-unlabeled behavior" category using general postulates regarding change.

Except for a few pioneers, therapists concerned with the treatment of psychosocial dysfunction have only recently become aware of the potential of learning theories as a theoretical base for treatment. There is now an increasing interest in the study of learning theories to assess their applicability to therapy. The following discussion of action-consequence is an attempt to illustrate how one learning theory may be used as a theoretical base for the treatment of psychosocial dysfunction.

---

*Thomas E. Clayton,*Teaching and Learning* (Englewood Cliffs, N. J.: Prentice-Hall, Inc., 1965), p 45.

THEORETICAL BASE

Acquisition of Behavior   As indicated in the introductory remarks, the action-consequence frame of reference is founded upon operant conditioning.[1] Operant conditioning is a theory which describes and make predictions about learned behavior. Learning is here defined as:

> . . . a process by which an activity originates or is changed through reaction to an encounter situation provided that the characteristics of the change in activity cannot be explained on the basis of native response tendencies, maturation, or temporary states of the organism (e.g., fatigue, drugs, etc.).[2]

The theory of operant conditioning states that behavior is acquired or learned through action directed toward the environment. Performances which alter the environment are learned and are in turn changed by their effect on the environment. These are referred to as *operant behaviors.* For example, the child is given approval by his mother when he picks up his toys. The frequency of such behavior—picking up the toys—increases because of its effect on the environment-mother's approval. The adolescent uses the jargon of his peer group because such behavior insures a positive response from the peer group. This same jargon may not be used in the home because the parents respond to the use of other language in a positive manner.

The "learning" concept is not used in the theory of operant conditioning. Behavior is described, instead, in terms of *frequency;* frequency being the number of times a given performance is emitted by the individual. The secretary who spends most of her workday typing, taking dictation, answering the phone, and filing has a high frequency of work-oriented behavior. The secretary who spends a good deal of her time in the coffee shop, talking with coworkers and making personal telephone calls, has a low frequency of work-oriented behavior. The word "learning" will sometimes be used, however, for ease of presentation. The reader is asked to keep in mind that, as used here, it refers to alteration of an individual's repertoire in terms of either an increase or decrease of specific behavior. The concept *teach* will be used to refer to a process specially designed to facilitate learning.

In operant conditioning, the term *reinforcement* is used to identify the process whereby the frequency of a performance has increased because of a

---

[1] For a more detailed discussion of operant conditioning, see C. Ferster and M. Perrott, *Behavior Principles* (New York: Appleton-Century-Croft, 1968); B. Skinner, *Science and Human Behavior* (New York: The Macmillan Company, 1953); J.Dollard and N. Miller, *Personality and Psychotherapy* (New York: McGraw-Hill, 1950); H. Eysenck, *Behavioral Therapy and the Neuroses* (New York: Pergamon Press, 1960); and L. Ullman and L. Krasner, *Case Studies in Behavior Modification* (New York: Holt, Rinehart and Winston, Inc., 1965).

[2] E. Hilgard and G. Bower, *Theories of Learning* (New York: Appleton-Century-Croft, 1966), p. 2.

reinforcing stimulus. A *reinforcer* or *reinforcing stimulus* is any event which increases the frequency of a performance it immediately follows. In the above examples approval and a positive response are reinforcing stimuli.

Reinforcement generates a *class* of behavior. It is defined by its effectiveness in producing the reinforcer. For example, some students will read a textbook and underline major points; other students may make notes as they read; still others may read each chapter and attempt to summarize the content. All such behavior, though different in many respects, is called studying. It is a class of behavior that is reinforced by the experience of mastery, a high grade on an examination, or approval from others.

What will act as a reinforcing stimulus is dependent upon the *needs* of the individual. In operant conditioning, a need is defined as an event which alters behavior. This locates the need in the external environment rather than in the individual. Thus it can be observed. To illustrate: if a young boy mows the lawn because his father has promised to take him to the ball game, we say he has a need to go to the ball game. If the infant ceases to cry when he is picked up and fondled by the mother, we say he has a need to be fondled by the mother. If the individual spends considerable time learning a specific skill, we often say that he has a need for mastery.[3] If a need is already being gratified, or if the need is presently satiated, an event which would satisfy that need no longer serves as a reinforcing stimulus. Satiation occurs, for instance, when an adolescent's need for approval is being gratified by his peer group to such an extent that he does not experience a need for additional approval. Approval by the parents no longer serves as a reinforcing stimulus, and would not, therefore, lead to alteration of behavior.

Through the process of reinforcement an individual acquires a *repertoire of behavior*, which is defined as the supply of performances possessed by an organism. Each individual's repertoire is relatively unique, especially when we attend to the smaller nuances of behavior; each individual has a particular way of moving and expressing himself. In most cases an individual's repertoire is sufficiently large and varied to allow him to satisfy his own needs and to meet those demands of the environment that he perceives as appropriate.

An individual's repertoire changes over time both through the addition of new behavior and through the deletion of previous behavior This latter process often occurs because the relationship between behavior and the environment is altered. *Extinction* is the term used to identify the process whereby a performance decreases in frequency because the reinforcing stimulus no longer follows the performance. For example, the young girl who had previously flirted with other boys because her boy friend gave her increased attention when she did so, may no longer flirt if her new boy friend tends to ignore her when she flirts with others. Flirting is extinguished (at least for the present time) as a result of a decrease in attention from a significant person. Attention as the reinforcing stimulus does not follow the flirting behavior.

---

[3]Robert White, "Competance and the Growth of Personality," in L. Rabkin and J. Carr (eds.), *Sourcebook in Abnormal Psychology* (Boston: Houghton Mifflin Co., 1967).

New behavior may be added to an individual's repertoire by the process of *shaping*. For example, in learning how to feed himself, the child receives approval from the mother for picking up the spoon. In a sequential manner, reinforcement is given for getting cereal on the spoon; bringing the spoon to the mouth; eating the entire bowl of cereal without assistance; and eating without spilling cereal on the table, floor, or bib. When using shaping as a means of teaching a given performance, one begins with a behavior which is currently a part of the individual's repertoire. The individual's behavior is differentially reinforced as the performance moves in the direction desired. *Differential reinforcement* is the process of providing a reinforcing stimulus for one type of behavior and withholding a reinforcing stimulus when another type of behavior occurs. Thus, in teaching a child to eat with a spoon, the mother does not give reinforcement for getting cereal on the spoon once this skill has been learned, but gives reinforcement only for bringing the spoonful of cereal to the mouth. Differential reinforcement during the shaping process causes extinction of partial performances or crude approximations of the desired performance. *Reinforcing successive approximations* is a phrase that is frequently used in place of the term *shaping*. It is perhaps a more descriptive means of identifying the process. Many complex performances of the individual are learned through reinforcement of successive approximations.

Differential reinforcement is also used in a somewhat different manner in the acquisition of behavior. In this situation some behavior incompatible with emitting a previously reinforced performance is reinforced. For example, a work supervisor may have given covert approval to long coffee breaks and lunch hours. A new supervisor, being more concerned with getting work accomplished, reinforces attention to the work task and a high level of productivity. Attention to work and productivity is incompatible with long coffee breaks and lunch hours. With continued differential reinforcement, behavior desired by the supervisor will occur with greater frequency. The frequency of the undesired behavior will decrease because both performances cannot occur at the same time.

Reinforcing stimuli can be negative as well as positive. Negative reinforcing stimuli are referred to as *aversive stimuli*. A stimulus may be aversive because it signals reduction of positive reinforcement. A low grade on an examination is, for instance, an aversive stimulus; the positive reinforcer of the experience of competency or congratulations from one's classmates is unlikely to occur. A stimulus also may be aversive because it precedes or sets the occasion for other aversive stimuli. A mother's use of the word *no* is an example of such a stimulus; the child has learned that if he does not alter the behavior which gave rise to the mother's response of no that other aversive stimuli will follow. Aversive stimulus increases the frequency of behavior which removes the aversive stimulus. Negative reinforcement occurs, therefore, when a student learns a given subject in order to terminate the criticism of the teacher.

Aversive stimulus is also used in punishment. Punishment is said to occur when a given performance is followed by an adverse stimulus: for instance, withdrawal of permission to use the family car because an adolescent boy returned late from a date the previous night. Punishment has frequently been found to be ineffective for learning because it usually suppresses the emission of behavior but does not extinguish it. The frequency of behavior returns to its prepunished rate of emission when the aversive stimulus no longer follows the performance.

The behaviors arising from aversive stimuli are described as either *escape* or *avoidance*. Escape refers to behavior which terminates the aversive stimulus. Examples of escape behavior are, putting on dark glasses to diminish the glare from the sun, leaving a boring movie, taking an aspirin to relieve a headache. Avoidance is behavior which postpones the appearance of an aversive stimulus—if it is effective the aversive stimulus will not occur. Studying before an exam, inventing a good excuse for tardiness, taking care that food intake does not lead to weight-gain are all examples of avoidance. The major distinction between escape and avoidance is that in escape, response occurs in the presence of the aversive stimulus whereas in avoidance the response occurs before the appearance of aversive stimulus. Putting on gloves when one's hands feel cold is escape behavior; putting on gloves before one leaves the house is avoidance behavior.

Although the frequency of many performances is influenced by aversive stimulus, intensive aversive stimulus tends to disrupt large segments of the individual's repertoire. Fear of failure (threatened loss of positive reinforcement) may disrupt the student's usual study habits. The teasing, bullying behavior of a neighbor boy may cause the young child to discontinue leaving his yard to seek out playmates. Such disruption is referred to as a *negative emotional response* or *anxiety.* However, in operant conditioning theory, it is more useful to describe emotion as change in the frequency of behavior rather than as something that occurs within the individual. The continued presence or threat of aversive stimuli may lead to a marked weakening of the individual's total repertoire. Even those parts of the repertoire which had been learned through positive reinforcement may be effected. For instance, in the latter example, the social interaction skills previously learned by the child will not be reinforced positively if the child does not leave his yard. Indeed, if there is a sustained lack of positive reinforcement, the previously learned skills may be eliminated from the child's repertoire.

In addition to the disruptive effect of aversive stimuli, it has been found that aversive stimuli may lead to the learning of undesired behavior. If aversive stimuli are used in the attempt to add behavior to an individual's repertoire, some performance other than the one intended may be increased in frequency. This is particularly true if the performance is just as effectively used in order to terminate the aversive stimulus. For example, a husband may increase his frequency of playing golf to terminate his wife's nagging demands that he do some particular household repairs. The performance the wife wished to increase through the use of aversive stimulus was actually decreased. This example illustrates as well that the unintended performance is often incompatible with the desired performance. If criticism is used to shape verbal responses in a classroom situation, a decrease in the frequency of verbal responses often occurs. The fewer verbal responses emitted markedly interfere with the shaping process. In contrast to the use of aversive stimuli, positive reinforcement has an emotional impact that is likely to increase the frequency of performances that are useful and satisfying to the individual. The use of positive reinforcing stimuli is also more likely to increase the frequency of the desired performance.

Human behavior is a complex, progressive phenomena. Rather than a single performance, we usually observe an aggregate of behaviors which are eventually effective in influencing the environment in the desired manner. The two concepts, *chains of performance* and *conditioned reinforcer*, are useful in describing how complex behavior is acquired. A *conditioned reinforcer* is the actual reinforcer which maintains the frequency of a given performance. It has become paired with a primary reinforcer because it has preceded reception of the primary reinforcer. This process is similar to classical or Pavlovian conditioning. For example, being attractively groomed for a date is a conditioned reinforcer for applying makeup and pressing a dress because in the past being attractively groomed has preceded receiving approval from one's date. A poor grade on a quiz may negatively reinforce studying for the final examination because in the past poor quiz grades have preceded failure in an examination. As the examples indicate, both positive and aversive stimuli can come to be conditioned reinforcers.

The temporal delay between the conditioned reinforcer and receipt of the primary reinforcer may be considerable. However, the conditioned reinforcer must occasionally be paired with the reinforcer or the conditioned reinforcer will lose its capacity to act as a reinforcing stimulus. Observing one's own success in accomplishing a task is a conditioned reinforcer. However, if it is not occasionally paired with a primary reinforcer such as approval of significant others, perception of competent task completion will eventually lose its capacity to reinforce.

There are a number of patterns or ways in which reinforcement may occur. Such patterns are referred to as *schedules of reinforcement*. Schedules differ in two dimensions; number of performances and interval between reinforcements. There are four common schedules of reinforcement: (1) Fixed-ratio; which requires the same number of performances for each reinforcement; (2) Variable-ratio, in which the number of performances required varies for each reinforcement; (3) Fixed-interval, where there is a constant interval between reinforcements; and (4) Variable-interval, where there are different intervals between reinforcement. Variable-ratio and variable-interval schedules are sometimes referred to as *intermittent reinforcement* because the reinforcing stimulus does not occur in any recognizable pattern. Performances intermittently reinforced tend to have a high frequency and are difficult to extinguish from the individual's repertoire. For most individuals, behavior which gives rise to a positive response from others is on an intermittent reinforcement schedule.

A one-to-one fixed ratio schedule is referred to as *continuous reinforcement*. Such a schedule is often used in establishing a conditioned reinforcer and in the beginning phases of the shaping process. As continuous reinforcement rarely occurs in the environment of the adult, the developmental process of the individual is usually characterized by movement from a small fixed-ratio schedule to a much larger fixed-ratio schedule. Increasingly greater numbers of performances are necessary prior to reception of the reinforcing stimuli. Movement toward a large fixed-ratio schedule must be gradual or the learner is likely to stop emitting the desired response. An example of the normal alteration of a fixed-ratio schedule is illustrated when praise is given to a first grader for each word read correctly, while a college student receives a reinforcing stimulus only after having read and understood the content of several books.

Strain is used to describe a period of time during which no relevent behavior is emitted because the behavior required for reception of the reinforcing stimulus is excessive. Strain occurs when a performance is maintained on a very large fixed-ratio schedule. This is evident in the tendency of students not to study after taking an exam, and in an author's tendency not to write immediately after having completed a book. If the fixed-ratio schedule is too great for the individual, relevant behavior will cease to be emitted entirely. The extent to which the individual will continue to emit relevant behavior on a large fixed-ratio schedule is dependent upon the deprivation state of the individual, the degree to which the reinforcing stimulus terminates the state of deprivation, and the extent to which there has been gradual movement to a large fixed-ratio schedule. For instance, the doctoral candidate who knows that his future professional career is dependent on receiving his degree and has received reinforcement for increasingly greater periods of independent study is more likely to write his dissertation than the candidate who does not feel that his career will be greatly altered by the degree and has received reinforcement only for course work completed.

Complex human behavior directed toward the environment must be delicately tuned to environmental stimuli. This process is referred to as *stimulus control* or *discrimination*. Discrimination has occurred when a different frequency and/or form of a performance is evident in the presence of one stimulus and not evident in the presence of another. For example, the housewife responds differently to spilt water on her kitchen floor than to a broken milk bottle; wiping with a wet sponge is effective in dealing with water but a broken milk bottle requires use of a broom, dust pan, soap and water. Performances which change in response to small variations in the environmental stimulus are referred to as *fine-grain repertoire*. This is evident, for example, when one steers a car. Each movement of the steering wheel is influenced by variations in the road, other motor vehicles, pedestrians, traffic signs, and the route to be taken to the desired destination. Use of a fine-grain repertoire is also evident in a meaningful conversation between two people. Each person varies his response as the response of the other individual varies. Response of one individual acts as a stimulus for a response from the other individual. A fine-grain repertoire is, essentially, highly refined discrimination.

Acquisition of discriminatory behavior occurs through reinforcement of a response to one stimulus and nonreinforcement of a similar response to another stimulus. For example, in learning shapes, the child is successful when he puts the round block in the round hole and is unsuccessful when he attempts to put the round block in the square or triangular holes. Similarly, in learning to shave with a safety razor, the young man comes to vary the angle of the razor when shaving the different parts of his face because such variation leads to success.

Development of discrimination occurs most easily when the stimulus differences are originally gross and obvious and slowly move toward subtlety. In the study of a foreign language, for example, words which sound and/or appear very different are included in initial vocabulary lists. Words which are more similar appear on subsequent lists. The degree of discrimination between stimuli which the individual develops depends upon the extent to which the discriminatory behavior is reinforced. Thus the painter learns to discriminate fine differences between hues, tones and shades of colors. Artists working in other media do not need to acquire such fine discrimination.

Verbal behavior is acquired and used in a manner similar to any other kind of behavior. Because of its significance in human interactions, however, special attention will be focused on it here. Verbal performances are part of the behavioral repertoire of the speaker; although it is often more useful to explore these performances in terms of their effect on the listener. Verbal behavior is reinforced by the response of the listener—his response to the stimulus provides the reinforcing consequence. For example, when one says, "It's a lovely day," the verbal performance is reinforced by nodding, smiling, and verbal behavior indicating agreement. The speaker acts as his own reinforcing stimulus when his verbal behavior increases the frequency of a particular performance. If saying to one's self "I must study now" increases the frequency of studying, the sentence "I must study now" is a conditioned reinforcing stimulus for the speaker. Similarly if the statement "The car costs $3000" leads to depositing money in a savings account then the statement has come to be a reinforcing stimulus.

Verbal behavior may also act as a conditioned aversive stimulus if its emission has been followed by an aversive stimulus. The emission may be a thought or may have been spoken. When such a pairing takes place the frequency of the particular verbal behavior is decreased. Thus, if the individual has been told that it is wrong (disapproval) to think or say something, as for example, "I hate you," it is unlikely that he will think or speak in this manner. If the spoken phrase has been only negatively reinforced or punished, the phrase will remain in the individual's repertoire—but it will be used infrequently, if at all.

In the development of language, words come to be paired with actions, events, and experiences. This is easily seen in the child learning the cultural label for colors or animals. Events come to be labeled by the verbal and nonverbal behavior that occurs. The child learns the difference between a parade and a party, therefore, because the behavior which is and is not reinforced during these events differs. Internal experiences acquire labels in a similar manner. For example, the child may point to his head and say "hurt"; the parents respond by saying "You have a headache." If emission of the label leads to positive reinforcing stimulus this phrase comes to be used as a label for the experience.

Most adults use verbal behavior as a means of ordering environmental stimuli and as a guide for action toward the environment. Verbal behavior comes to be a conditioned positive or negative reinforcer. Thus, praise acts as positive reinforcement because it specifies behavior that brought about positive reinforcement in the past. In a work setting, the supervisor's statement, "That was a good job" acts as positive reinforcement because in the past it has been paired with a raise, increased responsibility, or more interesting assignments. Criticism acts as negative reinforcement because it specifies behavior that has led to negative reinforcement in the past. "That dress does not look good on you" is an aversive stimulus because not being attractively dressed may have led to being ignored by others, being laughed at or having dates with less-than-desirable men. Praise or criticism is an effective reinforcer for a given individual only if it has been paired with other positive or aversive stimuli. The person giving the praise or criticism must serve as a reinforcing stimulus for the individual as well.

There are several ways in which a speaker can alter the repertoire of a learner. A performance already in the learner's repertoire may be increased or decreased in frequency because of the stimulus presented by the speaker. If the desired behavior is not in the learner's repertoire it may be added through the process of shaping or chaining. The verbal behavior of the learner may be altered by the speaker through a process of rearranging existing verbal behavior so that new word combinations may occur. New verbal behavior is added by pairing the new word with the verbal behavior that is already a part of the learner's verbal repertoire. A definition of a new word, therefore, must be stated in the language of the learner; to tell the learner that a correlation is a measure of association is meaningless to the learner if "measure of association" is not part of his verbal repertoire.

The high frequency of many behaviors is maintained through the conditioned reinforcer of awareness of achievement or progress towards mastery. The successful student, for instance, continues to study because he is aware of his increasing competence in various subjects. This awareness is a conditioned reinforcer because it has been paired in the past with other primary reinforcers such as parental approval. If a given performance is not reinforced by awareness of achievement, such awareness may be developed by reinforcing various steps toward mastery. The individual may, for example, receive approval or be permitted to engage in some enjoyable activity after having completed a set amount of work.

An individual is said to have self control in a given situation when he alters the frequency of some performance in his own repertoire. This usually occurs through pairing verbal behavior with ultimate aversive or positive consequences of the behavior. The verbal repertoire at this time comes to be a conditioned reinforcer. For example, the housewife who does not like to iron may think of several ultimate positive consequences of ironing. This in turn increases the frequency of ironing behavior.

The behavior which an individual is able to learn is dependent upon the reinforcement available to him and upon his physiological makeup; a four-month-old child cannot learn to walk, for example, because his neurological structures are not sufficiently mature. Both the rate of learning and performances that can be learned are influenced by such things as neurological impairment, hormonal imbalance, and the presence of pathogenic chemicals in the body. Some behaviors may be learned in spite of or in order to compensate for physiological damage or deficit, but there is usually a limit beyond which learning cannot take place. In many cases, this limit cannot be determined prior to appropriate attempts to teach or learn specific behavior. The individual's capacity to learn is often underestimated by the self and others. The potential of the individual is often not realized because of faulty teaching methods.

The Acquisition of Deviant Behavior   In using operant conditioning concepts to describe psychosocial function and dysfunction, the behavior of the individual is taken as the focal point. The low frequency of certain behaviors and the high frequency of other behaviors is considered; hypothetical inner states and assumed mental apparatus are not utilized. The person is viewed in terms of his current repertoire and its controlling environment. A person is considered to be in a state of dysfunction when there is marked discrepancy between his repertoire and the repertoire required by his cultural group. There is typically a low frequency of behaviors which are effective in giving the individual satisfaction and/or in meeting the demands for living in a community.

There are several factors which are considered to be significant in causing a person to reach a state of dysfunction: bizarre or primitive behaviors may be maintained at a high frequency because other performances are not reinforced. The patient who stares vacantly out the window, rocks back and forth, or plays with his hands, may do so because the environment does not offer sufficient positive or negative reinforcement to encourage the emission of other behaviors. This process can be observed in a variety of situations where reinforcing stimuli are minimal. For example, at a dull lecture many persons can be observed daydreaming, doodling, playing with a rubber band or engaging in some other stereotyped behavior. Listening, the type of behavior desired in the situation, is not reinforcing because the lecture is not interesting. Other behavior, such as talking with others, would be negatively reinforced if it occurred. A similar response is seen in studies of sensory deprivation. When minimal reinforcing stimuli are available from the environment, persons are observed to engage in bizarre or primitive behavior. Maladaptive behavior may have a high frequency because it has been reinforced in the past; it continues to be maintained in the individual's repertoire because reinforcement was intermittent. Such a schedule of reinforcement tends to maintain behavior for a long period of time without further reinforcement.

Escape and avoidance behavior as previously defined arises from the effect of aversive stimuli. The individual's own thoughts (verbal repertoire) or nonverbal behavior often develop into conditioned aversive stimuli as a result of being paired with primary aversive stimuli. Through accidental reinforcement, the individual may have found that some bizarre or primitive behavior allowed him to escape or avoid aversive stimuli. For example, meticulous attention to dress, personal hygiene and organization of a coin collection may be reinforced by avoidance of sexual fantasies, which is a conditioned negative stimulus for some individuals. Similarly, continued dependency behavior may be used as an escape from the disapproval of an overly protecting mother. The mother's behavior would be interpreted as being maintained by the conditioned positive reinforcement of having someone in a state of dependency relative to her.

There may be a marked decrease in frequency of effective behavior because of strain. As previously defined, strain describes the effect on a performance which is reinforced on a large fixed-ratio schedule. Strain tends to occur when the environment has not provided for gradual movement from a small fixed-ratio schedule to a large fixed-ratio schedule. This phenomenon is particularly observable in the adolescent period. At this time there is often a marked increase in the number of performances required before reinforcement occurs. For example, if the individual has received money from his parents any time he wished to make a purchase, he may find it very difficult to sustain work-oriented behavior at a job. The number of performances required before receiving a paycheck and the number of paychecks he must receive before buying a particular item may be perceived by the individual as excessive. There would than be a low probability of the individual engaging in work-oriented behavior.

Continued existence in an environment where there are predominantly negative stimuli which the individual cannot escape or avoid leads to a decrease in the frequency of effective behavior. The individual experiences an inability to function and is observed to be unable to perform adequately. The aversive stimulus may be in the external environment. For example, the individual may be in a situation where he is threatened with unemployment because the factory he has been employed in for several years is about to close, has an intolerable home life because of his wife's continual nagging, and has been ostracized by his friends because of his liberal political views. If the individual has no behavior in his repertoire which will enable him to escape or avoid these considerable aversive stimuli it is very likely that effective behavior will decrease in frequency. The individual may also be immobilized by conditioned aversive stimuli which are a part of his own repertoire. A considerable number of his thoughts may have been paired with primary aversive stimuli. If the individual is unable to increase the frequency of behavior which will terminate these aversive stimuli, there will be a decrease in the frequency of effective behavior.

If the major part of an individual's repertoire is characterized by avoiding or escaping aversive stimuli, the individual is often unable to act effectively in his environment; the negatively reinforced behavior is incompatible with increasing the frequency of positively reinforced behavior. For example, the individual who becomes excessively involved with painting and sculpting in order to avoid meeting the demands of authority figures (a conditioned aversive stimulus) is unlikely to develop a high frequency of vocationally oriented skills.

The high frequency of usual behavior may be decreased when there is a sudden change in the environment. The change may lead to the removal of reinforcing stimuli and thus usual behaviors are no longer reinforced; this may occur, for example, at the time of retirement or when a parent's last child leaves home—reinforcement for a large part of the individual's repertoire is no longer available. Other behaviors must now be reinforced or the individual will experience marked difficulty in adjusting to his new life situation.

The individual may have a low frequency of effective behavior because the relevant performances were never established in his repertoire. For example, the individual who has had minimal contact with a peer group or who has received essentially no reinforcement for peer group interaction may not have the vaguest idea of how to relate effectively in a group. The individual who has received no reinforcement for independent behavior may not have the ability to do such things as purchase items from a store or make a simple meal.

In summary, a person in a state of psychosocial dysfunction is not receiving sufficient positive reinforcement to maintain an adequate frequency of behaviors which are effective in acting upon and interacting with the environment. Sufficient positive reinforcement is relative to each individual. The stimulus which is reinforcing and the optimal schedule of reinforcement is a matter of much individual variation. This is perhaps one of the greatest challenges to a therapist.

FUNCTION-DYSFUNCTION CONTINUUMS

The rest of this chapter and the following chapter are devoted to a description of the way in which operant conditioning is used as the foundation for a treatment process. The presentation is oriented toward the treatment of the adult patient who has been recently accepted as an in-patient or out-patient by a mental health facility. This orientation was selected merely for general presentation. It is felt that action-consequence is applicable to other age groups, health facilities, and patients whose primary diagnosis is not psychosocial dysfunction. Some alteration in evaluative procedures and techniques of treatment may be necessary to make this frame of reference appropriate for particular patients in a given setting.

A person is in a state of function if he exhibits a high frequency of adaptive behaviors and a low frequency of maladaptive behaviors, which allows him to successively engage in the activities of daily living, avocational pursuits, and work. A person is in a state of dysfunction if he exhibits a high frequency of maladaptive behaviors and a low frequency of adaptive behaviors which do not allow him to successfully engage in the activities of daily living, avocational pursuits, and work.

Adaptive behaviors are all those behaviors which are positively reinforced, effective in dealing with people and things, and perceived as acceptable by one's cultural group. *Maladaptive behaviors* are all those behaviors which are negatively reinforced, ineffective in dealing with people and things, or perceived as unacceptable by one's cultural group. A given behavior may be adaptive or maladaptive depending on how it is being maintained in the individual's repertoire and the situation in which it occurs. For example, a man may follow the recommendations made by his work supervisor out of fear of being fired (maladaptive behavior) or because he enjoys his work (adaptive behavior). A woman cleaning her house during the day is engaged in adaptive behaviors. Cleaning the house in the evening when her husband and children require attention is maladaptive behavior.

The phrase *activities of daily living* refers to caring for the self (personal hygiene, dressing appropriately, etc.), communication (using the telephone, writing, speaking, etc.) and travel (using public transportation, driving a car, etc.). *Avocational pursuits* refers generally to all those activities in which the individual engages that do not result in a monetary reward. They may be purely recreational in nature, such as reading a mystery or going to a party; or they may involve engagement in the public sector, such as volunteer work at a boy's club, political activities, or serving on a committee for improving the recreational facilities in one's neighborhood. *Work* refers to an individual's occupation—it is what one is or what one does. When an individual says that he is a student, factory worker, painter, housewife, or folksinger, he is stating the nature of his occupation. A given activity may be an activity of daily living, an avocational pursuit, or work, depending upon the situation. For example, preparing a meal would be an activity of daily living for a person living alone; it would be an avocational pursuit if it involved preparing a meal for company; it is part of the housewife's work.

For clarity in assessing the nature of activities of daily living, avocational pursuits and work, these activities are subdivided into two parts: independent manipulation of the nonhuman environment and shared manipulation of the nonhuman environment. *Independent manipulation* refers to using, handling, altering and caring for nonhuman objects. It includes such things as using the telephone, playing volleyball and laying bricks. *Shared manipulation* refers to the interpersonal relations which surround and are a part of manipulation of the nonhuman environment. For example, in using the telephone to request that one's landlord fix a leaking faucet, there is a certain tone of voice and words that are appropriate to the occasion. Playing volleyball involves cooperation with one's teammates and competition with the opposing team.

Whether an individual is in a state of function or dysfunction is relative to what is required of him in his expected environment.[4] *Expected environment* is a term used to identify the anticipated living situation of the patient after termination of treatment. The environment in which the patient will live may be a total institution, a sheltered environment, the pretreatment environment, a new unsheltered environment, or any combination of these. A *total institution* is a place of residence, work, and recreation where a large number of like-situated individuals, separated from the wider society, lead an enclosed formally administered round of life.[5] (Total institutions are state mental hospitals and institutions for the mentally retarded, for instance.) A *sheltered environment* is one in which the individual is protected from the usual demands of the social system—a half-way house, a sheltered workshop, or a boarding house in which many of the individual's needs are provided for by salaried employees. The pretreatment environment is the environment in which the patient lived prior to hospitalization or is living during the treatment process. A new, unsheltered environment is one in which the individual must meet the demands of the social system but in a setting which is different from the pretreatment environment.

The behavior needed by the patient in his expected environment is compared to the behavior that he exhibits at the beginning of the treatment process.

---

[4] Anne C. Mosey, *Occupational Therapy: Theory and Practice* (Boston: Pothier Brothers, Printers, Inc., 1968),

[5] Irving Goffman, *Asylum* (New York: Doubleday and Company, 1961).

Dysfunction is described in terms of what behaviors must be eliminated from the patient's repertoire and what behavior must be added so that the individual may function effectively in his expected environment. For example, if the individual is to return to an environment in which he is not required to wash, iron, and mend his clothes, the inability to perform these activities is not considered dysfunction.

No operational definition of function-dysfunction is provided in this frame of reference. There are no symptoms indicative of pathology. (Pathology is the specific behavior which is interfering with the patient's functioning in an adequate manner, or behavior not in the patient's repertoire which is required for adequate function.) For example, if a patient is unable to sustain attention to a task, this is not considered to be symptomatic of something else; it is dealt with directly in the treatment process; it is the dysfunction.

EVALUATION

Description of Process   Evaluation involves assessment of behavior: (1) that contributes to functioning; (2) that interferes with functioning; (3) that is necessary to acquire for adequate functioning. Performances are assessed relative to the activities of daily living, avocational pursuits and work currently required of the individual, or which are likely to be required of him in his expected environment. For example, a self-employed accountant who likes to read and watch television in the evening does not need to have great skill in making casual conversation with others. However, the homemaker who lives in a housing development where there is much time spent in visiting back and forth between apartments and gossiping in the courtyard needs to have at least some conversational skill. In order to make an accurate assessment of adaptive and maladaptive behavior, the therapist must gain information about the patient's current repertoire and his expected environment.

A procedure for the initial evaluation is outlined on pages 98-99. This frame of reference utilizes other evaluative procedures which is referred to as *secondary evaluation*. These procedures are different from the continual evaluation which occurs in all treatment processes. Secondary evaluations are more specific than initial evaluation and usually take place during treatment rather than prior to it; because they are so imbedded in the treatment process they will be discussed in the next chapter.

The procedure for initial evaluation has four parts: *interview, performance assessment,* a *questionnaire*, and *reading the reports of other staff members.* The initial *interview* is designed both to gain some information about the patient's repertoire and to help the patient and therapist become acquainted with each other. The therapist's concern, interest, and desire to help the patient are communicated at this time. Following the interview the patient is involved in the performance assessment, which has two parts: an individual task, and participation in a shared task. The *performance assessment* is designed to allow the therapist to observe those behaviors that are needed, to a greater or lesser degree, in order to participate successfully in most activities of daily living, avocational pursuits, and work. The *evaluation questionnaire* is designed to allow the patient to communicate his difficulties in functioning and what he would like to be able to do. It is usually filled out by the patient prior to his involvement in the individual task of the performance assessment. The therapist may wish to go over the questionnaire with the patient to help him complete those parts he was unable to complete independently. The therapist may also want some additional information. For example, if the patient circled "volunteer work" in the "avocational experience" section, the therapist may ask the patient to describe the work that he did. In reading the reports of other staff members, the therapist is primarily concerned with the patient's current life situation and behavior. Information about sources of positive and negative reinforcers is sought. Any data regarding the patient's cultural group is also useful to the therapist.

A Behavioral Survey with a key for its interpretation is given on pages 104-108. It is presented as a guide for the therapist in observing and reporting evaluative findings. The key provides a description of each category listed on the form through definition of behaviors which are considered to be maladaptive (1) and adaptive (4). The form is used in the following manner: a score of 1 through 4 is given to indicate placement of the patient on the continuum of described behavior. The score is entered in the "Present" column on the evaluation form. Judgment is made on the basis of the therapist's observation during the initial interview and performance assessment. Because the therapist is concerned with specific behavior, a "Comment" column is provided for a statement of behavior actually observed by the therapist. The behavior listed in this column should be that behavior which the therapist used to determine the patient's score. For example, "wandered around the room, looked out the window" might be entered in the comment column after "Concentration." If the therapist is uncertain where the patient is on any of the listed continuums he should leave the "Present" column blank. It may be difficult, for example, to place the patient on the responsibility and reliability continuums using the suggested evaluative procedure. These areas may be assessed later during the treatment process. The "Behavioral Survey" should only be viewed as a guide; if observed behavior does not comfortably fit into one of the listed categories, the behavior and the extent to which it is adaptive or maladaptive should be indicated at the bottom of the form.

In identifying the expected environment, the therapist asks, "Where will the patient be and what will he be doing in a given amount of time from now?" The time used is the average length of time a patient receives treatment at the particular center where the therapist is working. It is often useful to make a notation of the activities in which the patient is likely to be engaged (daily living, avocational pursuits, and work). If sufficient information about the expected environment is not provided by the patient, or if the information provided does not seem reasonable, the therapist must make some tentative judgments. For example, if the patient is unable to state any job that would be of interest to him or names a job that is obviously beyond his ability, the therapist will identify some job that he feels might be appropriate for the patient. Judgment is based on the patient's age, sex, avocational experience, educational background, behavior exhibited in the performance assessment, what jobs are held by other persons who are in the patient's cultural group, and knowledge of jobs available. A category such as clerical work or working with children will be selected rather than a particular position. The area of work will, of course, be discussed with the patient as part of the treatment process. The job category is identified tentatively at this point only to help in the clarification of the expected environment. Other tentative judgments are also made regarding avocational pursuits. For example, a fifteen-year-old boy may indicate that watching television is his only avocational pursuit—considered to be maladaptive behavior in many cultural groups. The therapist then identifies what the majority of fifteen-year-old boys in the patient's cultural group are doing. In another situation the therapist might suspect, after reading the social worker's report, that the patient will not be returning to his family home. If it appears that the patient will be living alone or with a friend the therapist would include "shopping for and preparing simple meals" as one of his activities of daily living.

The therapist should be as specific as possible in delineating what the patient's life situation will be and in identifying the behavior necessary for satisfactory functioning. The behavior needed is relatively easy to identify if the therapist is familiar with the environment, the patient's cultural group, and the requirements of the social roles which the patient will be taking. The therapist may seek information about behavior required for unfamiliar social roles by talking with the patient, social worker, vocational counselor, the patient's family or friends, or through a visit to the given environment to observe interaction in the unfamiliar role at first hand.

The purpose of identifying the patient's expected environment at this early stage of treatment is to help in judging whether a given behavior is adaptive or maladaptive. For example, if a young woman is approximately at the "2" level of self-assertion, and if it appears that she will return to her job as a bookkeeper, then the therapist would not identify this behavior as maladaptive. However, if a man wished to return to his job as a car salesman, then a "2" level of self-assertion would usually be considered maladaptive.

Based upon the behavior needed by the person in his expected environment, the therapist places a score of 1 through 4 in the *Future* column of the Behavior survey. There is often a tendency to score this column higher than is necessary. The question, "What does this patient absolutely need to be able to do to get along in his expected environment?" should be used as a guide. When the score in both the *Present* and *Future* columns are the same, the patient's behavior in that category is considered to be adaptive. Discrepancies in scores indicate the presence of maladaptive behavior in the patient's repertoire. If the patient requires behaviors that are not listed on the Behavioral survey the nature of the behavior and the extent to which it is required should be indicated on the bottom of the form.

The Evaluative Procedures   *Interview*   The following interaction is suggested for the initial interview: the therapist visits the new patient on the ward—if he is an out-patient, invites him to the room where treatment will take place—and explains the general purpose of therapy and the role which is expected of the patient in the evaluation and treatment process. The therapist gives the Evaluation Questionnaire to the patient and asks him to complete it prior to the first evaluative session. The patient is encouraged to ask questions and is provided with forthright responses and reassurance. Though concerned with giving information and observing behavior, the therapist should encourage casual conversation and perhaps even conduct a tour of the treatment facilities. The interview usually ends with an appointment being made for a more formal evaluative session.

Performance Assessment   The *individual task* is structured in the following manner: The patient is asked to engage in a simple activity; adequate directions and the necessary tools and materials are provided. The therapist gives help and support as needed. This part of the procedure may take place with only the therapist and patient present or several patients may be evaluated at the same time. After the patient has completed the task or has completed as much of it as he is able to do, the therapist asks the patient whether or not he liked what he was doing, what parts of the task he most enjoyed and least enjoyed, and what he thinks of the results.

Shared Task   Six to eight new patients are involved in the shared tasks; they are asked to do a simple activity which requires collaborative interaction. Any necessary tools and materials are provided or made readily available. In this activity, however, the therapist does not participate in the group. (His role as observer should be explained to the patients.)

EVALUATION QUESTIONNAIRE[6]

I   Identification

Name

Address

Age

Marital Status

a. With whom are you presently living? Give relationships, age occupation.

b. What is your present weekly income? What is the source of this income?

II Education

a. Grade school attended? Years completed?

b. High School attended? Years completed? Type of course taken (vocational, commercial, college preparatory)?

c. College attended? Years completed? Major?

d. Other education (e.g., trade school, business college)?

e. Do you intend to return to school?

III Activities of Daily Living

(Please circle those items which you have performed in the past and check those items you either feel you will need to do in the future or that you would like to be able to do.)

a. Prepare your own meals _____
    Shop for food _____
    Care for your clothes (wash, iron, mend) _____

---

[6] This questionnaire was derived from various patient-oriented assessment forms developed at New York State Psychiatric Institute under the supervision of G. Fidler, Hillside Hospital, and from the work of J. Matsutsuyn.

Buy your clothes _____
Drive a car _____
Use public transportation _____
Clean your living quarters _____

IV Avocational Experiences

(Please circle those activities you have enjoyed doing in the past and check those activities that you would like to do in the future.)

swimming	_____	modern dancing	_____
table games	_____	sketching	_____
(poker, chess, bridge)		painting	_____
photography	_____	gymnastics	_____
drama groups	_____	boxing	_____
discussion groups	_____	wrestling	_____
choral groups	_____	cooking	_____
woodworking	_____	baseball	_____
reading	_____	basketball	_____
playing musical instruments	_____	football	_____
listening to music	_____	tennis	_____
social dancing	_____	golf	_____
pool	_____	skiing	_____
sewing	_____	sculpture	_____
bicycling	_____	electronics	_____
social drinking	_____	knitting	_____
going to parties	_____	calisthenics	_____
movies	_____	watching TV	_____
union activities	_____	casual conversation	_____
bowling	_____	gardening	_____
lectures	_____	fixing things	_____
attending a class to learn	_____	shopping	_____
how to do something		PTA	_____
poetry	_____	church organizations	_____
going out to a restaurant	_____	volunteer work	_____
or bar		community action	_____
political organizations	_____	groups	

List any other activities. _____

V Work Experience

a. What are your past work experiences, starting with your last job? Please give dates of employment, kind of business, job title and duties, wages and the reasons for leaving the job.

b. Which of the jobs you have held did you like the most? Why?

c. Which of the jobs you have held did you like the least? Why?

d. What work skills do you have (e.g., typing, operating a special kind of machine, telephone repair, keypunch operator)?

e. What three jobs do you feel at this time would be most interesting to you?

VI Personal Data

a. What do you consider to be your outstanding abilities, talents, and strong points?

b. In what ways does your present method of thinking, feeling and acting interfere with the things you would like to do?

c. What do you see yourself doing a year from now? Five years from now?

Reading the Reports of Other Staff Members   The following questions may be used as a guide in reading reports:

1. What are the activities required of the patient in his pretreatment environment?

2. What alterations appear to be needed in the environment? (E.g., is it likely that the patient should or will have to change his place of residence?)

3. What is the patient doing and/or not doing that is interfering with his functioning?

4. What adaptive behavior is highly valued by the patient's cultural group? Does the patient place a similar value on this behavior?

5. What aversive stimuli seem to be maintaining the patient's maladaptive behavior?

6. What positively reinforcing stimuli seem to be maintaining the patients' adaptive behavior?

7. Has there been a recent loss of a major positive reinforcer?

BEHAVIORAL SURVEY

Patient _____

Therapist _____

Date _____

Behavior	Comments	Present	Future
General Behavior			
Appearance Coordination Bizarre Behavior Hyperactivity Hypoactivity Affect Responsibility Reliability			
Task Behavior			
Engagement Concentration Directions Activity Neatness Attention to Detail Performance Standards Problem Solving Organization of Task Complexity Initial Learning Interest in Activities Interest in Accomplishment			
Interpersonal Behavior			
Independence Cooperation Self Assertion Attention from Others Response from Others Sociability Group Task Roles Group Social-Emotional Roles Group Norms			

Scale: 1 = exhibits maladaptive behavior most of the time
2 = exhibits maladaptive behavior some of the time
3 = exhibits maladaptive behavior occasionally
4 = no evidence of maladaptive behavior

Key for the Behavioral Survey[7]

General Behavior

Appearance

1 = Inadequate hygiene; dress inappropriate for age, sex, current fashions and occasion; clothes dirty and unironed.
4 = Adequate hygiene, dress appropriate for age, sex, current fashions and occasion; clothes clean and ironed.

Coordination

1 = Moves in a clumsy manner, has difficulty manipulating tools and materials.
4 = Able to engage in activities which require both fine and gross movements.

Bizarre Behavior

1 = Stereotyped activity (rocking, playing with hands, repetitive statements), appears to be talking to self, preoccupied with own thoughts, etc.
4 = Absence of above.

Hyperactivity

1 = Accelerated in speech and/or action.
4 = Speaks and acts at normal pace.

Hypoactivity

1 = Retarded in speech and/or action.
4 = Speaks and acts at normal pace.

Affect

1 = Minimal expression of affect or expression inappropriate to occasion
4 = Spontaneous expression of affect which is appropriate to occasion.

Responsibility

1 = Does not take responsibility for his own actions.
4 = Accepts responsibility for actions.

Reliability

1 = Cannot be depended upon to carry out a given activity, inappropriate use of tools and materials.
4 = Can be depended upon to perform in an acceptable manner.

---

[7] Many of these behavioral catagories and definitions are based on Fidler, 1963.

Task Behavior

Engagement

1 = Does not engage in activity.
4 = Readily engages in activity without encouragement.

Concentration

1 = Readily loses interest in a given task.
4 = Works at a given task with sustained interest and attention.

Directions

1 = Unable to carry out simple demonstrated, oral and/or written directions.
4 = Readily carries out relatively complex demonstrated, oral and written directions.

Activity Neatness

1 = Performs activities in a sloppy, careless manner.
4 = Performs activities in a neat and orderly manner.

Attention to Detail

1 = Overly concise to the point that it interferes with performance.
4 = Attends to detail according to the demands of the given activity.

Performance Standards

1 = Sets standards for performance (too low or too high) which are not compatible with acceptable results.
4 = Sets standards for performance compatible with acceptable results.

Problem Solving

1 = Adaptive behavior is disrupted when confronted with a problem in the context of an activity.
4 = Identifies and solves problems which arise in the performance of an activity; uses resources in an appropriate manner.

Organization of a Task

1 = Unable to effectively organize an activity even when tools, materials and directions are available.
4 = Organizes a task in a logical and efficient manner.

Complexity

1 = Can engage in simple tasks only.
4 = Able to engage in activities which require the use of a variety of tools and materials and which require several steps for completion.

Initial Learning

1 = Learns a new activity very slowly.
4 = Learns a new activity quickly and without difficulty.

Interest in Activities

1 = Engages in a variety of activities but shows no interest in the activities.
4 = Shows interest in and a liking for a variety of activities; readily explores new activities.

Interest in Accomplishment

1 = Task accomplishment and/or the end product are of minimal interest.
4 = Shows pleasure in task accomplishment and end product.

Interpersonal Behavior

Independence

1 = Relies on others for direction, guidance, decisions and emotional support.
4 = Self reliant in carrying out activities.

Cooperation

1 = Opposes directions, suggestions and constructive criticism.
4 = Willingly follows directions and tries out reasonable suggestions.

Self Assertion

1 = Passive, excessively compliant.
4 = Makes own wishes and desires known in an acceptable manner.

Attention from Others

1 = Verbally or nonverbally demands excessive attention from others.
4 = Seeks attention in an acceptable manner.

Response from Others

1 = Actions or speech evoke negative response from others.
4 = Actions or speech evoke a positive response from others.

Sociability

1 = Does not voluntarily join others in activities, unable to carry on a casual conversation.
4 = Readily and appropriately participates in group activities; spontaneously carries on conversation with others.

Group Task Roles[8]

1 = Does not take group task roles.
4 = Takes appropriate task roles.

Group Social-Emotional Roles[9]

1 = Does not take group social-emotional roles.
4 = Takes appropriate group social-emotional roles.

Group Norms

1 = Does not identify or comply with group norms.
4 = Identifies and complies with a majority of group norms.

---

[8] Task roles are oriented to the selection, planning and execution of the group task. The following roles are included in this category:
  1. Suggesting new ideas
  2. Asking for clarification of facts
  3. Asking for clarification of opinions or values
  4. Offering facts
  5. Spelling out suggestions
  6. Clarifying relationships
  7. Defining the position of the group with respect to its goals
  8. Comparing the accomplishments of the group to some standard
  9. Prodding the group into action
  10. Expediting group movement through the performance of routine tasks. (Parsons and Bales)

[9] Social-emotional roles are oriented to the function of the group as a whole and the gratification of members' needs. The following roles are included in this category:
  1. Praise, agreement and acceptance of the contributions of others.
  2. Mediation of differences between members
  3. Change in the behavior of the self so as to maintain group harmony
  4. Facilitation and regulation of communication
  5. Statement of standards for the group to achieve
  6. Noting, interpreting and presenting information about group process
  7. Going along with the movement of the group (Parsons and Bales)

Chapter 5
ACTION-CONSEQUENCE II

POSTULATES REGARDING CHANGE

Adaptive behavior is increased through the judicious use of positive and differential reinforcement in conjunction with the processes of shaping and building chains of performance.

Maladaptive behavior is decreased through the judicious use of nonreinforcement and reinforcement of adaptive behavior which is incompatible with the emission of maladaptive behavior.

Aversive stimuli may be disruptive to the total repertoire of the individual and may lead to the learning of unintended and undesirable behavior.

Conditioned reinforcers are developed through the pairing of primary reinforcers with the desired conditioned reinforcer.

Intermittently reinforced behaviors tend to have a high frequency and are difficult to extinguish from the individual's repertoire.

Large fixed-ratio schedules or reinforcement are typical for the adult and they are developed through gradual movement from small fixed-ratio schedules.

Discriminatory behavior and fine-grain repertoires are acquired through reinforcement of a response to one stimulus and nonreinforcement of a similar response to another stimulus. This occurs most easily when the stimulus differences are originally gross and obvious and slowly move in the direction of being more subtle.

The conditioned reinforcer of awareness of achievement is developed by reinforcing the steps which lead to achievement.

Pairing of verbal behavior with the ultimate aversive or positive consequences of a contemplated behavior enables the individual to develop self control.

The frequency of behavior can be increased or decreased only if it is emitted.

Language is acquired through the pairing of verbal sounds (words) with actions, events and experiences.

The verbal behavior of the learner may be altered by the speaker through a process of rearranging existing verbal behavior so that new word combinations may occur.

New verbal behavior is added by pairing the new word with the verbal behavior that is already a part of the learner's verbal repertoire.

The pairing of an aversive stimulus with a positive stimulus tends to eliminate the negative or feared quality of the previously aversive stimulus.

THE TREATMENT PROCESS

This section is divided into two parts: "Sequence" and "Application of Change Postulates." These two aspects must be combined and integrated in order for the reader to have a comprehensive view of the treatment process.

The two parts are interdependent and are separated only for ease in discussion. The ideas outlined below may at times appear either too vague or too specific, as indeed they may be, given a particular patient, therapist, and setting. A frame of reference is only a guide. That is all that it can be . . . and all it ought to be.

Sequence   The initial goal of treatment is selected in the following manner: If the patient has considerable difficulty in completing the individual task during evaluation, treatment begins in this area.[1] ("Considerable difficulty" means that the patient was unable to complete the task and/or he was given a score of 1 in most of the categories related to individual task accomplishment.) The immediate goal of treatment is to decrease the frequency of those behaviors which interfere with task accomplishment and to increase the frequency of behaviors needed for task accomplishment. The therapist asks the questions, "What behavior is interfering most with the patient's functioning?" and, "What behavior does the patient absolutely need for functioning?" The answers to these questions provide the therapist with the immediate goal, which is concerned, if at all possible, with those things which the patient identifies as causing him difficulty. For example, if the patient identifies his major problem as being unable to concentrate, this is where the treatment process should begin. (The therapist may identify other behavior as more central but these can be dealt with later.) If the patient is able to complete the individual task but has difficulty with the shared task, then treatment begins in this area. Questions similar to the two listed above are used to select the initial goal.

Activities used for helping patients acquire the capacity to carry out an individual task are usually ones which involve simple manipulation of the nonhuman environment. The criteria used for selecting an activity are characterized by the following statement: it allows the patient to express the maladaptive behavior which is to be decreased and to emit the adaptive behavior which is to be increased; it is compatible with the patient's age, sex, cultural group, current

---

[1] Operant conditioning does not provide information which would allow one to deduce sequential goal setting. Thus the suggestions offered are based on what I feel is reasonable rather than upon scientific postulates. In general, this is the sequence utilized at Hillside Hospital, although their treatment process is not described as being based on operant conditioning.

behavior, and interests. The first two criteria are important because only the frequency of emitted behavior can be increased or decreased. Behavior that does not occur cannot be altered. To meet the latter criterion, the therapist asks himself, "What is this patient able to do and what kinds of activities is he likely to enjoy?" This information is gained through reviewing the patient's behavior during the performance assessment, prior knowledge of activities which are typical in the patient's cultural group for individuals of his sex and age, review of the patient's avocational and work experiences, and discussion with the patient.

The process of matching patient and activity involves analysis of activities. Questions to guide analysis are: (1) What age group is usually involved in this activity? (2) Is the activity more typically performed by males or females? (3) What adaptive behaviors must be in an individual's repertoire in order to perform this activity successfully? (4) What maladaptive behaviors may be emitted in the context of this activity but will not grossly interfere with performance of the activity?

Shared task behaviors are learned in a group. The type of group utilized will depend upon the patient's current behavior and the behavior that is to be learned. In selecting the appropriate group for the teaching of shared task behaviors, the therapist will compare the patient's current repertoire to the classes of behavior which are required for successful participation in various types of groups. The patient is placed in a group which is most compatible with his current repertoire, but which also requires emission of the behavior that is the immediate goal of treatment. Treatment continues within the context of a given group until the patient has acquired all of the shared task behaviors required for adequate functioning in the group. If further shared task learning is necessary, the patient is placed in another group. This may be an entirely new group, or the original group as a whole may be altered in the direction of a more advanced level of performance.

Groups may also be used for the teaching of some individual task behaviors. However, this is done only if the patient has sufficient adaptive behaviors to be able to interact in a group setting. A one-to-one relationship is used for teaching individual task skills if the patient is unable to tolerate any group interaction, if his behavior is such that it continually disrupts the group, or if the patient requires the therapist's full attention.

When the patient has learned sufficient individual and shared task behaviors to engage in some activities of daily living, avocational pursuits, or work, the treatment goals are altered to include learning in these areas. Many patients, of course, have sufficient adaptive behaviors to begin treatment in these areas immediately. The initial focus will depend upon the patient's interests and what he needs to learn to function effectively in his expected environment. Two or three areas may be dealt with at the same time if the patient is able to learn several different behaviors simultaneously. Additional formal evaluation may be necessary at this time; these are the secondary evaluations previously discussed.

Activities of Daily Living   In addition to the activities of daily living listed on the Evaluation Questionnaire, the therapist is also concerned with such things as personal hygiene, appropriate dress, table manners, use of the telephone, and budgeting money. Observation of the patient will give the therapist information regarding personal hygiene and appropriate dress. Information about the patient's table manners may be sought from ward personnel. The patient's capacity to successfully engage in the other activities of daily living may need to be evaluated through observation of actual performance; if, however, the patient says he has no difficulty in activities of daily living and the therapist has no reason to suspect any problems, no further evaluation or treatment may be necessary. The therapist must, nevertheless, remember that many patients are unaware of inadequate functioning in this area or fearful of expressing difficulty with such common activities.

Ideally, evaluation of a patient's capacity to engage in activities of daily living takes place in his expected environment, preferable because the therapist is able to observe exactly where the patient is having difficulty. Also, the therapist is in a better position to estimate what behaviors are necessary for adequate function in his particular environment. The patient himself is also able to observe what he can and cannot do effectively. If it is not possible to evaluate a patient in his expected environment, a simulated situation in the mental health facility may be used. If such is the case, the particular procedures for evaluation are dependent to some extent upon materials and settings available in the institution—the therapist must often be ingenious in devising situations which allow him to gain sufficient information. The patient is evaluated only for those activities of daily living which he will be required to perform in his expected environment.

Some suggested evaluative procedures are as follows: (1) Ask the patient to demonstrate how he would wash his clothes using the washer and dryer on the patient's living unit. (2) Observe the patient ironing a shirt or blouse. (3) Ask the patient to sew on a button, mend a ripped seam and/or make a hem. (4) Observe the patient shopping for personal articles or food in the hospital canteen or a local store. (5) Have the patient prepare lunch. (6) Ask the patient to call the ward and tell the charge nurse that he will be late returning from his therapy session. (7) Ask the patient the appropriate price of common items that he might buy in a store. (8) Ask the patient to make out a grocery list for three days of meals for one person. (9) Provide the patient with appropriate maps of subway or bus routes and request that he tell you how he would get from one specific place to another.

Regardless of the evaluative procedure used, the therapist is concerned with identifying behavior which contributes to, interferes with, and needs to be acquired for adequate functioning. Behavior is assessed in connection with manipulation of nonhuman objects and the interpersonal interactions which must accompany such manipulation. For example, in evaluating the patient's ability to use a telephone, the therapist is concerned about the patient's ability to look up a telephone number, dial the phone accurately, ask to speak to a particular person, speak in a friendly coherent manner, and give the appropriate message.

Activities of daily living which the individual is able to perform are not of concern to the therapist unless there is a discrepancy between ability and actual performance of the activity in the patient's expected environment. In such a situation the therapist and patient must assess the environment together in order to determine why these activities are not being positively reinforced. Treatment of this problem is discussed in the following section.

When it appears that the patient is unable to perform one or several of his activities of daily living, learning these activities becomes a goal of treatment; the particular activity selected as the immediate goal will depend upon which one the patient believes to be most important for him to learn at the present time. If he is unable to give any opinion, the therapist may select one he feels is of particular importance.

From the evaluation process, the therapist has identified which portion of the activity the patient is able to perform, and has therefore gained information about his starting point. The therapist makes an analysis of the activity in order to assess the various behaviors which are necessary for adequate performance and identifies the gestalt of behaviors required, including assessment of behavior needed for manipulation of the nonhuman environment. If the activity involves a shared task, he lists and evaluates the interpersonal behaviors necessary to engage in this aspect of the activity. For example, in preparing a simple meal for one's self, no interpersonal behavior is necessary; shopping for food, however, involves interpersonal behavior relative to other shoppers, clerks, and the cashier.

As the patient acquires competence in one of his activities of daily living, the treatment process is focused upon others. The therapist is concerned not only with the patient's ability to carry out activities in the treatment setting—of far greater importance is the structuring of treatment so that the patient engages in activities of daily living in his expected environment. How this is done is described in the section on "Application of Change Postulates."

Avocational Pursuits   A review of the patient's Evaluation Questionnaire will provide information about the patient's avocational pursuits, and additional information may be gathered from the patient and other staff members. Taking the patient's age, sex, and cultural group into account, the therapist must decide whether the avocational pursuits in which the patient has indicated he would like to participate are appropriate: "Are these activities typical for an individual of the patient's age and sex in his cultural group?" "Will they provide the type of satisfactions most people receive from avocational pursuits?" In making this assessment, the therapist must take care not to use his own personal values as the sole means of judging the appropriateness of the patient's avocational pursuits, for this is an area of great individual difference. (A patient may not, on the other hand, entertain the idea of participating in a particular avocational pursuit he might enjoy because he is well aware that his repertoire does not contain the behaviors necessary for competent participation in the desired activity.)

The patient and therapist must discuss the issues and attempt to come to some agreement regarding the patient's future avocational pursuits. If the patient's past avocational pursuits appear to be appropriate and satisfying to the patient and if he indicates no desire to engage in new or different pursuits, no treatment needs to take place in this area. If the learning of new or different avocational pursuits is indicated, however, the therapist may offer some suggestions. Such suggestions should be based upon the therapist's knowledge of the patient's cultural group, the patient's current adaptive behavior and the behavior it appears that he has the potential to learn, the interests he has shown during the treatment process, and, pragmatically, the "kind of person the patient seems to be."

Suggestions made by the therapist may have little meaning to the patient; he may lack information about the activities mentioned or he may not be aware of the kinds of activities which he might enjoy. In this case it is useful for the patient to engage in *exploratory behavior*. Exploratory behavior is a trial engagement in a particular activity in order to discover whether or not that activity will lead to positive reinforcement or has the potential for being positively reinforcing.

Treatment in the area of avocational pursuits begins with the learning of a new activity in which the patient has expressed some interest. Again the therapist makes an analysis of the gestalt of behaviors necessary for successful engagement in the activity. For example, in an analysis of basketball, the therapist is concerned with the individual's actual manipulation of the ball, his maneuvers, his observance of the rules of the game, his cooperation with team members, and with his attitude toward competition. Other factors must be taken into consideration as well. If the therapist finds that the only place to play basketball in the expected environment of the patient will be in an athletic club, the behavior necessary for admission (filling out application forms, having a personal interview, etc.) and behavior necessary for acceptance by other club members must be part of the repertoire to be developed.

The therapist shares this analysis with the patient; together they assess what required behaviors are currently in the patient's repertoire and what behaviors need to be acquired, and on the basis of this evaluation the immediate treatment goals are set. The specific goal selected will depend upon the behavior the patient and therapist decide is essential and within the patient's capacity for learning at the present time. For example, the patient may be overwhelmed at the thought of learning how to participate in an interview, but may feel comfortable learning how to cooperate with team members.

The initial learning of avocational pursuits usually takes place in the treatment setting. After the individual has acquired the more basic behaviors, continued learning takes place in the patient's expected environment or one similar to that environment. Through reinforcement of involvement in avocational pursuits by the therapist, the patient acquires sufficient adaptive behaviors for him to receive reinforcement in his expected environment. Elaboration and refinement of behaviors may take place wholly through reinforcement from the expected environment or in conjunction with reinforcement by the therapist and fellow patients.

Work   Treatment in the area of work or occupation is dependent upon the patient's work experience and the extent to which he possesses work skills which are needed in his expected environment. Several common situations will be discussed.

If the patient has a job to which he wishes to return, or had a job in the not too distant past and wishes to return to a similar job, the therapist evaluates the patient in the light of that specific job. With the help of the patient, the therapist analyzes the position to determine what behaviors are necessary for successful employment in this type of work. Both manipulation of nonhuman objects and the personal interaction required are taken into consideration. In turn, the patient's current behavior is assessed relative to job requirements. The Behavior Survey may be used as a guide.

If there is minimal discrepancy between the patient's behavior and behavior required for the job, no treatment may be necessary in this area. If, however, the therapist suspects for one reason or another that the patient may have difficulty with this job, or if the patient feels he is not ready to return to work, or if the environment in which the patient's behavior has been observed is not sufficiently similar to the job environment, further evaluation is required. The evaluative procedure should take place in a situation as similar as possible to the anticipated work situation—an appropriate hospital or community job, a sheltered workshop, or, in the case of a homemaker, the actual home setting may be used. If necessary, a simulated work situation in the treatment facility may provide adequate information. The behaviors required for the job are compared to the behavior exhibited by the patient; and, if the patient does not exhibit the necessary behaviors, treatment is oriented to the learning of these behaviors.

Another approach is necessary if the patient's present behavior is grossly different from the behavior necessary for satisfactory employment in the job in which he expresses interest. When the patient is unaware of this great discrepancy, the patient's understanding of his own capacities and limitations relative to work would become the immediate goal of treatment. The treatment setting used would be one that was somewhat similar to the job desired by the patient. Treatment essentially involves the pairing of verbal behavior with nonverbal behavior relative to performance.

When the patient indicates through his verbal repertoire that he has gained some awareness of his capacities and limitations the therapist and patient discuss more suitable jobs. The therapist may suggest various types of work which he feels would be appropriate for the patient. His suggestions are based on his knowledge regarding the patient and the requirements of various jobs. When possible, suggestions would also be based upon data gathered from various vocational tests previously taken by the patient. As in discussion of avocational pursuits with the patient, a period of exploration may be necessary. The patient may engage in trial use of various machinery, or become involved in different jobs in the hospital, a sheltered workshop, or in the treatment facilities. When possible, the patient engages in trial jobs in his expected environment. During the process of participating in these trial jobs, the patient and therapist continue to discuss the appropriateness of various jobs and, ideally, come to some agreement upon the type of job it now appears the patient would enjoy and be capable of performing adequately. The agreed-upon job and the patient's present behavior are again compared to assess the need for further learning.

The therapist must determine which behavior he will be concerned with in the treatment process and which behaviors need to be acquired through formal training. "Formal training" here refers to an academic setting or a vocational training program. The therapist is usually concerned with teaching adaptive behaviors relative to jobs which require no particular prior training, the shared task aspect of jobs which require formal training, and preparation for engaging in formal training. To illustrate: if it has been decided that the patient is to prepare for a job as a salesperson in a department store, the therapist would provide experiences which would allow the patient to learn the necessary behaviors for this type of job. However, if it has been decided that the patient is to prepare for work as a secretary, the therapist provides experiences which would allow the patient to learn such shared task behaviors as making superficial conversation, appropriate dress, some deference to authority, how to ask another person to go out to lunch, pleasant telephone manners, organizing tasks relative to priorities, etc. Learning of many of the above-listed behaviors would also prepare the patient for a formal training program oriented toward learning typing and shorthand. Although the therapist may engage the patient in simple typing and shorthand exercises, this would be done primarily to help the patient learn necessary shared task behaviors and to facilitate her adjustment in the formal training program.

If the patient has not worked recently—or has never worked for any extended period of time—a different kind of work evaluation may be necessary prior to trial exploration of jobs. It is suggested that the patient be placed in some work situation which appears to be compatible with his current repertoire and interests (as assessed through discussion, the performance assessment, and the Evaluation Questionnaire). The therapist is concerned with evaluating behaviors relative to functioning in a general work situation. The following categories are offered as a guide:

1. Alter behavior appropriately on the basis of constructive criticism
2. Follow written and oral directions
3. Sustain attention to work tasks
4. Organize tasks relative to priority
5. Perform tasks in normal amount of time
6. Work at increased speed when required
7. Return to work when interrupted
8. Carry on appropriate conversation when working
9. Interrupt work task and carry on appropriate conversation
10. Complete forms
11. Plan work day so that required amount of work is accomplished
12. Come to work on time
13. Work a normal work day
14. Evoke a pleasant response from others

15. Follow the norms of the work setting
16. Give assistance willingly

In addition, the therapist attempts to determine what type of work may be appropriate for the patient. Questions like "What can he do" and "What aspects of the work does he appear to enjoy?" may be useful.

If the patient is deficient in many work-related behaviors, the treatment process is directed toward the learning of these behaviors. The immediate goal is selected on the basis of the most maladaptive behavior and on the behavior the patient is interested in adding to or eliminating from his repertoire. A situation similar to the one used for evaluation, or a somewhat different work situation, may be used in the treatment process. The criterion for selecting the appropriate setting is the same as the criterion for selecting any activity for treatment: it should allow the patient to emit the adaptive behavior which is to be increased and the maladaptive behavior which is to be decreased—and be acceptable to the patient. After the development of some work-related adaptive behaviors, the therapist and patient discuss the appropriateness of various jobs. Trial exploration of jobs may be necessary. The treatment process then proceeds as outlined above.

A patient who has had many unsatisfactory jobs may or may not be able to identify the behavior which has interfered with successful involvement in work. An evaluation procedure such as the one I have already outlined may be needed. If the patient has accurately delineated his areas of difficulty, however, a less extensive evaluation is needed. The behavior which the patient wishes to add to his repertoire and the behaviors he wishes to eliminate become the immediate goal of treatment.

The patient is ready to go out and seek employment or to participate in a formal training program when there is minimal discrepancy between the behavior required for satisfactory employment or formal training and the patient's repertoire. However, the process of looking for a job, obtaining employment, and gaining admission to a formal training program may require special behaviors which are not readily available to him. His repertoire must therefore be assessed in the light of behavior required for these activities. Treatment is directed toward acquisition of these behaviors if this is found to be necessary. Whether treatment continues after the patient has obtained employment or is involved in a formal training program is dependent upon the extent to which the patient is receiving positive reinforcement from his expected environment. Treatment continues until the patient's work-oriented behavior is sustained through positive reinforcement from the expected environment.

Treatment in the area of work is greatly facilitated and enhanced by collaboration with vocational counselors, social workers, persons involved in supervising hospital jobs and sheltered workshops, academic and technical educators, personnel from private, state, and federal employment agencies, and persons involved with allocating funds for the education and training of the handicapped. When these services are available to the therapist, the treatment process is planned and implemented as a joint, cooperative venture. The role of all those involved is clearly delineated so that treatment will be as efficient and expedient as possible. Even if such personnel are not readily available to the therapist, it is suggested that he seek out someone in one or more of these fields, for the time necessary for locating such persons and establishing a working relationship with them is well worth the effort.

Application of Change Postulates   In using action-consequence as the basis for treatment, the therapist is concerned with decreasing the frequency of maladaptive behaviors and with increasing the frequency of adaptive behaviors. The treatment process is directed not only to learning in the clinical setting but, more importantly, to establishing a repertoire of performances which is maintained through the patient's interaction in his expected environment. For example, the therapist may teach the patient to function in a hospital job as the initial step in helping him to secure gainful employment in the community. Only if the treatment process has been properly organized and applied will learning in the clinical setting influence what the patient does in his expected environment. Treatment, then, is guided by those postulates which are concerned with the development and continued maintenance of a repertoire of adaptive behavior.

The concept of reinforcement is central to the theory of *operant conditioning*. This term is the name given to the process through which the frequency of a given performance has increased because it has been followed by a reinforcing stimulus. It is necessary for the therapist to identify something which will act as reinforcing stimulus for a particular patient. The reinforcing stimulus must be such that it can be manipulated—given and withheld—by the therapist solely on the basis of the patient's performance in therapy. For example, receiving privileges is a reinforcing stimulus for many patients in a hospital setting. However, if the patient's privilege status is altered by the team on the basis of the patient's total behavior in the hospital setting, it is obvious that privilege is not an effective reinforcer for the therapist to utilize. It is ineffectual for several reasons: the patient's adaptive behavior does not result in immediate reinforcement; it is difficult for the patient to understand exactly which modes of behavior are resulting in reception of the reinforcing stimulus; maladaptive as well as adaptive behavior may be reinforced; it is difficult to control or alter the schedule of reinforcement; and finally, in many settings alteration of status is used as a form of punishment. An increase in privilege status can be utilized as a reinforcing stimulus by the therapist if the patient's status is based solely upon his acquisition of a specified number of points. In a clinical setting oriented to this procedure, points or tokens are gained through emission of adaptive behaviors in a variety of different situations. These, in turn, are exchanged for privileges or purchase of small items. Utilization of this type of reinforcing stimulus requires considerable cooperation and coordination on the part of staff members.

Other reinforcers which may be available to the therapist are: tactile contact; nonverbal or verbal expression of approval; attention; food; cigarettes; money; engagement in a desired activity; task accomplishment; and attention and approval from other hospital personnel, peers or persons in the community.

Making an accurate judgment of the reinforcer which will work for a given individual is difficult. It is often necessary to use a trial and error approach during the initial phases of the treatment process. However, certain principles may be used for making some judgments: a child or person who acts in an immature manner will often respond to tactile contact and food; if the patient seems to seek approval from the therapist during evaluation, receipt of such approval may be an effective reinforcer; adolescents often respond to attention and approval from their peers; if an individual enjoys a certain activity, engagement in the activity may reinforce the desired behavior; attention from a particular staff member may be reinforcing for a patient who has formed a special attachment to the staff member. The ability to make an accurate selection of the reinforcer that will be effective increases as the therapist has an opportunity to treat many different patients.

Once the therapist has identified a reinforcing stimulus, it is utilized subsequent to the emission of that adaptive behavior stated as the immediate goal of treatment. For instance, if the immediate goal is to increase the patient's attention to other persons in the treatment setting, and the reinforcing stimulus is the therapist's nonverbal approval and attention, the therapist smiles and nods and perhaps goes and sits next to the patient each time the patient looks at others in the room or responds to another's remarks.

The immediate goal of treatment may also be concerned with eliminating or extinguishing a specific maladaptive behavior. When this maladaptive behavior is emitted in the treatment setting, the reinforcing stimulus is withheld. Thus, if sitting in the corner alone reading a magazine has been identified as maladaptive behavior, the therapist ignores the patient while he is engaging in this behavior and attention is given when the patient engages in any behavior other than magazine reading. In the beginning phases of treatment the therapist may have to watch very carefully so that he will be able to give positive reinforcement (attention) for such a tentatively adaptive behavior as looking up from the magazine. The therapist may even have to wait until it is time for the patient to go to lunch; attention would then be given as the patient returns the magazine to the rack or places it under his arm to carry to the dining room. The therapist must exert a considerable amount of self control in this type of situation, for he must not only wait for some evidence of adaptive behavior but he must also inhibit the seemingly natural reaction to give attention to the individual who is exhibiting maladaptive behavior. If attention is being utilized as the reinforcing stimulus and the therapist sits next to or talks with the patient while he is reading the magazine, magazine reading, as the maladaptive behavior, would be reinforced.

The treatment process begins at the level at which the patient is currently functioning; it begins with the behavior the patient is currently able to emit. It is, therefore, impossible to attempt to engage a patient in the creation of a non-human object when he is only capable of getting out of bed through the application of almost continuous external reinforcement. Only behavior which is emitted by an individual can be subject to reinforcement. *Shaping* is one of the processes utilized to help the patient move from a position of emitting very primitive or simple behavior to a position in which he is able to engage in relatively complex performances. The procedure begins with reinforcement of behavior which is currently a part of the individual's repertoire. Behavior is differentially reinforced when the performance moves in the direction of the desired performance. Eventually only that class of behavior which is effective in carrying out a given individual or shared task will be reinforced. For example, if the therapist is concerned with helping a patient give appropriate attention to detail, any attention to detail is reinforced initially—once this behavior is established in the individual's repertoire, minimal attention is no longer reinforced. Instead, reinforcing stimuli are given for additional or more concentrated attention to detail. This process is continued until the patient gives the degree of attention to detail which is appropriate for a given task.

The activities selected for use in the shaping process are important. The activity is graded so that behavior currently available to the patient leads to successful completion of the activity. Using the example above, the initial activity selected would be one in which only minimal attention to detail leads to an acceptable end result. Activities requiring an increasingly greater degree of detailed work are provided as the patient acquires a higher frequency of this class of behavior. For example, the patient may start with an activity such as sorting different colored hospital forms. The activity might then be progressively altered to include collating multipage forms and then move on to alphabetical filing. Each change in the activity requires additional attention to detail.

The selection of an activity the patient is able to complete successfully allows for reinforcement of the behavior leading to successful completion as well as for adequate task accomplishment. Task accomplishment in itself may be reinforcing to the patient, particularly if there are obvious criteria by which success may be judged. For example, the criterion used to judge success in assembling a pair of moccasins from a kit is more obvious than the criterion used for judging the success of a charcoal drawing. The thought or statement of "I have done well" or "I have been able to complete a given task in an adequate manner" is often one of the most powerful sources of reinforcement.[2]

There are some patients, however, for whom task accomplishment is not a source of reinforcement. In the context of treatment the therapist regulates reinforcement so that it is provided as a result of successful task completion. This may not occur in the initial phases of treatment but should be provided for as soon as possible. Pairing task completion with an external reinforcer leads to the development of successful task completion as a conditioned reinforcer—considered to be an important part of the treatment process because task accomplishment is a type of reinforcer that the patient can carry with him into his expected environment. It will help to maintain adaptive behavior when no other means of reinforcement is available and allows the patient to be more independent or self-determining.

---

[2]Robert White, "Motivation Reconsidered: The Concept of Competence," in L. Rabkin and J. Carr (eds.), *Sourcebook in Abnormal Psychology* (Boston: Houghton Mifflin Co., 1967).

Shaping (differential reinforcement of approximations of desired behavior) may also be used in the teaching of a multidimensional performance. The therapist begins by reinforcing those aspects of the desired performance currently in the patient's repertoire. As the patient emits other behaviors which contribute to the total performance, these are reinforced. The previously emitted, more simple or lower level behaviors are no longer reinforced directly; they will be encouraged now only in combination with the more complex behavior. For example, in helping the patient to learn to prepare a simple meal, the most adaptive behavior the patient may be capable of emitting at the beginning of the treatment process is to enter the kitchen. Such behavior is reinforced and the therapist takes primary responsibility for meal preparation. Continued treatment is concerned with successive reinforcement of such things as watching the therapist, opening the soup can, going over to the stove to look at the soup, stirring the soup, getting out dishes and utensils, putting lettuce in the sandwiches, etc. As each specific behavior is established in the patient's repertoire, the therapist reinforces other behavior which leads to the total performance of preparing a meal. There is, therefore, progressive movement from the therapist preparing the entire meal to the patient taking over this responsibility, and the meal itself is altered over a period of time in the direction of becoming more complex. For example, the first few meals might simply consist of canned soup and crackers. Subsequently the patient and therapist might be involved in making peanut butter sandwiches, grilled cheese sandwiches, scrambled eggs, pancakes, and creamed chicken on toast. The preparation of each meal requires more complex behavior as the patient's ability to deal effectively with the various tasks increases.

Differential reinforcement of behavior is also effective in decreasing the frequency of maladaptive behavior. A class of adaptive behavior is reinforced which is incompatible with a specific class of maladaptive behavior. For example, an individual cannot usually emit behavior which leads to a positive response from others at the same time that he is emitting behavior which leads to a negative response. In applying differential reinforcement the therapist provides a reinforcing stimulus for behavior leading to a positive response and withholds the reinforcing stimulus when the patient emits behavior leading to a negative response. The frequency of the maladaptive behavior will decrease simply because it is incompatible with the reinforced adaptive behavior.

Another technique used in the treatment process is building chains of performance. *Chains of performance* are sequences of individual performances, each maintained by the stimulus it produces. Each individual performance is reinforced by the next performance in the chain. As mentioned in Chapter Four, chains of performance are taught by beginning at the end of the chain and reinforcing the final performance first. For example, in helping a patient to learn to shop in a grocery store, the therapist may begin the teaching process by taking the patient to a store and buying some item for the patient in which the patient has expressed interest—the item must be a source of reinforcement for the patient. The treatment process might progress backward over a period of time in the following manner: the patient pays for his own purchase, locates the item in the store and brings it to the cashier, takes responsibility for leading the therapist to the store (using public transportation if necessary), goes to the store alone, determines what is the best time to go shopping and makes a list of items to be purchased.

In building chains of performance, learning should be oriented toward the patient's expected environment if at all possible. The last performance in the chain should be reinforcing to the patient in a way that is independent from the therapist. To clarify: in the above example, the item initially obtained at the store was something that the patient wanted and would, therefore, serve as a reinforcer. The approval or attention of the therapist was not used as a reinforcing stimulus. (This is an important point because the therapist is concerned with teaching in such a manner that a chain of performance will be maintained after treatment is terminated. If the therapist is the primary reinforcing stimulus the chain is not likely to be maintained.)

Shaping and building chains of performance are similar since they begin with behavior the patient is currently able to emit. They are dissimilar because chaining begins with the final performance, whereas shaping leads to the desired final performance. Both processes may be used in helping the patient to develop complex behavior. For example, in teaching the patient to become an effective group member, shaping may be used to teach the patient to engage in casual conversation and chaining may be used to help the patient engage in decision making. In the latter situation, the therapist might begin asking the group to make a selection between two alternatives. Treatment moves progressively toward responsibility for decision making regarding a group task and the most efficient and effective manner of carrying out that task being taken by the group. In using either technique alone or both techniques in combination, the therapist must be very clear as to what behavior is to be reinforced and what sequence of learning is planned for the treatment process.

There are several techniques or initiating methods which the therapist may use in order to increase the probability of the patient emitting adaptive behavior so that it will be available for reinforcement. These methods may be used in the learning of individual or shared task behaviors. The method or methods selected are determined primarily by the extent to which the patient is able to alter his behavior on the basis of a verbal interchange. Pragmatically speaking, the therapist uses whatever initiating methods appear to be most successful with each particular individual or group.

The simplest and most primitive initiating method involves waiting until the patient exhibits an approximation of the adaptive behavior he needs to acquire. This behavior is differentially reinforced as it moves in the direction of becoming an effective performance. The therapist may also encourage imitation in order to initiate adaptive behavior in the patient. The therapist suggests to the patient that he do something in a manner similar to the therapist's performance or the performance of another patient. Imitation may also be encouraged by giving reinforcing stimuli for any imitated behavior. Once imitation is a part of the patient's repertoire, differential reinforcement is given for the emission of specific imitated behaviors. In another method, the therapist suggests that the patient act in a certain manner—the desired behavior is described. Another similar method involves pointing out ineffective behavior which the patient is emitting and suggesting that he experiment with other behaviors. Specific behaviors are not described. The patient is encouraged, instead, to try out various behaviors which he thinks will be more effective. Through trial and error the patient discovers the behavior that will lead to positive reinforcement. An initiating method which may be used in a group setting utilizes discussion of the behavior of self and others with mutual encouragement for appropriate and effective group behavior. A specific time may be set aside for this discussion—or it may occur whenever it appears to be needed. Adaptive behavior is discussed to give additional reinforcement to patients who have emitted the adaptive behavior and to emphasize this behavior as a model for those patients who are not emitting adaptive behavior in this area. Maladaptive behavior is discussed in order to point up the need for alteration in behavior—it is not subjected to criticism. Finally, the therapist may use role-playing exercises as an initiating method.

In the use of action-consequence as the basis for treatment, patients are utilized as ancillary therapists whenever possible. This is done particularly when treatment is taking place in a group setting. Patients are encouraged to give and withhold positive reinforcing stimuli on the basis of the behaviors exhibited by fellow group members. In order for patients to function as ancillary therapists, they must understand what behavior each group member needs to add to and delete from his repertoire at that specific time. They must also have sufficient self control to give and withhold reinforcing stimuli in an appropriate manner. If the therapist feels that a group of patients has the potential for acting as ancillary therapists, attention may be directed toward actualizing this potential during the initial phases of the group's interaction.

Aversive stimuli are used as little as possible in the treatment process. They tend to disrupt large segments of an individual's repertoire and may increase the frequency of behavior which is not truly adaptive in nature. Thus the therapist avoids *any* verbal or nonverbal threats regarding the withholding of positive reinforcers. Expression of disapproval is also to be avoided. It must be remembered, however, that there is a fine line between withholding approval and expressing disapproval. This is a subtle difference which needs to be mastered by the therapist. Effectiveness in this area is perhaps best judged by the honest exploration of subjective feelings. If the therapist experiences a negative feeling toward the patient—anger or vague feelings of disgust—then it is likely that the therapist is expressing disapproval as opposed to withholding approval. Another, more gross indicator is a patient's refusal to come to the treatment situation. He may well be avoiding aversive stimuli.

There seems to be an inclination to use punishment in a treatment process—so natural that the therapist may be unaware of using it to inhibit the emission of maladaptive behavior. Perhaps it is used so frequently because it is often so effective in the immediate elimination of undesirable behavior. Thus, the patient who is taken out of the therapy setting when he uses abusive language is likely to inhibit the emission of this behavior in a short period of time. (This is, of course, assuming that being taken out of the therapy setting is an aversive stimulus for the patient.) As mentioned in Chapter Four, punishment is usually ineffective in decreasing the frequency of a given behavior, for it suppresses the emission of the behavior but does not extinguish it. In order for behavior to be extinguished it must first occur, in order to be subject to nonreinforcement. Thus, using the above example, the therapist must allow the abusive language to occur and then withhold whatever positive reinforcer is being utilized in the treatment process. Admittedly, this method is slower in decreasing the overt emission of the maladaptive behavior and requires considerable fortitude on the part of the therapist. Realization of the effectiveness of this approach, however, may help the therapist to bear with the situation.

Punishment may be used occasionally in treatment in extreme circumstances—for instance, when no other method of treatment is effective in altering behavior which is physically harmful to self or others. It is questionable if this is ever really necessary. Concentrated and intense use of positive reinforcement is usually effective if the therapist is sufficiently tolerant to allow the reinforcer to have an impact upon the frequency of the maladaptive behavior. Often the environment must be arranged so that, although the patient may go through the motions of emitting physically harmful behavior, such behavior does not actually inflict injury. This is a difficult type of behavior to influence and requires the full cooperation of all staff members.

A major common goal of treatment for all patients is the maintenance of an adaptive repertoire through reinforcement from the expected environment. One way of approaching this goal is to assume that the patient has two relatively universal needs: (1) money, and (2) attention and approval from others. The therapist is concerned with helping the patient to establish a repertoire of behavior which will allow him to go into his expected environment, perform independent and shared tasks, and in turn receive money and/or attention and approval from others. In the transition from treatment situation to the community, the therapist continues to maintain the patient's repertoire until reinforcement is available from the expected environment. For example, the patient may have learned various homemaking skills in the treatment situation through reinforcement from the therapist, and from the conditioned reinforcer of perceiving a task well done. The therapist then reinforces her return home and use of these newly acquired or reacquired skills. The therapist continues to reinforce this behavior until the patient's husband, children, neighbors, mother-in-law (or whatever significant persons are involved in the home situation) perceive the patient's adaptive behavior and provide reinforcement for the behavior. These significant others essentially take over that portion of reinforcement which is needed from the environment in order to maintain the adaptive repertoire. The therapist's function as a reinforcing agent is then no longer required.

The process outlined above assumes that the behavior learned by the patient will lead to reinforcement from others in the home situation. The behavior must be, however, pertinent to the patient's cultural group as well. For example, the patient is unlikely to receive reinforcement for polishing pots and pans if this behavior is considered somewhat strange by the cultural group. Conversely, the patient may have acquired what is generally considered to be adaptive behavior, but significant others in the environment may be unable or unwilling to give reinforcement for this adaptive behavior. For example, a patient may have learned that one way of completing the vast number of necessary household chores is to send her husband's shirts to the laundry and to require her teenage daughter to iron her own clothes. The husband and the daughter may not initially be willing to give reinforcement for this behavior. If this occurs, the therapist must help the patient's family to understand the adaptive nature of the behavior and the important role their reinforcement will play in its maintenance. The therapist may even need to devote some time to reinforcing the families initial attempts to reinforce the patient.

There is another, somewhat different, approach to ensuring maintenance of an adaptive repertoire through reinforcement from the patient's expected environment. Using this approach, the patient and therapist discuss together what it is that the patient wants, how he personally and in his own unique way perceives his needs. The question is not so much, "What does the patient want to do?" as "What does the patient want to get from his doing?" The gratification of these needs is a potential source of reinforcement and a guiding thread for treatment. Essentially, then, the treatment process involves the learning of those adaptive behaviors which will allow the patient to gratify his needs (receive reinforcement) in his expected environment. The procedure outlined above, wherein the therapist gives reinforcement until the environment itself provides reinforcing stimuli, is utilized in this approach to treatment also.

The whole issue of reinforcement is considerably more complicated than indicated above. Without going into extensive discussion of theories relative to human needs, many patients experience only very primitive needs. (Indeed, it sometimes appears that a patient has no "normal" human needs.) We often use the terms "regressed" or "infantile" to describe these patients. Perhaps the best way of explaining such a phenomenon is to assume that the patient's needs have been paired with aversive stimuli, and experiencing the need has become a source of aversive stimuli. The patient has learned behavior which allows him to escape or avoid these conditioned aversive stimuli; needs are, therefore, no longer experienced. To engage such a patient in the treatment process takes considerable skill on the part of the therapist. The therapist must often try such approaches as sitting with the patient for a period of time; visiting the patient several times a day; bringing food, cigarettes or coffee; taking the patient for a walk, etc. It may take some time to get a response from the patient. ("Response" here refers to some indication that the therapist, something that the therapist does or some item the therapist gives to the patient is experienced as being pleasurable by the patient.) The response may be minimal and it will be necessary for the therapist to be an astute observer. Theoretically, what has occurred is the pairing of a positive stimulus with a latent or unexperienced need. The need has ceased to be an aversive stimulus through this pairing process and can, therefore, be experienced—although the patient, very likely, may not be able to express it verbally.

This connection between need and stimulus allows the therapist to proceed cautiously with the treatment process. It is necessary for the connection to be relatively firm; if, for example, after bringing a patient a candy bar every day for two weeks, the therapist observes that the patient's face registers pleasure when he sees the candy bar, the therapist might be tempted on the next day to require some additional adaptive behavior prior to giving the patient candy. This may be a mistake. It is usually better to wait, continuing to bring candy to the patient for several more days before providing candy contingent upon alteration of behavior. The connection between need and stimulus is initially very fragile—it must be nurtured and allowed to gain strength.

The reinforcer utilized at the beginning of the treatment process will, of course, vary from patient to patient. It may be very primitive (food or the indication of approval through touching or hugging the patient); or it may be more advanced (being permitted to attend the Friday night movie in the hospital); or it may be on an even higher level (spending the weekend at home or perceiving a task successfully completed). As may be evident, reinforcing stimuli are being placed on a hypothetical continuum, at one end of which are reinforcers that are unlikely to be available in the community; at the other end are reinforcers that are probably available in the patient's expected environment. A continuum is suggested in order to focus the therapist's attention upon developing conditioned reinforcers as part of the treatment process—accomplished through the pairing of a lower level reinforcer with a higher level reinforcer. The treatment situation is structured so that the lower level reinforcer is provided subsequent to the stimulus or event which is to serve as the higher level reinforcer. It is important that the conditioned reinforcer should not be too dissimilar from the primary reinforcer. For example, the initial reinforcer may be cigarettes, with the following sequence of conditioned reinforcers: therapist's approval, approval of other staff members, approval of fellow patients, approval from coworkers in a hospital job, and approval from fellow employees at a job in the community. Tokens may be used to develop money as a conditioned reinforcer. (The extent to which it is necessary to develop conditioned reinforcers and the sequence used will, of course, vary from patient to patient. The major concern of the therapist is to be sure that there are events or objects in the patient's expected environment which will serve as reinforcers for the patient's adaptive behavior.)

A word of caution is necessary regarding use of approval and attention of staff members and patients as reinforcing stimuli. In many hospital settings patients and staff members tend to reinforce behavior which would be considered maladaptive in the community. "You have to act sick to get any attention" is regrettably true in many settings. The staff often stresses that "patients should act like patients."[3] It is frequently necessary for patients and staff to identify the norms by which they judge behavior and what behavior is actually being reinforced before this potentially powerful source of reinforcement can be utilized in the treatment process.

---

[3]A. Stanton and M. Schwartz, *The Mental Hospital* (New York: Basic Books, Inc., 1954).

Another factor which must be taken into consideration in the treatment process is the *schedule of reinforcement*. "Schedule of reinforcement" refers to variation in the number of performances which must be emitted prior to reinforcement and to the time interval between reinforcement. The initial phase of treatment for many patients is characterized by a small fixed-interval schedule. There is a small set amount of time between reinforcements. Movement toward a larger fixed-interval schedule must be gradual; if it is not sufficiently gradual the patient may feel that the reinforcer is not worth the effort—he will cease to emit the desired adaptive behavior. For example, in helping a patient to learn to attend to a task, the therapist may provide reinforcement for as little as one minute of attention. The schedule for the following week might be two minutes of attention. If it is necessary to begin with one minute of attention, it is unlikely that the patient would respond to a five-minute schedule in the second week of treatment. The initial schedule and the rate at which the schedule is increased would depend upon the patient. He is often able to give a clear indication regarding an appropriate original schedule and rate of schedule change. The ultimate ratio between time and reinforcement utilized toward the end of the treatment process should approximate the schedule of reinforcement available in the patient's expected environment. The word "approximate" is used deliberately, in order to indicate that, although the schedule should be somewhat similar to the one available in the expected environment, treatment should be structured so that the ratio is variable. The time interval between reinforcements should vary from one occasion to the next. There are two reasons why a variable interval or intermittent schedule is preferable: (1) this schedule is more typical of schedules available in the community and (2) behaviors maintained on this type of schedule tend to occur frequently and are, therefore, more difficult to extinguish.

The above statements also apply to a ratio schedule. Treatment often begins with a one-to-one fixed ratio. This is called *continuous reinforcement*, because a reinforcer is given each time the desired behavior occurs. The schedule is altered during treatment so that an increasingly greater number of performances is necessary before the patient receives a reinforcing stimulus. This type of reinforcement schedule is used both in shaping and in building chains of performance. The eventual use of an intermittent ratio schedule is preferable for the same reasons given above.

The development of discriminatory behavior is an essential part of the treatment process. *Discriminatory behavior* is variation in the frequency and/or form of a performance in the presence of one stimulus which is not evident in the presence of another stimulus. Many patients tend to act in a similar fashion in many dissimilar situations. At one point in time or in some limited situations this behavior may have been or may be adaptive, yet is maladaptive when it is emitted in many other situations. Discriminatory behavior requires that the individual be aware of stimuli in the environment. He must perceive the situation so that he may select and initiate behavior which will lead to reinforcement in that particular situation. Discriminatory behavior is learned through reinforcement of a response to one stimulus and nonreinforcement of a similar response to another stimulus. A paired relationship between the stimulus and the response is developed over time. The individual learns to connect stimulus and appropriate response and act on the basis of this connection.

In helping a patient to develop discriminatory behavior or a fine-grained repertoire, the treatment situation is structured so that stimulus differences are initially gross and obvious; as treatment continues, stimuli differences become more subtle. For example, in helping a patient to learn to use tools in an appropriate manner, the therapist may need to begin treatment by presenting such dissimilar tools as a hammer and pliers. Eventually the patient might be required to use different size screwdrivers in an appropriate manner. In helping the individual to function in a work setting, the therapist might initially teach the patient the difference between an appropriate response to his work supervisor and an appropriate response to fellow workers. Treatment may progress so that the patient learns how to respond to a work supervisor when he is giving directions as opposed to conversing with him in the lunch room.

The number and variety of situations in which most persons are required to interact is so great that it would be difficult to teach anyone how to act in all situations. Thus, the therapist helps the patient to learn to observe the situation prior to action. The patient is helped to learn cues that will facilitate selection of appropriate behavior. This is particularly important in acquiring skill in interpersonal interaction. The patient is helped especially to observe nonverbal behavior as the basis for determining appropriate action. However, it must be remembered that helping a patient identify cues that will facilitate selection of behavior is effective only if appropriate responses to various cues are a part of the individual's repertoire.

In order to clarify the use of operant conditioning postulates in the treatment process, the function of *nonverbal* behavior has been emphasized. Verbal behavior can and often does play a significant part in the treatment process, for engagement in most shared tasks requires verbal interaction between participants. Verbal behavior is acquired in the same manner as nonverbal behavior: reinforcement is given for adaptive behavior, maladaptive verbal behavior is not reinforced. The principles of shaping, building chains of performance, and differential reinforcement are utilized as for nonverbal behavior.

Two other areas of verbal performance are important: (1) the therapist's use of his verbal repertoire to initiate patient behavior which may then be reinforced, and (2) the patient's control of his behavior through the use of his own verbal repertoire. The first area (touched upon earlier) is essentially concerned with the therapist suggesting a course of action to the patient. Pragmatically, this approach is used if and when it is effective in initiating patient behavior. Suggestions by the therapist are usually effective if the suggested behavior is already a part of the patient's repertoire, if the words used have previously been paired with the suggested action, and if the patient perceives the relationship between the suggested action and a reinforcing stimulus. The therapist, therefore, uses words that are familiar to the patient and suggests only that behavior which he knows the patient is capable of emitting. The suggestions should be accompanied by a statement of the positive consequences of engaging in the suggested behavior. This helps the patient to perceive the relationship between behavior and reinforcer. Outlining negative consequences which may result from not engaging in the suggested behavior should be avoided, for such an action involves the presentation of aversive stimuli—usually detrimental to the learning process.

Some therapists are hesitant to offer suggestions for adaptive behavior. They prefer letting a patient discover for himself what behavior leads to reinforcement. There are times when this is appropriate in that it gives the patient greater responsibility for his own learning process. At other times, however, it is more efficient to suggest behavior or, more accurately, to suggest several alternative means of handling a given situation. For example, the therapist may tell the patient that she must dress in a particular manner for a job interview. The kind of dress considered suitable for a job interview would be discussed. This may be done in general terms, or with reference to the patient's own wardrobe. The actual selection of clothes would be left up to the patient. A patient may not know what behavior is appropriate for a given situation. Many therapists have difficulty realizing that a patient may not have made a connection between a given situation and the most ordinary or simple behavior; this leads the therapist to speculate about why the behavior does not occur. Even though there may be other reasons, the therapist should first determine whether or not the patient knows what behavior is appropriate.

The other area related to verbal behavior is concerned with the patient's control of his behavior through the use of his own verbal repertoire. This process has been referred to as *self control*. The individual acts as his own reinforcing stimulus when his verbal behavior increases the frequency of adaptive behavior. The verbal repertoire which leads to self control is concerned with delineation of the consequences of emitting specific classes of behavior. The mechanics of this process are as follows: an environmental stimulus gives rise to covert verbal behavior (thoughts) which state the usual consequences of responding to that stimulus in a given manner. If these statements are concerned with positive reinforcement the individual is motivated to engage in the behavior. "Motivated" is here used only to indicate that behavior which has led to need satisfaction in the past is likely to do so in the future. To illustrate, a patient may have experienced deprivation of breakfast as a consequence of not getting out of bed at a prescribed time. (It is here assumed that eating breakfast is a reinforcing stimulus for this patient.) If the patient says something like, "If I don't get up I won't be able to eat," and gets out of bed because of this covert verbal behavior, the individual is influencing his own actions. The performance of getting out of bed is then self-controlled.

An individual gains control of his own behavior through pairing of a stimulus event with a verbal repertoire which states the consequences of responding to the event in an adaptive manner, and through pairing of the verbal repertoire with the actual consequences of action. The consequence of responding in a particular manner must be powerful enough to influence response, and must be intimately related to the particular need system of the individual. Whether a specific consequence is sufficiently powerful can often be determined only after the fact. If thinking about the ultimate consequence leads the individual to emit adaptive behavior, the consequence is sufficiently powerful.

Helping a patient to develop self control involves identification of the stimulus event and discussion regarding the positive consequences of engaging in particular adaptive behavior in response to that event. The therapist assists the patient in defining specific, concrete consequences that are clearly related to the patient's personal need system. Such consequences as, "It's good for me" or "People expect me to do this sort of thing" are usually not effective; a verbal repertoire such as, "I will be able to get an apartment", "My wife will want to have intercourse with me" or "I will be able to wear a bikini bathing suit," are likely to be more effective. There is, of course, considerable individual difference in the specific consequences which will influence behavior. The therapist helps the patient to recall past consequences of emitting adaptive behavior in response to the stimulus event. In some cases the actual consequence may have to be experienced repeatedly in the present for the patient to make the connection between a verbal statement of the consequence and the actual consequence.

The therapist is also concerned with ensuring that the statement of consequences follows immediately upon perception of the stimulus event. At times, the treatment process is oriented toward developing this paired relationship. For example, if the patient is unable to tolerate criticism, he may be placed in many situations where he is criticized by a number of people. He is first assisted and then asked to independently state the consequences of responding to the criticism in an adaptive manner. The purpose of this exercise is to ensure that a nonverbal statement of consequences follows the stimulus event.

At times, a therapist may be tempted to help a patient identify the aversive consequences which follow the emission of a particular maladaptive behavior—indeed, this is often an effective means of helping the individual to gain self control. However, aversive stimuli in this context can be just as detrimental to learning as it has been shown to be for other aspects of treatment. Its use, therefore, should be avoided if at all possible. It may take somewhat longer to identify positive consequences and to build the chain of stimulus event-verbal statement of consequence-action, but engagement in adaptive behavior will ultimately be more satisfying to the patient.

Self control of all behavior in all situations may not be possible for every patient. It is an assumed goal of treatment which will be reached to a greater or lesser degree by each patient. Time and effort should be devoted to developing self control even with those patients who the therapist feels are not capable of learning in this area. An attempt should be made, at least. The extent of control the individual has over his own behavior influences both his ability to function effectively in the community and his feelings about himself.

Specific verbal and nonverbal behavior may be aversive stimuli for a given patient. This has occurred through pairing of the stimulus events with other more primary aversive stimuli. The individual may not dare to think and/or express certain ideas, or he may be markedly fearful of getting involved in various situations. This latter state is often referred to as a *phobic response.*

When such behavior interferes with functioning effectively in the community it must be dealt with in the treatment situation. Effort is directed toward breaking the connection between the conditioned aversive stimulus and the primary aversive stimulus. This is done through pairing the conditioned aversive stimulus with a positive reinforcer. The shaping technique is often used. Successive approximations of the feared behavior are sequentially reinforced until the individual is able to emit the actual feared behavior. For example, an individual who is fearful of expressing any negative or angry feelings may be placed in a situation which tends to arouse negative feelings in most people. The therapist initially reinforces even the smallest indication of anger. As treatment continues, reinforcement is given for increasingly greater expression of anger as well as for appropriate expression of anger. Treatment for another patient who fears riding on a subway may involve sequential reinforcement of the following: talking about going on the subway, walking to the subway station, going into the subway station and standing on the platform, going for a ride to the next stop and finally taking a subway to a desired destination. Helping the patient to develop a verbal repertoire regarding the positive consequences of emitting the feared behavior is also a useful technique in this area of treatment.

Several factors considered significant in causing an individual to reach a state of dysfunction were outlined in Chapter Four; these hypothesized causes for emission of maladaptive behavior have not been mentioned in this section because treatment techniques are essentially similar regardless of the assumed process through which maladaptive behavior has come to be a significant part of the individual's repertoire. The therapist is concerned with the patient's current repertoire, the way in which it may be altered, and the development of adaptive behaviors which will lead to positive reinforcement in the patient's expected environment. The past has been, it cannot be altered. The patient and therapist are turned toward the future.

To summarize, action-consequence is a theoretical frame of reference which describes therapy as the process of teaching those behaviors which are necessary for adequate functioning in activities of daily living, avocational pursuits, and work, through application of principles deduced from the postulates of operant conditioning. It states that a person moves from a state of dysfunction to a state of function by receiving positive reinforcement for adaptive behavior and non-reinforcement of maladaptive behavior. The treatment situation is arranged so that adequate and appropriate reinforcement occurs. The treatment process begins by making use of the adaptive behaviors available to the individual. Shaping and building chains of performance are the primary techniques used. Any reinforcement and schedule of reinforcement that is successful in decreasing or increasing a given behavior is initially implemented by the therapist. The ultimate goal is the maintenance of adaptive behavior by positive reinforcing stimuli which are available in the patient's community.

Chapter 6
RECAPITULATION
OF ONTOGENESIS I

"Just as medical research was organized around concepts of pathology, so to-day we would do well to organize our efforts anew around the concept of growth. Those sciences that can help us to understand and nurture human growth—biological, behavioral and social sciences alike—should find ways of joining forces as the growth sciences. Let them make their knowledge relevant to those who are practitioners of the nurturing of growth. . ."

J. Bruner, quoted in Maya Pines, *"Why Some
3-Year-Olds Get A's—and Some Get C's"**

Recapitulation of ontogenesis is an example of a developmental frame of reference.[1] Briefly, an individual is able to interact effectively and with satisfaction to himself and others through learning those adaptive skills which are characteristic of a mature, well-adjusted individual. Adaptive skills develop in an interdependent, stage-specific manner through interaction in various growth-facilitating environments. A person is considered to be in a state of dysfunction when, in one or several adaptive skills, he has not attained a level relatively typical for his age and/or the level needed for effective and satisfying interaction in his environment. Treatment is directed toward the learning of required skills. This learning takes place through patient-therapist-nonhuman environment interactions, which allow the individual to progress sequentially through those stages of development which he had not attempted or never completely mastered. Interactions in the treatment process are synthesized in such a way that they simulate the specific growth-facilitating environments believed to be responsible for the learning of adaptive skills in the normal developmental process. It is through acquisition of adaptive skills that man is able to attain a true state of human-ness and to find and give satisfaction and joy.

New York Times Magazine, July 6, 1969.

[1] As far as I am able to reconstruct the process, this frame of reference came into being through an attempt to integrate some of the ideas of Ayres, Azima, Fidler, and Sechehaye.

THEORETICAL BASE

Adaptive Skills   Adaptive skills are learned patterns of behavior. The term "adaptive" is used to indicate that these skills are acquired and utilized by the individual so that he may satisfy his inherent needs and the needs of others, interact with the environment in order to attain personal goals, and knowledgeably select those environmental demands he wishes to meet. "Adaptation" is used here in the sense of creative use of the environment—not in the sense of conformity. The statement that adaptive skills are learned is made to differentiate the process of their acquisition from maturation. Maturation is the physical growth of the organism and the physical changes which take place during its life cycle.

The listing and definition of adaptive skills is an attempt to give some order and structure to the complex process of human development and mature functioning. Seven adaptive skills have been identified, as well as the subskills which sequentially form the foundation for each mature skill. The subskills delineate the developmental stages of each skill; when all of the subskills have been acquired the individual is said to have reached full maturity in a particular adaptive skill.

The following outline gives a brief definition of the seven adaptive skills. The subskills or stages which constitute each skill are listed in the sequence in which they are usually learned. Some of the subskills consist of more than one part. These various parts are referred to as *components*. The components of a subskill are not considered to be sequential except in a few instances which are identified in Chapter Seven.

A. Perceptual-Motor Skill

The ability to receive, integrate and organize sensory stimuli in a manner which allows for the planning of purposeful movement.
  1. The ability to integrate primitive postural reflexes, to react appropriately to vestibular stimuli, to maintain a balance between the tactile subsystems, to perceive form and to be aware of auditory stimuli.
  2. The ability to control extraocular musculature, to integrate the two sides of the body and to focus on auditory stimuli.
  3. The ability to perceive visual and auditory figure-ground, to be aware of body parts and their relationships, and to plan gross motor movements.
  4. The ability to perceive space, to plan fine motor movements and to discriminate auditory stimuli.
  5. The ability to discriminate between right and left and to remember auditory stimuli.
  6. The ability to use abstract concepts, to scan, integrate, and synthesize auditory stimuli; and to give auditory feedback.

B. Cognitive Skill

The ability to perceive, represent, and organize objects, events and their relationships in a manner which is considered appropriate by one's cultural group.

1. The ability to use inherent behavioral patterns for environmental inter-action.
2. The ability to interrelate visual, manual, auditory and oral responses.
3. The ability to attend to the environmental consequence of actions with interest, to represent objects in an exoceptual manner, to experience objects, to act on the bases of egocentric causality, and to seriate events in which the self is involved.
4. The ability to establish a goal and intentionally carry out means, to recognize the independent existence of objects, to interpret signs, to imitate new behavior, to apprehend the influence of space, and to perceive other objects as partially causal.
5. The ability to use trial and error problem solving, to use tools, to perceive variability in spatial positions, to seriate events in which the self is not involved, and to perceive the causality of other objects.
6. The ability to represent objects in an image manner, to make believe, to infer a cause given its effect, to act on the bases of combined spatial relations, to attribute omnipotence to others, and to perceive objects as permanent in time and place.
7. The ability to represent objects in an endoceptual manner, to differentiate between thought and action, and to recognize the need for casual sources.
8. The ability to represent objects in a denotative manner, to perceive the viewpoint of others, and to decenter.
9. The ability to represent objects in a connotative manner, to use formal logic, and to work in the realm of the hypothetical.

C. Drive-Object Skill
The ability to control drives and select objects in such a manner as to ensure adequate need satisfaction.
1. The ability to form a discontinuous, libidinal object relationship.
2. The ability to form a continuous, part-libidinal object relationship.
3. The ability to invest aggressive drive in an external object.
4. The ability to transfer libidinal drive to objects other than the primary object.
5. The ability to invest libidinal energy in appropriate abstract objects and to control aggressive drive.
6. The ability to engage in total and diffuse libidinal object relationships.

D. Dyadic Interaction Skill
The ability to participate in a variety of dyadic relationships.
1. The ability to enter into association relationships.
2. The ability to interact in an authority relationship.
3. The ability to interact in a chum relationship.
4. The ability to enter into a peer, authority relationship.
5. The ability to enter into an intimate relationship.
6. The ability to engage in a nurturing relationship.

E. Group Interaction Skill

The ability to be a productive member of a variety of primary groups.

1. The ability to participate in a parallel group.
2. The ability to participate in a project group.
3. The ability to participate in an egocentric-cooperative group.
4. The ability to participate in a cooperative group.
5. The ability to participate in a mature group.

F. Self-Identity Skill

The ability to perceive the self as an autonomous, holistic, and acceptable object which has permanence and continuity over time.

1. The ability to perceive the self as a worthy object.
2. The ability to perceive the assets and limitations of the self.
3. The ability to perceive the self as self-directed.
4. The ability to perceive the self as a productive, contributing member of a social system.
5. The ability to perceive the self.
6. The ability to perceive the aging process of the self in a rational manner.

G. Sexual Identity Skill

The ability to perceive one's sexual nature as good and to participate in a heterosexual relationship which is oriented to the mutual satisfaction of sexual needs.

1. The ability to accept and act upon the bases of one's pregenital sexual nature.
2. The ability to accept sexual maturation as a positive growth experience.
3. The ability to give and receive sexual gratification.
4. The ability to enter into a sustained heterosexual relationship.
5. The ability to accept physiological and psychological changes which occur at the time of the climacteric.

The Adaptive Skills Developmental Chart (Figure 1) indicates the sequential, interdependent nature of skill component learning. It illustrates the approximate age at which the various subskills are developed. The outline may not be accurate for a given individual in regard to actual sequence of such skill learning or the age at which the subskill is acquired.

Although there is some overlapping between the adaptive skills and subskills, for our purpose here each adaptive skill and subskill is considered to be an identifiable unit which is nevertheless interdependent with the other identified units.[2] The various adaptive skills have, each in turn, been described as the skill

---

[2]The characteristics of adaptive skills are fully discussed in John Flavell, *The Development Psychology of Jean Piaget* (New York: D. Van Nostrand Company, Inc., 1963); J. Pearce and S. Newton, *The Conditions of Human Growth* (New York: Citadel Press, 1963); J. Bruner, *Studies in Cognitive Growth* (New York: John Wiley and Sons, Inc., 1966), and *Towards a Theory of Instruction* (Cambridge: Harvard University Press, 1966); and in J. P. Guilford, *The Nature of Human Intelligence* (New York: McGraw-Hill Book Co., Inc., 1967).

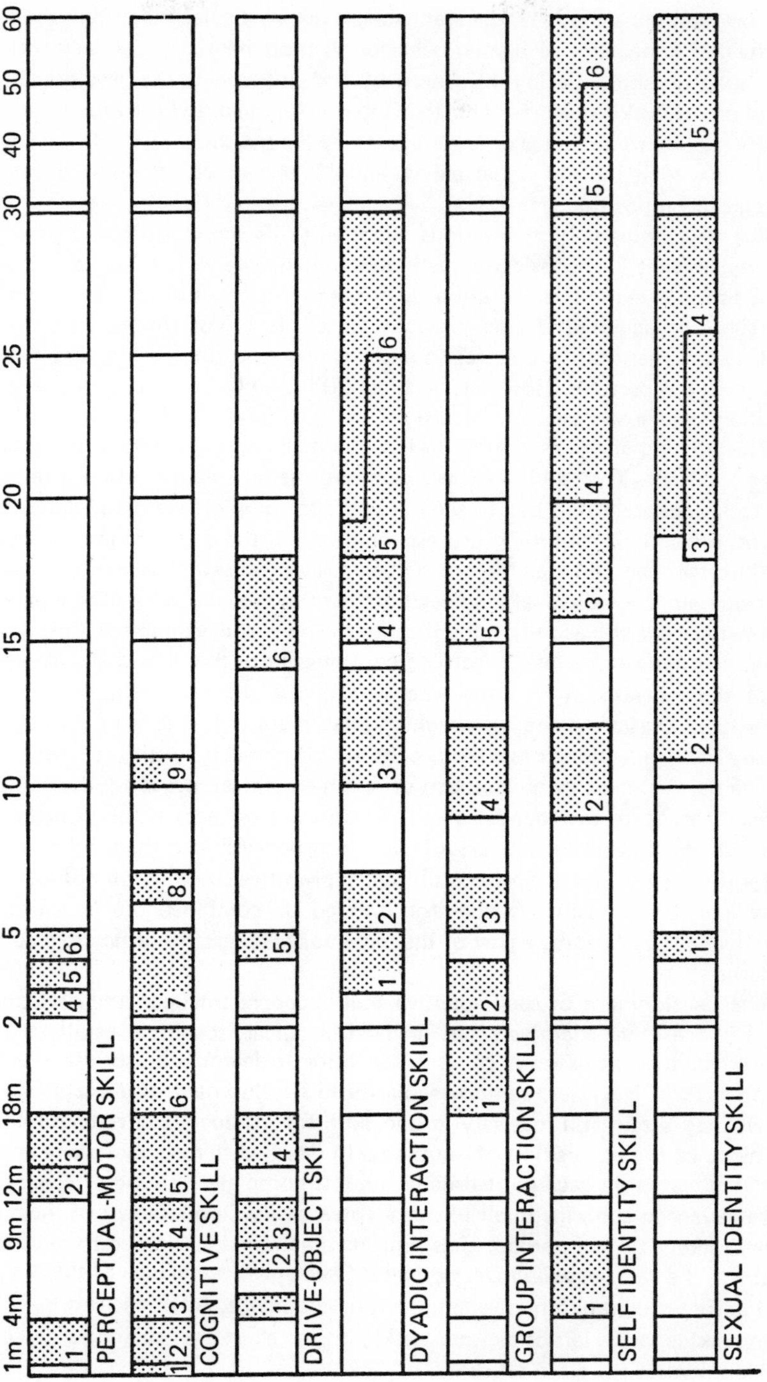

Figure 1. ADAPTIVE SKILLS DEVELOPMENTAL CHART

most crucial for function and the foundation upon which all other skills rest. This orientation, although understandable, is not particularly useful in the search for further knowledge of human behavior. A more heuristic approach is to view each adaptive skill as being influenced by and influencing the development and use of all other skills; and further, that the development and use of each adaptive skill is shaped to a greater or lesser extent by (1) the social and cultural environments in which the individual exists, and (2) the individual's past and current biological composition.

The development of the various adaptive skills shows sufficient qualitative differences that it is considered justifiable to delineate various stages of development for each skill. The subskill acquired at each stage is different in form from the subskills acquired during previous stages. It is not simply a matter of a continuous quantitative change; something new and different is added to the individual's repertoire. However, each subskill usually becomes more refined as the individual grows toward maturity.

The learning of adaptive subskills is sequential, and the sequence is considered to be invariant. Thus all individuals must successfully learn the first subskill of a particular adaptive skill before they are able to complete learning relative to the second subskill. The learning process required for the development of a specific subskill may be initiated before a lower level subskill has been completely learned; thus the individual may begin to learn the second subskill of a particular skill while he is still acquiring the first. In the normal developmental process, the sequential nature of subskill learning continues until the individual has acquired all of the subskills which constitute a particular adaptive skill. There is much individual variation in the age at which a given subskill is learned; yet there are usually minimal and maximal limits considered normal by a cultural group.

The development of an adaptive skill is hierarchical; the subskills acquired at a given time form the foundation or the capacity for acquisition of higher level subskills. Previously learned subskills are incorporated into the subskill which is currently being learned. Sequentially more primitive subskills are not lost to the individual, but remain available for isolated or combined use in appropriate situations. They become a part of the individual's repertoire of possible behavior patterns.

The development of each adaptive skill is dependent upon the development of all of the other adaptive skills. In most instances, specific subskills of one or several adaptive skills must be acquired prior to learning a subskill of another adaptive skill. However, some irregularity in development may occur. An individual may attain full maturity in one skill, for instance, and remain relatively deficient in the acquisition of another skill. Marked deficiency in one adaptive skill is undesirable because it usually inhibits complete learning of sequentially more advanced subskills in all of the adaptive skills. Development of these other skills is likely to be retarded, thus limiting the individual's capacity to function. Figure 1, the *Adaptive Skill Development Chart*, gives some idea of the hierarchical, interdependent nature of component development. All of the subskills of the various skills to the left of a given subskill on the chart are usually learned before development of the given subskill.

Adaptive skills are believed to be universal, and not specific to particular cultural groups.[3] The identified adaptive skills are described in such a manner that they are believed to be sufficiently general to include behavior required by most cultural groups. However, subskills may be manifested in a somewhat different manner in different cultural groups. The development of adaptive skills is influenced by membership in cultural groups and subgroups; cultural group affiliation to some extent determines whether the individual attains full maturity in the various adaptive skills. The environment may facilitate the full maturation of some skills and only partial maturation of others. This is dependent upon the requirement of the cultural group, for it is the group that determines the adequate level of adaptive skill development for its members.

The level of development in each of the adaptive skills somewhat influences the social roles assigned to the individual by the cultural group. Roles which demand full maturation of several or all adaptive skills are usually reserved for persons who have attained such a level of development. Membership in cultural subgroups may be permitted only if the individual has acquired specific subskills. The subskills utilized in a given social role sometimes vary from culture to culture. For example, in one culture the father role may demand the ability to participate in a nurturing relationship, whereas this may not be required in another cultural group. Individuals who, by choice or circumstances somewhat beyond their control, move into a new cultural group are often required to learn additional subskills. An individual is usually only able to gain full membership in a new cultural group by learning and/or utilizing subskills required by the group for adequate interaction in social roles.

Relationship of Adaptive Skills to the Theoretical Base of Object Relations Analysis The theoretical base of recapitulation of ontogenesis is similar in many respects to that of object relation analysis. It is suggested that the reader review this section with the following ideas in mind:

The ability to select and invest psychic energy in objects for the purposes of need satisfaction is considered learned behavior. This aspect of mature functioning and the sequential development of this skill is described in the drive-object skill. The relationship between needs, drives, and objects is, in part, the theoretical base for the drive-object skill. However, an additional need is proposed—the need for mastery of adaptive skills.[4] The mastery need motivates and

---

[3]For discussion of cultural similarities and differences see Ira Brown, *Understanding Other Cultures* (Englewood Cliffs, N. J., Prentice-Hall, Inc., 1963); L. Coser and B. Rosenberg, *Sociological Theory* (New York: The Macmillan Company, 1957); George Mead, *Mind, Self and Society* (Chicago: The University of Chicago Press, 1934); Talcott Parsons, *The Social System* (New York: The Free Press of Glencoe, 1951); F. Reissman, J. Cohen, and A. Pearl, *Mental Health and the Poor* (New York: The Free Press of Glencoe, 1964); and in Jack Weller, *Yesterday's People* (Lexington: University of Kentucky Press, 1966).

[4]A. Jean Ayres, *Perceptual Motor Dysfunction in Children* (Ohio Occupational Therapy Association Conference, 1964); and Robert White, "Motivation Reconsidered: The Concept of Competence," in L. Rabkin and J. Carr, (eds.), *Sourcebook in Abnormal Psychology* (Boston: Houghton Mifflin Company, 1967).

facilitates subskill learning. It directs or nudges the individual to seek out and use environmental interactions which will lead to subskill learning. As will be discussed in detail later, gratification of the need for mastery reinforces learning. The mastery need is not considered hierarchical, as are the other listed needs, but rather as ever-influencing the individual's behavior. It merges with the self-actualization need when this latter need is the predominant motivating force of the individual.

Affect is inherent to the human organism and is not learned. However, the capacity to experience some of the various affects is dependent upon the development of adaptive skills.[5] For example, satisfaction and fear are not dependent on learning, hate cannot be experienced until the individual has acquired the ability to work in the realm of the hypothetical (ninth cognitive skill), and love cannot be experienced until the individual has successfully formed a chum relationship (third dyadic interaction skill).

Man as a willing being is part of the theoretical base for recapitulation. However, again, the capacity for mature conscious willing is dependent upon adaptive skill learning. The development of the drive-object skill and cognitive skill are particularly important.

The concepts *conscious, preconscious, personal unconscious* and *collective unconscious* form part of the theoretical base of recapitulation. The phenomena of complex formation and repression is accepted. However, complexes are believed to be the result of deficient adaptive skill learning. Similarly, those complexes which reflect unknown aspects of the self are also assumed to arise from adaptive skill learning deficits. The inherent human responses which occur when complexes are held in the unconscious (denial, transference, etc.) are a part of the theoretical base of recapitulation. As in object-relation analysis, these responses are believed to reflect both sides of the conflict, assist in keeping the complex unconscious, and in some small way gratify the need (or needs) which are part of the complex. The predetermined nature of complexes can perhaps be better understood when it is viewed in relation to adaptive skills. Since these skills are universal, lack of adequate learning, a relatively common human phenomena, is reflected in archaic memory traces.

Cognition, discussed as a characteristic in the theoretical base of object-relations analysis, is considered in this frame of reference as a learned adaptive skill. Definitions of the processes of perceiving, representing, and organizing stimuli are accepted and utilized. The terms "exocept," "image," "endocept," and "concept representation," and primary, secondary, and tertiary organization are considered to develop in a sequential manner (to be discussed in greater detail later). They reflect to a great extent, the progressive development of cognitive skill.

The theoretical base of recapitulation utilizes the concept of symbolism and the nature and function of symbol formation as outlined in object relation analysis. However, another function of symbolism only touched upon in object

---

[5]Silvano Arieti, *The Intrapsychic Self.*

relation analysis, is of some importance in recapitulation: symbols produced by the self or objects invested with symbolic meaning are able to gratify needs.[6] This is particularly true of the physiological need for the reduction of sexually induced tensions and the love and acceptance needs. The need-gratifying function of symbols is seen in the normal developmental process. The intrusive behavior seen so predominantly in young boys, for example, is considered to be an attempt to gratify, in a symbolic manner, sexual impulses which are not able to be gratified directly. Similarly, a child's transitional objects (a blanket, particular soft toy, a pillow, etc.) symbolize mother and thus gratify in part the need for mother love. The potential of symbols as need-gratifying objects is utilized in some aspects of the treatment process based upon recapitulation.

That part of the theoretical base of object relations analysis which is not a part of the theoretical base of recapitulation of ontogenesis is the idea that an individual can move from a state of dysfunction to a state of function through the bringing of complexes to consciousness and integration of this previously unconscious content with conscious content. In recapitulation, complexes are seen as a result of faulty adaptive skill learning and treatment is, therefore, directed toward alteration of this faulty learning. Unconscious complexes are symptoms which will no longer be troublesome when adequate adaptive skill learning has occurred.

Growth-Facilitating Environments and Learning   The theoretical base of recapitulation also makes use of concepts and postulates of the action-consequence theoretical base. Adaptive skills are learned through interaction in growth-facilitating environments. A *growth-facilitating environment* is characterized by appropriate environmental elements and learning interactions; *environmental elements* are specific human, nonhuman and abstract objects which must be available in the environment in order for adaptive skill learning to take place.[7] *Learning interactions* are those interactions which may be described by the postulates of operant conditioning. The following example may clarify the difference between these two concepts: in the learning of the first group interaction skill (the ability to participate in a parallel group), the environmental elements might be outlined as: (1) the presence of others who are non-threatening to the self, (2) the opportunity to engage in individual tasks which are within the capacities of the self, and (3) relative satisfaction of physiological, safety and love and acceptance needs by significant others through other dyadic interactions. The learning interaction might be described as differential reinforcement of attention to tasks in the presence of others. Reinforcement may be offered by the above-mentioned "others," through gratification of the esteem needs or some other need. Environmental elements are specific to the learning of

---

[6]H. and F. Azima, "Outline of a Dynamic Theory of Occupational Therapy," *American Journal of Therapy*, Vol. XIII, No. 5 (1959); M. Sechehaye, *Symbolic Realization* (New York: International Universities Press, 1951); G. and J. Fidler, *Occupational Therapy: A Communication Process in Psychiatry.*

[7]Anne C. Mosey, *Occupational Therapy: Theory and Practice* (Boston: Pothier Brothers, Printers, Inc., 1968).

each subskill of the various adaptive skills, whereas learning interactions are general in character, since they are required for the learning of all subskills of the various adaptive skills.

The concept of environmental elements adds another dimension to learning which is not included in action-consequence. Recapitulation, in addition, identifies the gratification of mastery, physiological, safety, love and acceptance, esteem and self-actualization needs as primary reinforcers. Needs are seen as being located within the individual. Operant conditioning describes the learning process and the sequence of that process. The concept of adaptive skills identifies that behavior which is (or can be) acquired in the process and the sequential manner in which behavior is learned.

The learning of a subskill of the various adaptive skills usually moves from tentative trial behavior, to active experimentation with and practice of the subskill, to retreat into marginal awareness.[8] The end result of this process is called *subskill integration* or *integrative learning*. Although the subskill may continue to be refined, it is now a functional part of the individual's total repertoire. *Retreat into marginal awareness* or *preconscious* refers to the process through which the subskill becomes automatic; the individual need not be conscious of the subskill in order to use it in meeting personal needs and the demands of the environment. However, the subskill is not repressed, since the individual has the ability to bring it into awareness should the need arise—once a subskill is learned in an integrated manner, the individual's attention and energy are freed to be used in the acquisition of additional subskills or other environment interactions.

Some individuals are unable to acquire all the adaptive subskills in an integrative manner. Subskills—or some of their components—may either not be learned at all, or they may be learned by rote. *Rote learning* is superficial acquisition of a behavioral pattern and it requires conscious effort on the part of the individual to utilize the pattern.[9] Behavior tends to be somewhat divorced from the feelings of the individual. If, for example, an individual has integrated the ability to satisfy the social-emotional needs of other members of a group, his interaction in groups is spontaneous and requires little conscious effort; he has a sincere desire to satisfy the needs of others and derives pleasure from doing so. If the individual has learned this component by rote, considerable thought and effort is necessary in order for him to recognize and meet the needs of others. Since he may not have any real desire to engage in this type of interaction and does so only because it is expected or demanded of him, there is often a hollow, unnatural quality to the behavior.

Use of subskills learned by rote requires the expenditure of considerable energy which could be expended more appropriately in further skill learning or productive environmental interaction. It is possible, however, for rote learning of

---

[8]T. Parsons and R. Bales, *Family, Socialization and the Interaction Process* (New York: Free Press of Glencoe, 1951); J. Pearce and S. Newton, *The Conditions of Human Growth.*

[9]A. Jean Ayres, *Perceptual Motor Dysfunction in Children.* J. Pearce and S. Newton, *The Conditions of Human Growth.*

a subskill to permit integrated or rote learning of other subskills; but the foundation upon which these new subskills rest is not stable. Subskills learned by rote are fragile and easily affected by internal or external stress; in such a situation the individual is unable to make use of these subskills and utilizes previously integrated subskills instead. The individual thus functions at a lower or more primitive level.[10] Integrated subskills are much more resilient to stress. The stress situation must be of a catastrophic nature—prolonged deprivation of external stimuli or injury to the central nervous system, etc.—before integrated components are adversely affected. Rote learning of subskills may account for the appearance of normal development in an individual who is actually experiencing difficulty in acquiring mature skills.

There may be several factors which account for lack of learning or rote learning of subskills: Generally, these factors fall into two categories: (1) abnormality in the individual's physiological makeup or in the maturation process, or (2) the environment may have been deficient in providing those environmental elements and learning interaction necessary for the development of the various subskills. Either of these major factors may retard the development of a subskill or make learning essentially impossible. When a subskill is not learned at the usual time in the developmental process, therapeutic intervention or marked environmental change ordinarily must occur for the nonintegrated skill component to be learned. The specific reason for a subskill not being learned—or being learned by rote—is unclear; it does appear, however, that the number and severity of the factors just described play an influential role.

FUNCTION-DYSFUNCTION CONTINUUMS

The seven adaptive skills are the function-dysfunction continuums of concern in the recapitulation frame of reference. An individual is said to be in a state of function when there is evidence of integrated learning of those adaptive subskills which are needed for successful participation in his expected environment; he is said to be in a state of dysfunction when there is evidence of a lack of integrated learning of those adaptive subskills.

As in action-consequence, function and dysfunction are relative to the individual's expected environment and the social roles required of him within that environment. (*Expected environment* refers to the probable environment in which the patient will live after termination of treatment—a total institution, a sheltered environment, the pretreatment environment, a new unsheltered environment or any combination of these.) The adaptive subskills which are needed for satisfactory interaction in required social roles are assessed. Comparison of these required adaptive subskills to the adaptive subskills which are

---

[10]Gerald Caplan, *Principles of Preventive Psychiatry* (New York: Basic Books, Inc., 1964); Howard Parad, *Crisis Intervention* (New York: Family Service Association of America, 1965).

currently a part of the individual's repertoire is made in order to determine function and dysfunction on the various continuums.

Behavior indicative of function and dysfunction relative to the seven adaptive skills will be outlined in Chapter Seven. This behavior may be divided into three types: (1) the ability or inability to successfully participate in individual and shared tasks which require use of the various adaptive subskills, (2) evidence of those inherent responses which occur when there are unconscious complexes, and (3) symbols produced by the individual. The symbols produced by an individual, as mentioned in the discussion of object relation analysis, tell us about the objective situation of the individual, providing, among other things, information regarding complexes. Complexes are considered in recapitulation to be caused by deficient adaptive skill learning, symbol production, therefore, reflects both adequate and inadequate adaptive skill learning. Also used in recapitulation is the fixed meaning of symbols outlined in object relations analysis. However, interpretation is made in this case in connection with skill development rather than to complexes.

EVALUATION

There are two parts to evaluation: (1) assessment of the individual's current adaptive subskill learning and (2) assessment of the expected environment. Unfortunately, most of the suggested procedures for evaluating skill learning (outlined in Chapter Seven) are relatively vague and unsystematized, and therefore offer only a few clues to assist the therapist in the evaluation process. It is important to understand the processes behind delineation of behavior which is indicative of learning or lack of learning. The therapist must ask himself, "How might an individual act who had acquired a given subskill, and how might an individual act who had not acquired a given subskill?" Understanding this process, the therapist is in a position to assess whether or not the listed behavior seems reasonable and to use this information in a knowledgeable and flexible manner.

The procedure involved in assessment of the patient's expected environment is similar to that outlined in action-consequence, although the interpretations which the therapist makes are somewhat different. After identifying the social roles required of the patient, the therapist attempts to determine which adaptive subskills the individual needs to engage in these social roles.

Some therapists have found that the *Adaptive Skill Developmental Chart* is useful for summarizing evaluative findings. A perpendicular red line is drawn to the right of the most advanced subskill the patient has learned in each adaptive skill; a perpendicular blue line is drawn to the right of the most advanced subskill of each of the adaptive skills which the patient needs for successful participation in his expected environment. (For a young person this blue line is often drawn to indicate his current chronological age.) This is a graphic way of delineating the patient's current status as well as the ultimate goals of treatment. Treatment is then directed toward the sequential learning of all of those subskills which fall between the red and blue line.

POSTULATES REGARDING CHANGE

The major change postulate of recapitulation states that adaptive subskills are learned through participating in growth-facilitating environments. On the basis of this postulate, the therapist synthesizes various patient-therapist-nonhuman environment situations which simulate the specific growth-facilitating environment which is necessary for the learning of a given subskill. The environmental elements required for the learning of each subskill and techniques which may be used to simulate these elements in the treatment setting are outlined in the following chapter.

The learning interaction part of growth-facilitating environments are general and not specific to a particular subskill. The change postulates used are identical to those listed in action-consequence. (It is suggested that these be reviewed at this time. Application of the postulates will not be discussed in detail, for it is felt that the subject has been adequately covered in action-consequence.) The only difference in application is that in recapitulation the therapist is concerned with providing positive reinforcers for behaviors or approximation of behaviors which are the essence of the particular subskill being taught. Positive reinforcers are withheld for behaviors which are inconsistent with subskill learning. As in action-consequence, attention is given to shaping, building chains of performance, movement toward generalized reinforcers, adequate schedules of reinforcement, and to developing self control.

Another postulate regarding change is: the learning of subskills is interdependent and occurs in an invariant sequence; application of this change postulate delineates the sequence of the treatment process. The learning of the most primitive subskill which the patient has not learned is the initial goal of treatment. Treatment continues in this adaptive skill until the subskill level of the skill is equal to the subskill level of the next least developed adaptive skill, and treatment of this skill is then initiated. This sequence continues until the patient has acquired all of the subskills which he needs for successful participation in his expected environment. More than one subskill may be dealt with in the treatment process if these subskills are usually learned at approximately the same time in normal development. Reference to the *Adaptive Skill Developmental Chart* is useful for determining the appropriate sequence of subskill learning.

The final—but particularly important—postulate regarding change states that the need for mastery serves as a motivational and regulating force in the development of adaptive skills. This need allows the individual to experience what is good and right for him at any given time; if appropriate interactions are available, he will make use of them for continued learning. In essence, the treatment process involves tuning into or tapping this need for mastery. The therapist's clinical judgment, of course, continues to be important—it is his responsibility to select appropriate learning experiences; to provide the objects which may be necessary; to judge when the individual is able to move on to the learning of more advanced subskills; and to provide support, encouragement, and reinforcement. However, if the individual shows evidence of anxiety, resistance, or frustration, it is recommended that the therapist reassess the individual and the treatment situation. The activity may not be appropriate for the patient at this time. The treatment of adaptive skill dysfunction must be a profoundly collaborative experience if it is to nurture growth.[11]

---

[11]Perceptual Motor Workshop, Princeton, New Jersey (1969). Major contributors: A. Jean Ayres, Barbara Knickerbocker, Eleanor Messing, and Patricia Welbarger.

Chapter 7
RECAPITULATION
OF ONTOGENESIS II

The discussion of recapitulation in Chapter Six was general. It is necessary for further understanding to explore each of the adaptive skills in greater detail. This will be done in the following manner:

Theoretical Base   Additional theoretical information relative to each adaptive skill is provided when this appears to be required for adequate comprehension of the skill and skill learning.

Postulates Regarding Change   This section is included in the discussion of an adaptive skill when there are general postulates which are applicable to learning all of the subskills of the adaptive skill.

Evaluation   Some general suggestions regarding evaluation of each adaptive skill is provided. As mentioned, these suggestions are relatively vague. Much more work needs to be done in this area.

The Subskills   Each subskill, and, where necessary, each component of a subskill, is dealt with separately in this section. The subskill is defined if its meaning does not seem to be obvious. Behavior indicative of learning and lack of learning is provided. The change postulate specific to each subskill and component is also given. These postulates refer to interactions between the individual and his environment, which are believed to be responsible for the learning of the subskill or component in the normal developmental process. One must remember, however, that there is much that we do not know about normal development; and therefore these change postulates should be viewed as tentative—in many cases more educated guesses than tested and accepted hypotheses. Suggestions for applying the change postulate (simulating the specified interactions) in the treatment process are usually offered. However, some of the change postulates seem to be sufficiently self-evident that further discussion would be redundant.

PERCEPTUAL-MOTOR SKILL

Perceptual-motor skill[1] is the ability to receive, integrate and organize sensory stimuli in a manner which allows for the planning of purposeful movements, and requires the application of previously acquired information to current physical interaction with objects. For meaningful action to take place, the individual must know the physical properties of objects, the position of objects in space relative to self, the mechanical characteristics and capacities of his own body, and what actions will be effective when they are directed toward an object. This information is obtained through sensory stimulation arising from the individual's action upon the environment—and the environment's action upon the individual. The general parameters of perceptual motor skill are usually considered to be the reception and processing of information obtained through stimulation of the tactile, vestibular, proproceptive, auditory, and visual sensory mechanisms and the planning of gross and fine motor acts.

Perceptual motor skill, as outlined in Chapter Six, was presented as a singular unit which developed in six stages. This first view is a horizontal one of a human ability which has often been explored vertically as several relatively independent skills. Still, the phenomena of concern is similar. A. Jean Ayres, for example, has identified six perceptual-motor skills through factor analysis of the results of neuromuscular, perceptual, and cognitive testing. Statistical data indicates that these skills are functional units—to some extent independent from each other. The six skills are: (1) postural and bilateral integration, (2) apraxia, (3) tactile defensiveness, (4) language, (5) form and space, and (6) deficit of one body side. All of these skills (except tactile defensiveness) are considered to be stage specific.

Figure II indicates the relationship between the perceptual-motor skill outlined in Chapter Six and the six skills identified by Ayres. The shaded spaces under each skill listed at the top of the table identify the subskills which are fundamental to each skill listed on the left of the table. The components of the perceptual-motor subskills outlined in Chapter Six are listed on the left side.

---

[1] Reference works suggested for this section are: A. Jean Ayres, *Perceptual Motor Dysfunction in Children;* Kurk Goldstein, *The Organism* (New York: The American Book Company, 1939); Philip L. Harriman, *An Outline of Modern Psychology* (Littlefield, Adams and Company, Inc., 1963); D. O. Hebb, *Organization of Behavior* (New York: John Wiley and Sons, Inc., 1949); Henry Head, *Studies in Neurology, Vol. II* (London: Oxford University Press, 1920); Barbara Knickerbocker, "Guide to Understanding the Perceptual-Motor Training Program" (unpublished paper); L.Llorens and G. Beck, "Training Methods for Cognitive-Perceptual—Motor Dysfunction," *Normal Growth and Development with Deviation in the Perceptual-Motor and Emotional Areas* (proceeding of the Occupational Therapy Seminar, St. Louis, Mo., March 1966); Eleanor S. Messing, "Auditory Perception: What Is It?" (proceedings of the Association for Learning Disabilities) *Academic Quarterly,* 1967; Charles Nobach, *The Human Nervous System* (New York: McGraw-Hill Book Company, 1967); Perceptual-Motor Workshop, Princeton, New Jersey (major contributors: A. Jean Ayres, Barbara Knickerbocker, Eleanor Messing, and Patricia Welbarger); Paul Schilder, *The Image and Appearance of the Human Body* (New York: John Wiley and Sons, Inc., 1950); and Dean E. Wooldridge, *The Machinery of the Brain* (New York: McGraw-Hill Book Company, Inc., 1963).

Figure II

The relationship between the perceptual-motor adaptive skill and the six perceptual-motor skills identified by Ayres

	Subskills and Components of the Perceptual-Motor Adaptive Skill	Postural and bilateral integration	Apraxia	Tactile defensiveness	Language	Form and space	Deficit of one body side
		Six Perceptual-Motor Skills (Ayres)					
Subskill 1	Integrate primitive postural reflexes	1					1
	React appropriately to vestibular stimuli	2					2
	Maintain a balance between the tactile subsystems		1	1			
	Perceive form					1	
	Awareness of auditory stimuli				1		
Subskill 2	Control extraocular musculature	3					3
	Integrate the two sides of the body	4					4
	Focus on auditory stimuli				2		
Subskill 3	Perceive visual figure-ground					2	
	Perceive auditory figure-ground				3		
	Awareness of body parts and their relationships		2				
	Plan gross motor movements		3				
Subskill 4	Perceive space					3	
	Plan fine motor movements		4				
	Discriminate auditory stimuli				4		
Subskill 5	Discriminate between right and left	5				4	5
	Remember auditory stimuli				5		
Subskill 6	Use abstract concepts	6					6
	Scan auditory stimuli				6		
	Integrate and synthesize auditory stimuli				7		
	Give auditory feedback				8		

The vertical view of perceptual-motor skill is not utilized in recapitulation. However, it is often useful to keep this orientation in mind during evaluation and in planning the treatment process.

THEORETICAL BASE

General Concepts and Postulates   The organization of sensory input is dependent upon a neural system inherited from our phylogenetic past. Its structures are relatively fixed but retain some plasticity, especially in a younger individual. The brain has evolved from primitive neurological structures through interaction in an environment which required an increasingly greater degree of refined adaptive behavior. Adaptation to change is a key factor in the evolutionary process. The subcortical levels of the brain are older than the cortex and have been responsible for a considerable portion of perceptual-motor behavior—this remains true in the human brain. The cortex provides additional control but never loses its dependency upon subcortical structures. When cortical control is substituted for subcortical control, the individual is unable to engage in complex cognitive and social activities. The acquisition of perceptual-motor skill involves both the cortical and subcortical levels of the brain.

Perceptual-motor skill learning occurs through interaction between the individual and the environment. Of prime importance are the availability of adequate sensory stimulation and an opportunity for meaningful motor response to stimuli. ("Adequate stimulation" refers to an optional level of sensory input which is sufficiently intense as to trigger sensory receptors—but not so intense that it is overwhelming to the individual. There seems to be some individual difference in the optimal level. "Meaningful activity" refers to goal-directed actions; it is hypothesized that such action enhances integration of sensory stimuli.) Stimuli not used as the basis for directed activity are less likely to be held in memory and thus are less available as the basis for future action. The particular type of interaction between individual and environment needed for the development of each subskill is only now in the process of being identified. Observation of children, educated guesses, and trial use of various interactions in the clinical setting are being employed to further our knowledge in this area.

In consideration of perceptual-motor skill, sensory perception and motor response are often treated separately. This is done, however, only to facilitate discussion; they are intimately related. Perception takes place in the neurological system and therefore cannot be directly observed; it must be observed indirectly through motor response. Motor response arises from sensory input and in turn provides sensory input.[2] *Perception* is the process of organizing sensations for

---

[2]Neurophysiological deficits leading to paralysis, athetosis, spasticity, etc., are not considered to be a part of the domain of perceptual-motor skills. Thus an individual who is lacking in one or several perceptual-motor skills is considered to have a deficient sensory system, which interferes with the functioning of an adequate motor system. An individual may have deficits in both the sensory and the motor systems. Each area is dealt with somewhat differently by the therapist. The usual therapeutic procedures may require alteration when there is this dual handicap. Exploration of deficit in the motor system and alterations in treatment procedures when there is both a sensory and motor deficit are outside of the scope of this text.

use, a complex process and thus more easily explored by breaking it down into some (and only some) of its component parts. Perception involves the recognition, discrimination, and memory of sensory stimuli. *Recognition* is the awareness of sensory input—not necessarily conscious awareness but rather stimuli getting through and being registered in the nervous system—at least momentarily. *Discrimination* refers to the process of distinguishing one stimulus from another. It involves being able to identify the origin of stimuli, the intensity of stimuli, and the foreground and background of stimuli received by one sensory system. *Memory* refers to the process of retaining information regarding a stimulus; it is remembering how something feels, looks, or sounds.

D. O. Hebb has formed some postulates about the neurophysiological aspects of perception. He states that repeated stimulation of specific receptors will cause the nerve cells of the association area of the brain to form engrams, which gradually alter the nerve cell. This structural change takes the form of an anatomical growth on the cell which facilitates future synaptic activity. If two different synapses are repeatedly activated at the same time, they will tend to become associated; activity in one facilitates activity in the other. Sensory neurons or sensory and motor neurons may become associated. The latter is likely to occur in the sensory-motor cortex where sensory and motor patterns coincide somatotopically. Sequential maturation of the central nervous system is dependent upon the successful function of integrative mechanisms. These, in turn, are dependent upon patterned stimulation and meaningful response to or use of stimuli. Repeated stimulation by a given stimuli source establishes engrams which allow for subsequent rapid perception and recognition of the stimulus source. Engrams for muscle movements are set only if the movement leads to a desirable or adaptive result. The brain appears to recognize that certain sensory information sent to the motor system was effective in bringing about adaptive movement.

All levels of the central nervous system are involved in perception. The cortex, although important, is not currently considered to be the most significant area; the brain stem, instead, appears to play a crucial role. This is understandable when we consider the relatively fine perceptual-motor skill of lower animals. Their cortical development is comparatively less advanced than the development evident in the human brain. Experimental studies indicate that the cortex is an organ of elaboration and refinement rather than a crucial participant in much perceptual and motor activity. There appears to be a relationship between the place in the evolutionary scale where a particular sensory system developed and the extent to which that system is dependent upon cortical function. Thus, the phylogenetically older tactile and vestibular systems require less cortical involvement than the auditory and visual systems, which are more recent developments in the evolutionary process.

Perception involves intersensory and interhemispheric integration. Information from two or more sensory systems are combined in the process of intersensory integration. Thus we can feel a rubber ball with occluded vision and still know what it looks like. We look at sandpaper and know that it feels rough.

Most of the useful information the individual has about himself and the environment has been gained through combining isolated stimuli from the various sensory systems. Integration occurs through the functioning of special neurons which connect various sensory systems. The connections take place at different levels in the nervous system. These special neurons not only promote intersensory integration but also enhance the receptivity of the connected systems. Thus, stimulation on one sensory system increases perception in other sensory systems. This phenomenon is observed in the difference between the golfer who "keeps his eye on the ball" and the one who does not. Interhemispheric integration involves the combining of sensory information from both sides of the body. What is seen, heard, and felt on the right side is combined with similar information from the left side. The structures responsible for this integration are tracts of axons which crisscross within the central nervous system. One of the largest aggregates of these interconnecting fibers is called the *corpus callosum,* which ties the two halves of the cortex together.

It appears that sensory stimuli are subjected to some type of evaluation. It is judged as injurious or noninjurious by the individual. Action is initiated on the basis of this judgment. Injurious stimuli are responded to by fight or flight. The individual responds to noninjurious stimuli by exploratory behavior. This process has been studied particularly in relation to the tactile system. The existence of two tactile subsystems has been hypothesized: (1) a protective system which warns the individual of impending danger and (2) a discriminatory system which conveys information about the environment. The protective system is considered to be phylogenetically older—and therefore stronger. The discriminatory system is believed to fulfill a checking or controlling function relative to the protective system. For adequate functioning, the two systems must be balanced so that the protective system is inhibited when the environment is safe for investigation and manipulation. Conversely, the discriminatory system must be inhibited when survival is threatened. Sometimes the two systems have never attained or have lost this functional balance and the protective system predominates. It is suggested that such imbalance arises from some malfunctioning of the central nervous system. When this type of malfunction is present there is a tendency for the individual to regress to a phylogenetic earlier response pattern, or to one which has greater survival value, illustrating the predominance of the protective system.

As stated earlier, these dual systems have been postulated relative to the sense of touch. However, there is increasing data to support the idea that all sensory systems possess this duality. Some individuals show evidence of a predominant protective system in connection with one or more of the senses; they feel discomfort and a desire to escape when certain types of stimuli are experienced. This is a negative reaction to stimuli, which is not considered injurious or unpleasant by the majority of the population. Thus, there may be a fight or flight reaction—not only to some types of tactile stimulation, but to certain kinds of sounds and odors also. A hypersensitivity to stimuli is often evident.

The *reticular activating system* appears to be particularly important to sensory perception and selection of motor responses.[3] This system is a more or less homogeneous network of cells that extends from the top of the spinal cord, through the brainstem and on up into the thalamus and hypothalamus. Afferent and efferent nerves which connect the brain with the periphery of the body have collateral fibers which terminate on reticular neurons. There are additional fibers which connect the reticular activating system to the cerebellum, several major areas of the cortex, the brainstem and the spinal cord. Essentially, all incoming and outgoing messages pass through the reticular system, which has often been referred to as a communication center.

The reticular activating system exercises control over consciousness. Experimentation has indicated that the only thing that arouses a sleeping animal is electrical activity in the reticular system. General anesthesia seems to cause loss of consciousness by deactivating the reticular neurons. The reticular system itself is activated by external sensory stimuli and thought processes. (The latter effect is illustrated, for instance, by the difficulty involved in going to sleep when we have something on our minds.)

The reticular activating system inhibits sensory perception. It is this system which reduces sensitivity to particular stimuli, filtering out uninteresting, irrelevant or extraneous stimuli, and permitting the individual to focus upon stimuli which are of immediate concern. The nerve signals activated by extraneous stimuli have less impact upon the central nervous system than signals arising from stimuli to which the individual is attending. Massive stimulation of one sensory system causes the reticular system to inhibit logical thinking and cortical reception of information from other sensory systems. Similarly, intensive thought processes or intellectual activity inhibits reception of external stimuli.

The reticular activating system is also influential in the selection of appropriate behavior patterns from the great number of patterns available to the individual. Its function is to inhibit some responses, while allowing other responses to be carried out. This may occur through selective activation of muscles; signals are sent which increase or decrease the magnitude of the muscular response. Responses are also controlled by inhibiting transmission of some sensory input and allowing other sensory stimuli to be transmitted.

Another way that the reticular system monitors muscular response is by shifting control from the cortical level to the cord level. A spinal reflex circuit regulates contraction so that the muscle will function appropriately for the work to be performed. These automatic circuits are often used to maintain stable postural positions while other parts of the body are engaged in various actions.

---

[3]The reader should not infer from the discussion which follows that malfunction of the reticular activating system is the cause of deficient perceptual-motor skill. The specific causal elements of perceptual-motor dysfunction are presently unknown. There is much study being done in this area. A report of these studies, however, is beyond the scope of this text.

Dean Wooldridge likens the recticular activating system to the central switching office of a telephone system. He goes on to say:

If we include in the function of the central switching station the task of assigning priorities—of deciding which incoming nervous messages are to be amplified and listened to, and which are to be minimized, ignored, or caused to wait their turn—we have a pretty good description of how the reticular activating system seems to work.[4]

No attempt will be made to give a detailed description of the sensory systems, but an outline of some of the pertinent factors which contribute to an understanding of perceptual-motor skill is necessary..

The tactile system is considered to be the oldest of the sensory systems. All animals, regardless of their position in the evolutionary scale, appear to be sensitive to touch. It is interesting to note that the nervous system arises from the ectoderm, the same type of tissue which forms the skin. This fact seems to account for two phenomena which have been repeatedly observed: (1) exploration of an individual's response to tactile stimulation seems to be one of the best ways of determining the presence or absence of perceptual-motor dysfunction and (2) predominance of the protective tactile system over the discriminatory system interferes with an individual's ability to utilize all of the other sensory systems.

The tactile system has special receptors which respond to light touch, pressure, pain, and temperature. It is this system which gives us considerable information about objects which come in direct contact with our body as well as information about all objects which we are able to manipulate with our hands. Tactile receptors are distributed over all parts of the body, but there is a higher degree of concentration in the hands and in the area which surrounds the mouth. The latter receptors are more mature at birth. Indeed, they provide the child with more accurate information about objects than manual manipulation during the first months of life.

The vestibular system is also considered to be one of the oldest sensory systems. It is usually identified as part of the proprioceptive system; still, it is treated separately in discussion of perceptual-motor skill because of the special role that it plays. The primary vestibular receptors are in the vestibule and semicircular canals of the inner ear. However, receptors in the spinal accessory muscles and extraocular muscles are also important in vestibular perception. The vestibular system provides the individual with information about his relationship to the earth and the effects of gravity. Through the vestibular system in conjunction with other systems man has learned both to use and to overcome gravity.

The proprioceptive system appears to stand midway in the evolutionary scale. It seems to have developed after the tactile and vestibular systems and before the

---

[4]Dean E. Wooldridge, *The Machinery of the Brain* (New York: McGraw-Hill Book Company, Inc., 1963), p. 70.

development of the visual and auditory systems. Proprioceptive receptors are found in the muscles, tendons, joints and viscera. They provide the individual with information about the position of his body parts in space and relative to each other. Two structures seem to be particularly important in proprioceptive perception: the Pacinian corpuscles and muscle spindles. The Pacinian corpuscles respond to pressure and are found both just under the skin and in the internal organs. They have a high threshold and are activated by heavy muscular exertion.[5] These receptors provide information regarding the state of the muscle and joint movement. The muscle spindles are stretch-sensitive receptors attached to the muscles. They play a significant role in regulating the degree of muscle contraction through a spinal reflex circuit. It is believed that the muscle spindle also provides information about the state of a muscle which is relayed to the midbrain.

The visual system has been studied extensively. We have considerable information about neural pathways, visual acuity, color perception, and deficits in the various visual fields. Little is known, however, about the mechanisms which underly those aspects of visual perception usually considered a part of perceptual-motor skill.[6] Attempts to treat inadequate perception of form and space have pointed to the importance of tactile, vestibular and proprioceptive perception in the organization of visual stimuli. It is undetermined whether this relationship is found in ontogenetic development or whether ancillary sensory systems are being used to compensate for visual-motor deficits.[7]

As with visual perception, there is considerable information regarding auditory acquity. Little is known, however, about the mechanisms which allow the individual to comprehend what is said and to give appropriate responses. Obvious lesions in the auditory cortex and other related areas interfere with auditory perception, but deficits are also evident in persons who have no identifiable neurophysiological impairment. Eleanor Messing defines auditory perception as "the ability to comprehend and relate auditory stimuli, with appropriate meaning and response, to stored auditory experiences which are retrieved through instantaneous scanning of the memory. It is meaningful interpretation and comprehension of heard sounds.[8]" Very little is known about the specific interaction between individual and environment which is responsible for the development of auditory perception; all that is really known is that an individual does not develop language or language comprehension unless there are others in the

---

[5]The Pacinian corpuscles under the skin respond to heavy pressure exerted on the surface of the body.

[6]These areas include form perception, space perception and visualization, directionality, visual figure-ground and disregard of one half of space.

[7]Perception of form and space is one of the least understood perceptual-motor skills. It appears to be superordinate to other subskills. However, it also seems to be somewhat of an independent entity since it can be found in the absence of other subskill deficiency.

[8]Eleanor S. Messing, "Auditory Perception: What Is It," Proceedings of the Association for Learning Disabilities, *Academic Quarterly*, 1967.

environment who use language. Such an environment, however, does not always lead to the development of accurate auditory perception. The improvement of impaired auditory perception, basically, involves teaching the individual how to listen to what he hears and to respond to this auditory stimulus in a purposeful, adaptive manner. This is done by providing specific micro-units of auditory stimuli to which the individual is able to respond.

POSTULATES REGARDING CHANGE

Perception in a given sensory system is enhanced by general sensory stimulation (vestibular, tactile, proprioceptive, visual, and auditory) which does not cause over-arousal, yet which is still sufficiently intense to be received by the central nervous system.

Intense, clearly delineated, repeated, and prolonged sensory stimuli increases perception.

Controlled input from the environment encourages adaptive response.

Adaptive movement is enhanced by increased proprioceptive and tactile stimulation of the receptors associated with the involved muscle groups.

Purposeful activity increases sensory perception and adaptive motor responses. A purposeful activity is characterized by active response to stimuli, the arousal of interest, and a feeling on the part of the individual that he is doing something which is important and significant to the self.

Increasingly refined and integrated sensory motor-acts are developed by the grading of motor acts from gross to fine.

Discriminatory responses are learned by grading stimuli events from gross to fine.

Long-term memory of stimuli is enhanced by graded time between stimuli event and required response.

Activities which have become automatic for the individual facilitate maintenance of attained skill but do not bring about further skill development.

EVALUATION

There are several standardized tests available for perceptual-motor evaluation. These are particularly useful in evaluating children, since norms have been established for various age levels. The tests are sometimes used for the evaluation of adolescents and adults; one must be cautious in interpreting these results, however. Some of these standardized tests are:

The Ayres Space Test by A. Jean Ayres, Ph.D., OTR, published by Western Psychological Services, 12035 Wilshire Boulevard, Los Angeles, California 90025, 1962. Age range 3 through 10 years.

Southern California Motor Accuracy Test by A. Jean Ayres, Ph.D., OTR, published by Western Psychological Services, 1964. Age range, 4 through 7 years.

Southern California Figure-Ground Visual Perception Test by A. Jean Ayres, Ph.D., OTR, published by Western Psychological Services, 1966. Age range, 4 through 10 years.

Southern California Kinesthesia and Tactile Perception Tests by A. Jean Ayres, Ph.D., OTR, published by Western Psychological Services, 1966. Age range, 4 through 8 years.

Southern California Perceptual-Motor Dysfunction Tests by A. Jean Ayres, Ph.D., OTR, published by Western Psychological Services, 1968. Age range, 4 through 8 years.

Marianne Frostig Developmental Test of Visual Perception by Marianne Frostig, Ph.D., published by Consulting Psychologists Press, 1961, 1963. Sold through Follett Publishing Company, P.O. Box 5705, Chicago, Illinois. Age range, 2 years 6 months through 8 and 10 years.

Winter Haven Perceptual Copy Forms Test, published by Winter Haven Lions Club, Winter Haven, Florida, 1965. Age range, 6 years through 8 years, 6 months.

Developmental Test of Visual-Motor Integration by Keith Berry, Ph.D. and Norman Buktenica, published by Follett Publishing Company, 1967. Age range 3 years through 15 years.

The Illinois Test of Psycholinguistic Abilities by Samuel Kirk, Ph.D. and James McCarthy, Ph.D., published by University of Illinois Press, Urbana, Illinois, 1961, 1968. Age range varies with tests from 2 years, 1 month through 10 years, 11 months. Revised Edition.

Symbols produced by the individual may give clues regarding perceptual-motor function and dysfunction. Such symbols may be particularly evident in drawings of the human figure; any deletion, distortion or emphasis of body parts should be noted. However, it appears that symbols offer only general information relative to perceptual-motor skill learning. Specific information regarding nonintegrated subskills and components is perhaps best gained through selecting or designing evaluative procedures which elicit the behaviors indicative of learning and lack of learning outlined in the following section.

THE SUBSKILLS

1. *The ability to integrate primitive postural reflexes, to react appropriately to vestibular stimuli, to maintain a balance between the tactile subsystems, to perceive form, and to be aware of auditory stimuli. (1 month—4 months)*[9]

---

[9]There is some evidence that primitive postural reflexes are integrated before the individual learns to react to vestibular stimuli in an appropriate manner.

a. Integrate primitive postural reflexes

The primitive postural reflexes of concern here are the tonic-labyrinth reflexes (flexion of arms and legs in the prone position and extension in the supine position) and the tonic neck reflexes (extension of the arm toward which the head is turned, flexion of the other arm, and a similar or opposite reaction in the lower extremities). These reflexes are believed to be integrated when the individual does not exhibit any evidence of the tonic neck reflex or trunk rotation when the head is passively turned, vertical movement of arms when asked to hold arms out in front of body with eyes closed, or difficulty in maintaining a pivot prone position (extension of neck and extremities when in the prone position). These reflexes are considered to be unintegrated if the individual exhibits the above-mentioned behaviors.

Primitive postural reflexes are integrated through taking positions which are directly opposite from the reflex position. The ability to take the opposite position is facilitated by vestibular stimulation. It also appears that stimulation of the pressure receptors of the chest and stomach when an individual is in a prone position leads to assumption of the pivot prone position. Flexion of the neck in a supine position tends to cause flexion of the extremities. These reactions themselves appear to be reflexive in nature.

One treatment method that has been found to be effective involves the use of a scooter board (thorax-sized board on wheels).[10] Maintaining a prone position on a scooter necessitates extension of neck and extremities. This position may be further facilitated by rolling down an inclined plane (increases vestibular stimulation) and pressure stimulation of the back extensors. The supine tonic labyrinth reflex may be inhibited by taking a supine position on the scooter board or a swing. The tonic neck reflexes are integrated through eliciting the reflex and then taking a standing or kneeling position with the arm opposite from the way in which the head is turned in an extended position which supports the body. The arm on the side of the body toward which the head is turned is maintained in a flexed position and the position taken by the legs is dependent upon their reflex reaction. There should be extension of the leg which is receiving increased flexor tone from the tonic neck reflex. The turned-head position is facilitated by holding a towel between chin and shoulder, which also provides increased tactile stimulation. The need for equilibrium reactions in maintaining these positions enhances integration of the reflexes. The individual should engage in activities which promote inhibition of the postural reflexes several times a day. It is recommended that they be preceded by or take place concurrent with vestibular stimulation. Such

---

[10]The methods to be suggested are primarily oriented to the treatment of children. The principles underlying these methods may be used for selecting appropriate activities for adolescents and adults. However, little work has been done in utilizing recapitulation as the basis for treating perceptual-motor deficit in adolescents and adults. It is not known whether it is an effective method of treatment.

stimulation can be gained from swinging, spinning, twirling, rolling, etc. The activities listed below for developing equilibrium reactions are also useful for integration of postural reflexes.

b. React appropriately to vestibular stimuli

Appropriate reaction to vestibular stimuli is often referred to as *the development of balance* or *adequate equilibrium reactions*. An individual reacts appropriately to vestibular stimuli when he is able to maintain one and two legs standing balance with eyes open and closed, easily retain balance when his center of gravity is shifted, and stabilize trunk and proximal body parts when using distal parts to carry out an activity. Absence of these reactions indicates lack of learning in this area.

The development of appropriate reactions to vestibular stimuli occurs through repeated attempts at making bodily adjustments in response to alteration in vestibular stimulation.

Some methods which have been used for treatment of dysfunction in this area are activities which involve rolling in a barrel (lined with a rug in order to increase tactile stimulation), self-initiated spinning or swinging;[11] maintaining balance on a large beach ball while in a prone, supine, sitting and kneeling position;[12] scooter activities (independent or with another person pulling the scooter at an increasingly greater speed); balance on a rocking board in kneeling, sitting and standing positions; sliding down an inclined plane kneeling on pieces of slick paper; balancing on a T-stool; walking on different types of stilts; and walking on a rail. Activities selected to increase equilibrium reactions are structured so that the individual's attention is distracted from the act of balancing itself. This enhances integration at a subcortical rather than at a cortical level. Activities which require co-contraction of postural muscles while distal parts are involved in the performance of a task are particularly helpful in enhancing integration.

c. Maintain a balance between the tactile subsystems

Balance between the protective and discriminatory tactile subsystems is the ability to differentiate between injurious and noninjurious tactile stimuli and to inhibit the appropriate system on the basis of this information. An individual has learned this aspect of perceptual-motor skill when he is able to tolerate stimulation of light touch receptors, accept tactile stimulation initiated by others, locate point of tactile stimulation, perceive double tactile stimulation, identify simple geometric shapes drawn on the back of

---

[11]Passive swinging or spinning may be used in the initial phases of treatment to assist in subcortical reception of vestibular stimuli. Some individuals with deficit in this area appear to have a very high threshold for vestibular stimuli; there is a need for massive input. Self-initiated spinning or swinging should be used later in the treatment process as this both arises from adaptive behavior and promotes adaptive response. Sensory-motor integration is therefore increased.

[12]The therapist holds on to the individual's hands or feet until he has gained sufficient skill to safely engage in the activity without assistance.

the hand (*graphesthisia*), and identify shapes through manual manipulation. An individual has not learned this aspect of perceptual motor skill if the behaviors listed above are absent. Other indications of nonintegrated learning are hyperactivity; feelings of discomfort and desire to escape when certain types of tactile stimuli are experienced; hypersensitivity to pain, cold, sounds, and odors; unreasonable anger or belligerence; and the seemingly uncontrolled desire to touch objects.

A balance between the tactile subsystems is acquired through stimulation of those tactile receptors which respond to pressure (probably the Pacinian corpuscles), as opposed to light touch. This tends to inhibit the protective system. In addition, the individual must have an opportunity to experience many different kinds of noninjurious tactile stimuli. Stimulation of the hands, forearms, and face promotes perception because of the rich supply of tactile receptors located in these areas.

Treatment for deficiency in this aspect of perceptual-motor skill involves massive stimulation of the tactile receptors, especially those receptors which respond to pressure. A rough cloth or brush of appropriate stiffness is usually used to stimulate receptors on the face, forearms and hands. This may be done by the therapist, but the preferred method is for the individual to give tactile stimulation to himself. This method is recommended for two reasons: (1) the individual is less likely to respond in a negative manner to self-stimulation, and (2) stimulation can be initiated several times a day. Many individuals who lack a balance between the protective and discriminatory tactile subsystems find that self-stimulation has a soothing, organizing effect at those times when they are feeling anxious, upset or jumpy. Other areas of the body may also be stimulated by rubbing or brushing. Additional stimuli are provided by using various textured carpets and rugs during floor activities. The barrel and beachball mentioned earlier may be lined and covered with carpeting or furry rugs. When facilities are available, water play, swimming, water hose activities, hot and cold showers, and covering the body or body parts with sand provide additional tactile stimulation. Such stimulation occurs concomitantly with purposeful motor activity, and should be perceived as safe and predictable by the individual. Tactile stimulation is not utilized if there is evidence of hypertonicity. If stimulation gives rise to pallor, an increase in heart or respiratory rates, or a strong negative reaction, it is discontinued or altered in such a manner that the above-listed responses do not occur.

d. Perceive form

Form perception is the ability to recognize different, simple forms, and is considered to be a part of an individual's repertoire when he is able to draw, copy and match geometric figures; identify forms through manual manipulation; and distinguish similarities and differences in size and shape. Lack of the above abilities indicates deficient learning in this aspect of the first perceptual-motor subskills.

Form perception is acquired through visual, tactile (manual and oral), and proprioceptive exploration of objects. Although visual stimuli are important in the treatment of form perception deficiency, perception is enhanced when visual stimuli is integrated with information gained through tactile and proprioceptive receptors (the receptors in the extraocular muscles being especially important). Thus, treatment is initially directed toward manual manipulation of objects concomitant with visual inspection. Objects should be clearly differentiated one from another and have distinctive characteristics. As tactile receptors in and around the mouth may provide more accurate information than receptors in the hand, the individual is encouraged to mouth objects if he is so inclined. Two-dimension form perception is facilitated by accentuating the boundaries of forms. The therapist provides line drawings of geometric shapes and simple pictures of familiar objects which are heavily outlined in black, and the patient is encouraged to follow the outline of the drawings with his eye while he traces the outline with his finger or a pencil. Drawing also provides stimulation of the receptors involved in form perception. Ontogenetically, the child progresses from drawing horizontal lines, to vertical lines, to circles, to curved lines, to diagonal lines. This sequence is utilized in planning activities in the therapeutic situation. (Initially the therapist may provide dots to guide the individual's drawing.) Treatment may also involve cutting out various geometric figures and simple pictures. Another aspect of form perception is perception of an object as a whole rather than as isolated parts. To facilitate this learning, the therapist demonstrates how a group of stimuli can be organized into larger units. The various characteristics of objects and their going-together relationships are pointed out. The individual is eventually provided with activities which allow him to practice identifying wholes when only parts are observed. As the individual begins to gain facility in form perception, activities are introduced which involve identifying, discriminating similarities and differences, and matching objects after brief inspection. Selecting pictures that are slightly different or a different view from the stimulus object is also useful.

e. Be aware of auditory stimuli

Auditory awareness is the comprehension of environmental sounds. Research seems to indicate that the infant has an inherent hypersensitivity to the sounds coming from his own body; attention to these sounds must therefore be inhibited so that the child is able to attend to environmental sounds. An individual is considered to have acquired auditory awareness if he appears to be attending to environmental sounds; and, conversely, inattention indicates a deficit in auditory awareness.

Auditory awareness is acquired through interaction in an environment where there are sounds which are perceived as pleasant by the individual and through the reception of positive reinforcers subsequent to attention to those sounds.

In the treatment process, auditory awareness may be enhanced by presenting recordings of distinct and pleasant common sounds. Reinforcers are given when the individual appears to be attending to the sounds. As treatment progresses the individual may be requested to identify the object which produces the sounds.

2. *The ability to control extraocular musculature to integrate the two sides of the body, and to focus on auditory stimuli. (12m-14m)*[13]

   a. Control extraocular musculator
      In acquiring this aspect of perceptual-motor skill the individual gains control of those muscles which are responsible for eye movement. Function and dysfunction in this area are indicated by the ability or lack of ability to maintain visual pursuit of objects.

      Development of ocular control is facilitated by attempts to focus on stationary and moving objects. Objects outside of the individual's present field of vision cause him to move and visually grasp the sound source.

      The treatment of extraocular control deficit involves the use of activities suggested for the treatment of inadequate equilibrium reactions. While engaging in these activities the individual may be required or requested to focus on various stationary or moving objects; visual focus on different sources of sound may also be built into the activity. Any interaction which involves visual pursuit of objects increases integration of this component; playing tag with flashlights in a darkened room, for instance, is an ideal activity.

   b. Integrate the two sides of the body
      This aspect of perceptual-motor skill is often called *interhemispheric integration* or *bilateral motor coordination*. When developing this capacity, the individual becomes aware of and learns to coordinate the two sides of the body. The difference between the dominant and nondominant sides of the body, although present, is not extreme; an individual who has integrated the two sides of his body is able to cross the body midline visually and manually without hesitation and perform bilateral activities with ease. Learning is indicated as well by evidence of only a small amount of discrepancy between right and left sides of the body in terms of sensory perception and motor response (the evaluator should note body side differences in all procedures used to assess perceptual-motor skill). An individual who has not integrated the two sides of his body will not exhibit these characteristics. Additional behaviors indicative of dysfunction in this area are seeming disregard for one half of space or one half of the body.

      Integration of the two sides of the body is acquired through reciprocal movement of the extremities, bilateral activities, and activities which require manual and visual crossing of the midline of the body.

---

[13]There is some evidence that control of extraocular musculature is acquired prior to integration of the two body sides.

Treatment of deficit in this area begins with such gross reciprocal activities as creeping, crawling, clapping, bicycling, playing with hulahoops, jumping with two feet, and swimming. Bilateral activities which require joint use of two hands are used next (for instance, moving large objects, hitting a suspended ball with a cardboard tube held at either end, and batting a ball). Complementary bilateral activities and unilateral activities are initiated as the individual's skill increases. Concurrent with use of the above activities, the individual is involved in tasks which involve movement away from, toward, and across the midline of the body. Blackboard activities and calisthenics which require these types of movement are suggested. Special attention should be given to increasing tactile and proprioceptive stimulation (for instance, rubbing body parts and use of weighted cuffs). When there is evidence of marked perceptual and motor deficit on one side of the body emphasis is placed upon this neglected side. If there is evidence of poor motor planning on one side of the body, the methods outlined below for the development of motor planning are utilized in the treatment process.

c. Focus on auditory stimuli
Auditory focus is the ability to locate the direction of sound and to determine the distance between self and sound source. Function and dysfunction in this area are indicated by the ability—or inability—to identify the location and distance of sound sources.

It is believed that this aspect of perceptual motor skill is acquired in the normal developmental process through the receiving of positive reinforcers for accurate identification of sound source, location, and distance.

In treating auditory focus deficit, the individual is provided with positive reinforcers for locating sounds relative to the self. This may be done by asking the individual to locate sounds which have been produced in various parts of the room. Sounds may be produced electronically or by individuals situated in different places. The individual may also be asked to tell which of two sounds are closer or farther away.

3. *The ability to perceive visual and auditory figure-ground, to be aware of body parts and their relationships and to plan gross motor movements. (14m-18m)*[14]

a. Perceive visual figure-ground
Visual figure-ground refers to the capacity to select out of a gestalt of visual stimuli that which is of particular importance at a given time. It involves the ability to focus on some visual stimuli to the exclusion of others, and to reverse this process.

---

[14]Awareness of body parts and their relationships appears to be developed before the individual acquires the ability to plan gross motor movements.

Acquisition of this capacity is indicated by the ability to identify super-imposed and imbedded pictures of objects; individuals who do not have this capacity are unable to perform this task.

It is not precisely known how the ability to distinguish between visual figure-ground is developed. It appears to be a function of the recticular activating system, since it involves inhibition of some visual stimuli and focus on other visual stimuli. It has been suggested that the reticular system develops the dual capacity of inhibition and focus through develop-ment of the integration of postural reflexes, adaptive responses to vestibu-lar stimulation, and the balancing of the protective and discriminatory tactile systems. The ability to distinguish between visual figure-ground can be learned at the cognitive level by practice in the identification of figures out of an increasingly more complex or confusing background. It is ques-tionable, however, whether this learned splinter skill can be transferred to perception of visual stimuli in situations other than figures on a piece of paper.

In the treatment of visual figure-ground deficit the individual is asked to trace around line drawings. The activity is altered over time so that there is a decrease in the homogeneity of the background and an increase in distracting elements. (A stimulus object may be used to help the individ-ual identify the appropriate foreground figure.)

b. Perceive auditory figure-ground

Auditory figure-ground is the ability to pay attention to those sounds which are pertinent to a given situation while screening out background noises. Function or dysfunction in this area is indicated by marked distrac-tion by extraneous auditory stimuli.

There is little knowledge of how auditory figure-ground develops—it, also, appears to be a function of the reticular activating system. The re-ception of positive reinforcers has been suggested as the basis for learning.

In the treatment process auditory figure-ground is developed by provid-ing positive reinforcers for responses to a particular sound, word or phrase in the presence of other minimally distracting sounds. The activity is graded so that there is variation in the complexity, intensity and distracta-bility of both the foreground and background sounds.

c. Aware of body parts and their relationships

This aspect of perceptual-motor skill is sometimes referred to as *body scheme*. It involves knowledge of the various body parts, their static rela-tionship to each other, and the relationship of parts during movement and in different postural positions.

An individual who is aware of body parts and their relationship to each other is able to identify various fingers when they have been touched by an examiner (vision occluded), name the various body parts, state the relationship between parts, and identify the position of his body parts without aid of vision. Dysfunction in this area is indicated by the inability to engage in the behaviors listed above.

Awareness of body parts and their relationships is acquired through purposeful movement and observation of the body of self and others. It involves integration of tactile, proprioceptive and visual information.

Some treatment activities deduced from the above postulates are: movement of body parts through their full range of motion with assistance from the therapist, without assistance and against resistance; imitation of the therapist's movements; visual inspection of the self, another person or a representation of the human body accompanied by identification of body parts and discussion regarding the relationship of one part to another; drawing around body parts; sculpting and drawing the human body and putting together a representation of the human body; identifying various objects and textures with vision occluded, sand play, and finger painting (primarily for adequate finger identification).

d. Plan gross motor movements

Gross motor planning is the ability to carry out large movements in a skilled and coordinated manner. This ability and the ability to plan fine motor movements is sometimes referred to as *praxia. Apraxia,* the inability to plan motor acts in a skilled manner, may be differentiated from disorders caused by upper-motor neuron deficit. Such a deficit interferes with the execution of a planned motor act. Adequate gross motor planning is indicated by the ability to successfully engage in activities which require gross motor actions, skillfully carry out nonstereotyped gross motor activities, and imitate postures taken by an examiner. Deficit is indicated by the inability to successfully engage in the activities mentioned above.

The individual acquires the ability to plan gross motor movements through participation in gross activities which require increasingly more precise and complex planning for their proper execution.

There are several suggested methods for treatment of gross motor planning dysfunction. Activities are graded from "simple" to "complex." Initially, the therapist may take the individual passively through the motions which are required, which will increase sensory input and thus facilitate planning. Proprioceptive input is further increased by co-contraction of postural muscles and weighted cuffs. The motions required in the activities should be nonstereotyped or unusual actions which the individual does not ordinarily perform; the therapist, for instance, would not have the individual walk up a flight of stairs—he may request, however, that the individual go up the stairs backwards. Once a particular motor activity is learned or does not require the individual's attention, it is no longer useful for treatment and a new activity or some modification must be introduced. The therapist, initially, suggests various gross motor activities; later the individual is asked to make up his own motor tasks, describe the task to the therapist and then execute the task. Self-initiated activities require planning prior to action and thus facilitate the development of this aspect of perceptual-motor skill. Some activities which are useful for the develop-

ment of gross motor planning are: modified rolling, crawling, walking, and
scooter board activities; obstacle courses involving hopping, jumping, walking, crawling, and climbing; rhythm bands, circle games, body stunts, ball
games, gymnastics, "Simon Says", postural imitation, and pantomimes of
common tasks. Although subcortical levels are involved in the learning of
motor planning, the motor cortex is of particular importance. In treatment
directed toward enhancing motor planning, therefore, the individual is
engaged in activities which require his full attention. The therapist may
need to remind the patient to focus on what he is doing.

4. *The ability to perceive space, plan fine motor movements, and to discriminate
   auditory stimuli. (2y-3y)*

   a. Perceive space
   Space perception involves the ability to use space concepts as the basis for
   movement, visualize what an object would look like if it were moved into
   a different position, and understand the three-dimensionality of objects.
   Integration of this aspect of perceptual-motor skill is indicated by the
   ability to return the hand to a position similar to a position previously
   assumed with the help of the examiner (without the aid of vision) and
   immediate and accurate response to directions or questions which require
   understanding of space concepts. Lack of learning is indicated by difficulty in the performance of these tasks.
       Space perception is developed through movement of the body through
   space. Space concepts (up, down, under, around, etc.) are learned first in
   relation to the self. They are learned as the individual moves himself
   relative to stable objects and as he moves objects relative to each other.
   These concepts are later translated to static and dynamic objects as they
   exist in space. Learning something first in relation to the self and then in
   relation to external objects is often referred to as the *autocentric-allocentric principle.* Visualization of space is enhanced and consolidated through
   its integration with information gained from the vestibular and proprioceptive systems. The vestibular system is particularly important because it
   provides direct information to the visual system regarding the existence of
   space.
       The initial phase of treatment in this area involves activities which
   require movement of the body through a variety of limited spaces and
   around various objects. Some examples are: going through obstacle
   courses, jungle-gym activities, games requiring placement of the body in
   given spaces, parallel bar activities, and scooter-board activities. These
   tasks are performed both with vision and with vision occluded. The individual is encouraged to visualize in his mind the size, shape and position
   of a given space prior to movement relative to the space. As treatment
   continues, the individual is involved in activities which require the accurate
   placement of objects external to the self. Such activities as putting things

together, sorting, beanbag toss, ball games, and building with blocks or other objects may be employed. Space concepts are used for planning and initiating action. For example, the individual might be asked to identify the relationship of one body part to another, move his body or other objects according to special directions, and identify similarities and differences in size. Locating objects in space is another facet of space perception. Thus activities involving going to or explaining where a familiar object is located, explaining how to get from one place to another and locating places or objects on a map may be used. The ability to identify distance, conceptualize approximate distance and compare different distances is important. Examples of tasks which facilitate learning in this area are: measuring with a ruler; physical movement of various distances (foot, yard, mile, etc.); and identifying whether A or B is closer to or farther away from C.

b. Plan fine motor movements

Fine motor planning is the ability to carry out highly refined and integrated movements in a skilled and coordinated manner. Adequate fine motor planning is indicated by the ability to successfully engage in activities which require fine motor responses, imitate intricate and refined postures taken by the examiner, and return his hands to a position previously assumed with the help of the examiner (without the aid of vision). Deficit is indicated by the inability to successfully complete such activities.

The individual acquires the ability to plan fine motor movements by engaging in refined activities which require increasingly more precise and complex planning for their proper execution.

The treatment principles and methods outlined above for enhancing gross motor planning apply as well to the development of fine motor planning. Some appropriate nonstereotyped activities are: hand puppets, tracing, jacks, paper folding, ring toss, peg boards, sewing cards and various crafts.

c. Discriminate auditory stimuli

Auditory discrimination is the ability to comprehend the difference between various sounds, syllables, words, phrases, and sentences. It also involves perceiving the appropriate sequence of these language components. An individual is in a state of function in this area if he gives relevant responses arranged in a manner which is considered acceptable by his cultural group, and in a state of dysfunction if he gives irrelevant responses or responses which involve reversals, omissions, or transposition of sounds, syllables, words, phrases, or sentences.

Auditory discrimination is developed through reception of positive reinforcers for identifying similar and dissimilar sounds and proper word arrangements.

Suggested treatment methods deduced from this postulate are: providing a stimulus picture and asking the individual to select from pictures of several objects those objects which begin, rhyme, and end with the same sound as the stimulus object. A similar method may be used in oral presentation of a stimulus word. Rather than pictures the individual may be asked to select words from memory.

5. *The ability to discriminate between right and left and to remember auditory stimuli. (3y-4y)*

a. Discriminate between right and left

Right-left discrimination involves the ability to perceive a horizontal sequence and to identify the difference between reversed images. This ability is sometimes referred to as *directionality*. It is prerequisite to learning how to read, since it involves the ability to consistently scan written lines from left to right and to tell the difference between letters (e.g., to distinguish between *b* and *d*).Function in this area is indicated by consistent, accurate recognition and reproduction of letters; left-right directionality in reading; and accurate identification of right and left. Dysfunction is indicated by vertical (and very occasionally horizontal) reversal of letters; inconsistent left-right directionality in reading; and difficulty in identifying right and left.

Discrimination between right and left appears to be developed by activities which require manual and visual crossing of the body midline. It is thus closely related to integration of the two sides of the body. It can be taught on the cognitive level, but it does not appear to be learned in this way normally.

In teaching this aspect of perceptual-motor skill, the therapist utilizes methods similar to those outlined for the treatment of deficit in integrating the two sides of the body. In addition, the therapist is concerned with structuring activities which facilitate right-left discrimination. These activities usually require the individual to identify and actively use a specific extremity in the performance of a task. For example, the individual may be asked to pick up all of the yellow blocks with his right hand and the green blocks with his left, to follow a color-coded pattern on the floor using his right and left feet as indicated by the therapist and respond to directional commands in the context of a game. Additional stimulation such as weighted cuffs on the right or left wrist and ankle or different colored string tied on the extremeties may be used. Activities are graded so that there is a decrease in the external cues available to the individual. An attempt is made to help the individual get a feel for right and left. If these methods are only partially effective, additional training involving the use of higher cortical levels is initiated. The individual is engaged in activities which require eye and hand movement from left to right and the identification of identical and reversed line drawings.

b. Remember auditory stimuli

Auditory memory is the ability to remember what is said and the sequence in which it is presented; it is especially important in comprehending and carrying out verbal directions. Function and dysfunction are indicated by the ability or inability to accurately respond to verbal directions; remember over a period of time what someone said; order words in a manner acceptable to one's cultural group; and correctly label things, people and places. When there is deficit in auditory memory, the individual may use substitutes or functional definitions for labeling. The ability to remember auditory stimuli appears to be acquired through shaping and differential reinforcement.

Auditory memory may be increased in the treatment process by giving the individual simple, one-step instructions, then two-step directions, etc. This process continues until the individual is able to follow complex oral directions given in an uninterrupted sequence. Practice in responding to time concepts, using acceptable word order in speaking, labeling objects and events, and remembering what someone said over an increasingly greater time span is also beneficial.

6. *The ability to use abstract concepts; to scan, integrate and synthesize auditory stimuli; and to give auditory feedback. (4y-5y)*[15]

   a. Use abstract concepts

The *ability to use abstract concepts* is evident when responses are based upon the typical classification system used by one's cultural group. This ability has been learned when the individual recognizes similarities and differences in the size, shape, color, quantity, movement, direction, sequence, and time components of objects and events. Conversely, the inability to recognize similarities and differences indicates dysfunction in this area.

The ability to use abstract concepts correctly is acquired through practice in the classification of objects and events in the various ways in which they are classified by one's cultural group.

In the treatment process, the use of abstract concepts is taught by assigning to the patient activities which involve categorizing and labeling objects and their relationship to one another. The individual is helped to recognize, differentiate and remember the various characteristics of objects which are usually used as the basis for abstract concept formation. The multiple relationships between objects are learned from activities which require identification of these various relationships. It appears that many abstract concepts are first acquired relative to the self and later applied to objects and events that are external to and distant from the self. An example of how this autocentric-allocentric principle is used in the treatment process is evident in a method used to teach the concepts of time and sequence. The individual initially participates in a recognizable series

---

[15]It appears that auditory scanning is acquired before auditory integration and synthesis and that auditory feedback is acquired last.

of events concomitant with verbal statement of appropriate time concepts (for instance, *first, second after, before* etc.). Activities such as paper sculpting, eating a meal, making a cake, or a simple woodworking project can be used. In the next treatment phase, the individual is required to order a series of events or actions in which he is not immediately involved—he may be asked to describe the events of a day or week in the order in which they occurred, or retell a story in proper time sequence. Finally, time-measurement tools are used to order events or guide action. Activities which involve use of a play clock, practice in telling time, and use of a calendar are suggested. Methods which make use of this autocentric to allocentric orientation can be employed in the teaching of many abstract concepts.

b. Scan auditory stimuli

Auditory scanning is the ability to comprehend the general impression of what is said; it involves classifying and organizing auditory stimuli. Function and dysfunction in this area is indicated by the ability or lack of ability to abstract and categorize information presented verbally.

Auditory scanning appears to be learned through receiving positive reinforcers for accurate response to relatively complex verbal information.

Treatment of auditory scanning deficits is similar to the process outlined above for deficient use of abstract concepts. However, there should be a predominance of auditory stimuli. The individual is given considerable practice in identifying *who, what, when, where* and *how* from verbal presentations.

c. Integrate and synthesize auditory stimuli

Auditory integration and synthesis is the ability to comprehend words and phrases which have multiple meanings. Learning in this area is indicated by accurate response to and use of words and phrases having many different meanings. Dysfunction is indicated by inaccurate response to and use of these words and phrases.

Interaction in an environment in which there is considerable use of words and phrases which have multiple meanings and reinforcement of correct response and use, appears to account for learning in this area.

The treatment of auditory integration and synthesis deficit, therefore, involves practice in the identification and accurate use of synonyms, autonyms, homonymns, and analogies.

d. Give auditory feedback

Auditory feedback is the ability to reproduce auditory stimuli in speech. Function in this area is indicated by language production which is easily comprehended by others; dysfunction is indicated by circumlocution (evasive speech), speech impairment (which does not appear to be caused by a deficiency in organic structures basic to speech) and gross grammatical errors.

The capacity to give adequate auditory feedback is acquired through an opportunity to engage in linguistic output which leads to the reception of positive reinforcers.

A suggested sequence of graded activities for the treatment of auditory feedback deficit are: naming objects, repeating simple stories (with and then without the aid of pictures), making up a story about a picture with particular attention to proper sequence (a beginning, middle and end), and recall of objects seen or described (graded so that there is an increase in the number of objects remembered and the length of time between stimulus objects and response). The therapist emphasizes appropriate word selection and sentence structure.

COGNITIVE SKILL

Cognition[16] has been defined in Chapter Three as "the process of perceiving, representing and organizing stimuli." The various aspects of cognition were discussed without reference to their sequential development. In this chapter, cognition will be explored as a stage specific, learned human ability. Mature cognitive skill is defined as "the ability to perceive, represent and organize objects, events, and their relationship in a matter that is considered appropriate by one's cultural group." Although there are some cultural differences, mature cognitive skill is usually considered to be the use of denotative and connotative concept representation and secondary process organization for conscious thought and shared communication.

Exocept, image and endocept representation are acquired in the process of developing mature cognitive skill. These types of representation remain available to the individual. Some perceptions continue to be stored as exocepts, images and endocepts. Even after the development of mature cognitive skill many persons prefer to use a lower level type of representation. Thus an individual may use image representation more frequently than connotative representation. This in no way indicates that the individual has a lesser degree of cognitive skill, for he is able to use connotative representation when necessary. The reason for his preference for one type of representation to another is unknown. However, it does appear that effectiveness and efficiency influence the

---

[16]Complete discussions of cognitive skills can be found in the writings of Jean Piaget, the primary authority in the field; Silvano Arieti, *The Intrapsychic Self;* Jerome Bruner, *Studies in Cognitive Growth* (New York: John Wiley and Sons, Inc., 1966) and *Towards a Theory of Instruction* (Cambridge: Harvard University Press, 1966); John Flavell, *The Development Psychology of Jean Piaget* (New York: D. Van Nostrand Company, Inc., 1963); D. Ford and H. Urban, *Systems of Psychotherapy;* J. P. Guilford, *The Nature of Human Intelligence* (New York: McGraw-Hill Book Company, Inc., 1967); L. Llorens and G. Beck, "Training Methods for Cognitive-Perceptual-Motor Dysfunction"; Maya Pines, "Why Some 3-Year Olds Get A's—and Some Get C's"; H. S. Sullivan, *The Interpersonal Theory of Psychiatry* (New York: W. W. Norton and Company, 1953); Clare Thompson, *Psychoanalysis: Evolution and Development* (New York: Grove Press, 1957); Len S. Vygotsky, *Thought and Language* (Cambridge: The M.I.T. Press, 1962).

type of representation selected for solving a particular problem. In learning to ski, for example, most persons find that use of exocept representation is more effective than image representation. It may be possible to use connotative representation to think about redecorating a room, but most persons find it easier and more efficient to use image representation.

Movement from primary process organization to secondary process is not completed until the individual has acquired all of the cognitive subskills. The various aspects of secondary process organization are acquired at different times. For example, the ability to distinguish what is internal and external to the self is learned before deterministic causality. Tertiary process organization will not be considered in the discussion of cognitive skill because it is not felt to be necessary to adequate environmental interaction. It is a relatively rare ability acquired by only a small percent of the population. It is, however, considered to be a learned ability which can only be acquired after the individual has developed all of the cognitive subskills. Secondary process organization must be completely integrated before it is possible to engage in tertiary process organization.

EVALUATION

No standardized tests are available for assessing the extent to which an individual has successfully completed the various stages of cognitive skill. Specific evaluative techniques are in such a primitive stage of development that I feel that it would be useless to describe them here. (However, it is suggested that the reader explore the works of Arieti, Piaget, Bruner and Guilford in order to obtain some idea of the work that has been and is being done in this area.) Behavior indicative to subskill learning and the absence of learning is provided to assist the reader in developing appropriate evaluative tools.

As in the case of perceptual-motor skill, symbols produced by the individual give clues about cognitive skill learning. Symbols do not appear to give specific information regarding the learning or lack of learning of the various subskills and components, however. The manner in which the individual uses symbols which refer to the unconscious, consciousness, order, confusion, mind, the thinking function, representation, and relation to the nonhuman environment provide clues regarding cognitive development.

THE SUBSKILLS

1. *The ability to use inherent behavioral patterns for environmental interaction. (0-1m)*

The inherent behavioral patterns of concern here are sucking, grasping, crying, gross bodily movements and recognition of and attention to visual and auditory stimuli. We cannot be certain whether or not this is an acquired or an inherent subskill. Lack of inherent behavioral patterns is more likely due to neurological deficit than to inadequate learning. The first of the two reasons for describing the subskill here is that it provides a base for considering the other subskills. This is particularly true in regard to causality and acquisition of new responses. At this stage of development temporal contingency between two events is interpreted as one event causing the other, and the individual's own actions are perceived as responsible for all external happenings. As will be discussed later, inherent behavior patterns which lead to pleasurable consequences tend to be repeated and consolidated into new behavioral patterns. The second reason for describing this subskill is that it does appear to be developed further through environmental interaction.

This subskill is considered integrated when the individual is able to locate the nipple with some facility, has a strong grasp and sucking response, cries and is stimulated to cry when he hears another baby cry, is able to move body parts in a gross and vigorous manner, and appears to attend to visual and auditory stimuli. Nonintegration is indicated by the absence of the above-listed behaviors.

Inherent behavior patterns are believed to be enhanced through the availability of objects and events which permit, elicit, and sustain the behavioral patterns.

In the treatment process, poor sucking and grasp responses may be altered by providing objects which are suitable for sucking and grasping. Borrowing from neurological theory discussed in the theoretical base for the treatment of perceptual-motor dysfunction: stimulation of the tactile receptors located around the mouth and in the palm of the hand also increases sucking and grasp responses. Looking and listening responses may be increased by the presence of a variety of pleasurable stimuli. Unrestrictive clothing and the tactile and vestibular stimuli which are a part of playful interaction with another enhances gross and vigorous movements of body parts. Although it seems somewhat strange to speak of *increased crying response*, consistent response to the needs which generate the crying relates crying to environmental interaction. It appears that an infant sometimes cries simply for the sake of crying rather than in response to an experience of need deprivation: allowing such crying—within reason—may indeed be a way of enhancing the crying response.

2. *The ability to interrelate visual, manual, auditory, and oral responses.* *(1m-4m)*

In this stage of development, some of the inherent behaviors mentioned above are organized into patterns. Behaviors which indicate that the subskill has been learned are: anticipatory sucking in response to visual, positional, or auditory cues; more active looking and the ability to follow objects in motion; more active listening and seeking the source of auditory stimuli; smiling response to the human face; vocal responses when alone and in the presence of others; evidence of intentionality in thumb sucking; anything placed in the hand is usually inspected and brought to the mouth; anything placed in the mouth is grasped; attempts to grasp objects in visual field; and imitation of actions which are a part of behavioral repertoire (does not imitate new actions). Lack of several of the above behaviors indicates that the subskill has not been learned.

The patterns of behavior which are a part of this subskill appear to be learned because they are need-satisfying. The environmental elements required are: objects which provide visual, auditory, and tactile stimulation; objects which can be manipulated, grasped and sucked; and playful interaction with a limited number of others who experience such playing as pleasurable.

Treatment of deficiency in this subskill, essentially, involves supplying the above-listed environmental elements during the majority of the time an individual is awake.

3. *The ability to attend to the environmental consequence of actions with interest, to represent objects in an exoceptual manner, to experience objects, to act on the bases of egocentric causality, and to seriate events in which the self is involved. (4m-9m)*

a. Attend to the environmental consequence of actions with interest.

This component of the third cognitive subskill refers to the repetition of certain motor acts which influence the surrounding environment—the first active exploration of the world. Prior to this time, attention has been directed primarily toward the individual's own body or the very near environment. Learning of this component is indicated by intense study, manipulation, and rotation of objects; experimental actions directed toward objects; attention-getting behavior; deliberate and systematic imitations of behaviors already in the individual's repertoire; and repetition of imitated actions in order to reproduce it in others. The absence of these behaviors indicates lack of learning.

This component is acquired through the opportunity to explore and interact in an environment which is interesting, consistent in response, influenced by the actions of the individual, and one which stimulates mutual imitation.

The treatment environment must contain objects which are interesting to the individual. The therapist must sometimes be quite ingenious to find such objects—particularly in the treatment of an adult. Exploratory and manipulative behavior often needs to be encouraged if it does not occur spontaneously. Objects must be such that they can be manipulated in a number of ways without damage to them. There should be no set rules for manipulation—this must be a free experience. Activities selected allow the patient to observe readily his effect on the objects involved. This is particularly important in regard to the therapist's response. The patient must be able to observe his impact upon the therapist; and therefore, the response of the therapist must be as consistent as possible.

b. Represent objects in an exoceptual manner

Exoceptual representation is memory of stimuli in terms of the action response to the stimuli or action directed toward the stimuli. Integration of this component has taken place when the individual initiates an appropriate motor response to unfamiliar objects which are similar to objects in his usual environment. An example of such learning would be the child who picks up a toy car which he has never seen, runs it back and forth on the table and perhaps makes a motor-like sound. This also indicates acquisition of a primitive idea of class. In the above example the child has grouped car-like objects into one category, and responds in a similar manner to all such objects. Learning of this component is also indicated by evidence that the individual recognizes that the intensity of a given act will influence the intensity of the result. Lack of learning is indicated by absence of the above-mentioned response.

This component is learned through interaction with many objects which belong to the same class and objects which respond to variation in the intensity of action directed toward them.

Treatment, essentially, involves providing the types of objects mentioned in the postulate and encouraging the patient's interaction with these objects.

c. Experience objects

This component refers to the individual's ability to recognize that objects have some permanence. (However, it is not until the next stage that the individual recognizes that objects exist in their own right, independent from the individual's actions.) Learning of this component is indicated by anticipation of the ultimate position of a moving object from observation of its trajectory, searching for lost objects (the individual, however, will act as if an object no longer exists if it is covered while he watches), and anticipation of whole object when only a part is seen. The individual has not learned this component if the above behaviors are not present.

It seems that this component is acquired through the opportunity to manipulate and become familiar with a number of objects.

In the treatment process there should be emphasis upon manipulation. Although vision is important, information received through proprioceptive and tactile receptors are particularly important in acquiring the ability to experience objects.

d. Act on the bases of egocentric causality

Egocentric causality is the belief that one's own actions are completely responsible for object response. There is a quasimagical quality about this type of causality. For example, a child acts as if pressing his father's nose causes his father to stick out his tongue—the intentionality of the father is not recognized. It is also seen in the phenomena of knocking on wood to avoid the occurrence of an unwanted event. Behavior which indicates learning of this component is the use of gestures in order to influence the environment, the gestures being essentially unrelated to the response desired.

This component is learned through playful interaction in which various magical gestures frequently lead to specific responses which are experienced as pleasurable by the individual.

The therapist applies this postulate by repeatedly making responses which may be experienced as pleasurable by the patient when the patient initiates a given behavior. There is no attempt to teach reality-oriented cause and effect in this aspect of treatment. The magical, playful quality of this component must be kept in mind.

e. Seriate events in which the self is involved

This component refers to a primitive idea of before and after, relative to events in which the individual's own actions are a part of the sequence. This can be seen, for example, when a child indicates displeasure or confusion when his mother gives him a cracker at the beginning of a meal when he is used to receiving a cracker at the end of the meal. The child has acquired some idea about a typical sequence of events, as indicated by his response to alteration of the sequence. Learning of this component is evident when the individual exhibits awareness of a specific order in events in which he has been repeatedly involved. Lack of awareness indicates dysfunction in this area.

This component is learned through interaction in an environment which involves a regular sequence of activities.

When teaching this component there must be recognizable routine of events in which the patient participates. A consistent sequence must be maintained.

4. *The ability to establish a goal and intentionally carry out means, to recognize the independent existence of objects, to interpret signs, to imitate new behavior, to apprehend the influence of space, and to perceive other objects as partially causal. (9m-12m)*

a. Establish a goal and intentionally carry out means

This component refers to the ability to establish a goal prior to action and to deliberately select and initiate actions which will lead to the goal. The goals of concern here are simple in nature—as are the means. For example, while a child is playing with a block, he may notice his pail across the room—he then walks to the pail and places the block inside it. An observer of this action receives an impression of unequivocal intentionality. Integration of this component is indicated by removal of objects in order to reach some desired object and the impression of deliberate selection of goals and means. (It is difficult, however, to describe specific behavior which causes an observer to attribute deliberateness to an act.) Nonintegration of this component will be seen by actions which seem to be inadvertent and unplanned.

This component is acquired through repeated opportunities to independently establish goals and select and carry out means.

In teaching this component, the therapist makes activities available in which the patient may engage without assistance. The patient must be allowed to manipulate objects in any way that he chooses. Intervention by the therapist is liable to hamper learning.

b. Recognize the independent existence of objects

Independent existence refers to an understanding that objects have permanence; their existence is not dependent upon the individual's manipulation or visual perception. Some writers describe acquisition of this component as "differentiation between the self and other objects." The independent existence of the self as well as other objects is recognized. Behavior which indicates learning of this component, for example, is removal of an object which covers or hides a desired object; lack of learning is evident when an individual acts as if an object no longer exists even though it is covered while he watches.

An individual learns to recognize the independent existence of objects by experimenting with momentary loss of contact with objects. An example of momentary loss is the mother and child playing peek-a-boo.

Some treatment activities deduced from this postulate are putting objects in a covered box and taking them out again, patient and therapist hiding objects under a towel or behind a screen, very simple hide-and-seek, and the therapist and patient hiding under a blanket.

c. Interpret signs

Interpretation of signs refers to anticipation of future events on the basis of a current event. An example of this ability is seen in the child who walks over to his stroller when he sees his mother take his jacket out of the closet. Acquisition of this component is indicated by sign recognition relative to familiar events in the environment and ease in identifying signs in a new situation. Lack of learning is indicated by lack of overt response to signs.

Sign interpretation is acquired through interaction in an environment where there is a regular sequence of events.

Treatment technique based upon this postulate are similar to those suggested for treatment of deficit in the ability to seriate events in which the self is involved. The treatment situation is arranged so that the therapist and patient engage in a consistent series of activities. The pattern of events which take place are similar from one session to the next.

d. Imitate new behavior

With acquisition of this component, the individual is able to observe simple behavior which is not a part of his usual repertoire and imitate the isolated behavior or behavior which is structurally analogous. An example of the latter is seen in the child who waves his arm when he observes his father moving his foot. Learning of this component is indicated by the ability to imitate simple new behaviors.

This component appears to be learned through interaction with human objects who engage in simple behaviors which are imitatable, given the individual's current perceptual-motor capacity, and encouragement of this imitation.

e. Apprehend the influence of space

This component is more exploratory behavior than an integrated ability. The knowledge acquired during this stage is consolidated and actively used in the next stage of cognitive development. Component learning of the apprehension of the influence of space is indicated by active study of differences in size, shape, perspective, and change in objects resulting from different positions of the head. Lack of component learning is indicated by the absence of this exploratory behavior.

This component is learned through interaction in an environment which encourages exploration of objects in space (the self as well as nonhuman objects) and the availability of a variety of object-space relations.

Some treatment techniques developed from this postulate are: activities which involve placing the body and body parts into various size shapes and around various size objects, encouraging the patient to move objects in space to study apparent size change, and activities which involve viewing objects from different positions.

f. Perceive other objects as partially causal

With the learning of this component, the individual realizes that the other objects are causal, but believes that the cause effect relationship is set in motion by his actions; the true volition of other people is not recognized. An example of such learning can be seen in the child who places his mother's hand on a top when he wants to see it spin. Acquisition of this component is indicated by the use of physical contact in an attempt to bring about desired events. Nonintegration of this component is indicated by the continued use of magical gestures in the effort to initiate pleasurable events.

This component is acquired through interacting in an environment in which physical contact is more effective in bringing about desired events than magical gestures.

Using this postulate in the treatment process, the therapist provides reinforcing stimuli for nonmagical gestures and withholds reinforcing stimuli for magical gestures. Shaping is often utilized in teaching this component.

5. *The ability to use trial and error problem solving, to use tools, to perceive variability in spatial positions, to seriate events in which the self is not involved, and to perceive the causality of other objects. (12m - 18m)*

a. Use trial and error problem solving

Trial and error problem solving is the active manipulation of objects to bring about a desired result. Goals are able to be reached by new and unfamiliar means. Learning is indicated by the ability to solve simple problems through active manipulation of objects. The objects required for solution must be available in the immediate environment. Lack of learning is indicated by disinterest in any activity which requires trial and error problem solving.

This component is learned through interaction in situations which require the use of trial and error problem solving.

In treating deficits in this area, the therapist provides interesting non-human objects that present problems which can be solved through active manipulation of objects and object parts.

b. Use tools

Tool use involves the manipulation of one object by application of another object rather than the hand—the child who uses a stick to retrieve a ball which has rolled under the couch, for example. Component learning is indicated by the use of objects in a tool-like manner when the desired result cannot be attained by use of the hand. Lack of component learning is indicated by disinterest in tasks which require the use of tools.

Tool use is learned through interaction in tasks which require the use of readily available tools and reinforcement of such activity.

c. Perceive variability in spatial position

This component refers to the realization that spatial positions are not fixed. Learning is illustrated by the child who rolls his ball under the bed and retrieves it by going around to the other side of the bed. This component also refers to the ability to reach a desired destination by various routes; if the most direct or obvious route is blocked, the individual is able to utilize an alternative route. Learning is indicated by the ability to retrieve an object by a route that is different from the trajectory of the object.

Perception of variability in spatial positions is acquired through exploration of the relationships between objects, space and movement.

d. Seriate events in which the self is not involved

This component refers to memory of the order of a simple sequence of events through observation of these events rather than through participation. Learning is indicated by the ability to repeat a simple sequence of acts after observing another person perform these acts. Lack of learning is indicated by the inability to repeat a sequence of demonstrated acts or confusion regarding the proper sequence.

This component is acquired through interaction in an environment in which there is an opportunity to practice sequential ordering.

e. Perceive the causality of objects

With the learning of this component the individual loses his sense of omnipotence; he recognizes that others are causal. The effect of gravity is also recognized. The individual perceives himself as a recipient of the causal activities of others. Learning is indicated by evidence that the individual understands that others as well as himself have a causal effect on the environment. Lack of learning is indicated by a feeling of omnipotence relative to other human objects, throwing down rather than dropping objects, and waiting for nonhuman objects to move spontaneously.

The individual acquires the ability to perceive the causality of objects through interaction in an environment where there is opportunity to observe the causal effects of others.

6. *The ability to represent objects in an image manner, to make-believe, to infer a cause given its effect, to act on the bases of combined spatial relations, to attribute omnipotence to others, and to perceive objects as permanent in time and place. (18 months - 2 years)*

a. Represent objects in an image manner
Image representation is memory of stimuli in terms of an internal, pictorial, quasi-reproduction. Learning of this component is indicated by the ability to engage in covert trial and error problem solving, to imitate an absent model, and to recognize that pictures of objects and real objects are related.

The interactions responsible for the learning of this component are unknown. However, reinforcement of covert problem solving may facilitate learning.

b. Make-believe
This component refers to the capacity to reenact familiar events by using inadequate objects and treating them as if they were adequate. There is differentiation of the "let us pretend" orientation from the real event. This ability to distinguish between the real and not real becomes more highly refined with continued maturation and learning. However, it is at this point that the basic ability is acquired. Learning of this component is indicated by the ability to engage in make-believe and to understand that it is make-believe. Dysfunction in this area is indicated by the treatment of inadequate objects as if they were adequate, disinterest in make-believe activities, or excessive engagement in such activities.

This component is acquired through an opportunity to engage in make-believe activities alone and with others, and interaction with another who enjoys make-believe, but who also reinforces recognition of the difference between make-believe and real events.

In teaching this component, the therapist must provide inadequate objects which are similar in some respects to adequate objects; these must be specific to events which are familiar to the patient. It is particularly important to be aware of cultural differences. The patient must be allowed to go through the entire process of make-believe without interruption by the therapist. For example, destructive behavior must be as readily accepted as more constructive behavior. Limiting any aspect of make-believe interferes with the patient learning the distinction between what is real and not real.

c. Infer a cause given its effect

This component refers to the ability to recognize that familiar inanimate objects do not act spontaneously. When apparently spontaneous movement does occur, the individual is either able to identify the cause or engage in activities which are likely to lead to identification of the cause. For example, if a ball rolls into a room where a child is playing alone, he is likely to go into the next room to see who initiated the ball's movement. Learning of this component is indicated by interest in locating causal sources; lack of learning is indicated by the acceptance of the spontaneous movement of inanimate objects—or actually attributing spontaneous movement to inanimate objects.

This component is acquired through interaction in an environment where cause and effect is readily apparent and where exploration of cause leads to reinforcing stimuli.

d. Act on the basis of combined spatial relations

With the learning of this component the individual is able to estimate roughly whether or not one object will fit into another and to manipulate objects so that they will fit into a given space. Acquisition is indicated by minimal overt trial and error behavior in activities which involve placement of objects of various sizes within matching spaces.

Combined spatial relations are learned through manipulation of objects in space.

On the basis of this postulate, the therapist provides objects which allow the patient to study the position-filling and displacement properties of objects.

e. Attribute omnipotence to others

Acquisition of this component appears to be necessary in helping the individual to clearly understand that he is not omnipotent. A beginning understanding of the causal effects of others was acquired in the last stage of cognitive development. However, some belief in self omnipotence continued to be present. Learning of this skill is indicated by the belief that others control natural phenomena (for instance, rain or the growth of flowers) and that others know the thought processes of the self; dysfunction is indicated by continued belief in the omnipotence of the self.

This component is probably acquired through interaction in an environment in which others are perceived as trustful and effective in manipulating the environment in a manner which is pleasurable to the individual.

f. Perceive objects as permanent in time and place

This component seems to be an integration of the other, more primitive components which are concerned with learning about the independent existence of objects and time and space relations. It is considered learned when an individual's conscious thought processes are characterized by recognition of temporal and spatial relationships and the relative absence of condensation and displacement. Lack of learning is indicated by confused temporal and spatial relations and frequent condensation and displacement.

This component appears to be learned through positive reinforcement of verbal and nonverbal behavior based upon culturally accepted temporal and spatial relations and nonreinforcement of condensation and displacement.

7. *The ability to represent objects in an endoceptual manner, to differentiate between thought and action, and to recognize the need for causal sources. (2y - 5y)*

a. Represent objects in an endoceptual manner

Endocept representation is memory of stimuli in terms of a felt experience. The nature and method of learning of this type of representation is not well understood. The only reason we believe it is learned at this age is from reports of experiences which occurred during this stage of the developmental process. The experiences are represented in an endocept manner; therefore, this type of representation must be available. Behavior indicative of endocept representation is primarily seen in the adult who is able to discuss the difference between an endocept representation and that which is communicated relative to the representation; a child at this stage of development does not usually have the verbal capacity to describe these differences. However, many persons are not aware of or able to communicate about their own endocept representation. At this point in our understanding we do not know how to evaluate for the presence or absence of this component, nor do we know how this component is learned. In fact, there is some question whether the learning of this subskill component is necessary for full maturation of cognitive skill.

b. Differentiate between thought and action

This component refers to the ability to recognize that conscious content and overt behavior lead to different consequences. Although unsubstantial phenomena (dreams, thoughts, fantasies) are still perceived as quasi-tangible reality they are seen as differing from action in the environment. In learning this component, part of the omnipotence ascribed to others is lost; the individual recognizes that others cannot read his thoughts. Learning is indicated by recognition that thoughts cannot directly influence the environment unless they are translated into action and awareness of the unreality of dreams and fantasies. Lack of learning is demonstrated by the continued belief that others are aware of one's thoughts, fear of fantasizing about actions which would be harmful of others, and a belief that thoughts influence others.

This component appears to be learned through interaction in an environment in which response to verbalized thoughts is different from response to action, and an environment in which response is based upon the action of the individual—rather than on the basis of assumed thoughts, desires or needs.

In establishing treatment techniques deduced from this postulate, the therapist must remember that verbalized thoughts are very different from actions even when these thoughts are concerned with injury to self or others. It is typical for many therapists to respond to patients on the basis of the deduced needs or desires of the patients—these deductions are often quite accurate and facilitating to the treatment process. In teaching this component, however, the therapist must take care to respond to the obvious meaning of verbal and nonverbal behavior only.

c. Recognize the need for causal sources
Through learning of this component, the individual comes to believe that there must be an identifiable cause for every effect. The cause ascribed to an effect, however, may be idiosyncratic and not related to cause and effect relationships considered acceptable by one's cultural group. Learning is indicated by the ability to identify a causal source for any suggested effect and by the apparent need for such identification. Lack of learning is indicated by the absence of the above-listed behaviors.

The learning of this component seems to be motivated by safety needs, in particular the need to have a limited number of unknowns in the environment. The component seems to be acquired through interaction in an environment in which requested causal relationships are given in language and detail that is comprehensible to the individual and in an environment in which a considerable amount of idiosyncratic causality is accepted by others.

8. *The ability to represent objects in a denotative manner, to perceive the viewpoint of others, and to decenter. (6y - 7y)*

a. Represent objects in a denotative manner
Denotative representation is memory of stimuli in terms of words which stand for or name objects—the word is perceived as part of the object or equivalent to it. Learning of this component is indicated by relatively accurate use of language; age level reading; action-oriented, pictorial, and concrete definitions of words; awareness of higher and lower level classification; the ability to form classes on the basis of similarities, and to add or subtract classes to form supraordinate or subordinate classes.

This component appears to be learned through interaction in an environment in which rich and extensive verbal behavior is emphasized as a means of communication.

In teaching this component it is important for the therapist to use extensive verbal communication and to reinforce the patient's use of accurate verbal communication; interactions which emphasize manipulation of the nonhuman environment may interfere with learning. Meaningful conversation is of prime importance. In the initial phase of teaching, it may be necessary for the therapist to select a topic for discussion. The therapist uses his knowledge of what might be interesting and stimulating to the patient(s) as the basis for selecting appropriate topics.

b. Perceive the viewpoint of others

This component refers to the ability to coordinate one's own perceptions with those of others. Learning is indicated by the ability to take the role of others (but not through imitation, as is typical in the play of young children), to perceive one's own point of view as only one of many possible points of view, and to be comfortable in considering various ways in which an object or event might be perceived. Lack of learning is indicated by egocentric, inflexible points of view.

The ability to perceive the viewpoints of others is acquired through human interaction in which the individual receives positive reinforcement for taking other's viewpoints into consideration.

Interactions in which argument and disagreement are nondestructive but frequent are useful for development of this component. A common example of such an activity is a group of young baseball players deciding whether Tommy had indeed touched third base. It is suggested that argument and disagreement take place primarily with peers, and there should be minimal interference or direction from the therapist. The opinion of an authority figure is often accepted without question or accepted only overtly. Neither process is conducive to learning.

c. Decenter

Decentration is the process of distinguishing several features or characteristics of an object. Learning is indicated by a balanced view of all characteristics of an object and use of this information in thinking and making judgments. Lack of learning is indicated by perception of a single outstanding characteristic of an object, concern with surface phenomena only, and stereotyped attitude and action toward a considerable number of objects.

Decentration is learned through interaction in an environment in which the individual receives reinforcement for recognizing and using many characteristics of objects.

Appropriate activities for teaching this component are ones in which the individual must consider several factors if he is to be successful in that activity. These activities should involve interaction with both the human and nonhuman environment.

9. *The ability to represent objects in a connotative manner, to use formal logic, and to work in the realm of the hypothetical. (10y - 12y)*[17]

   a. Represent objects in a connotative manner

    Connotative representation is memory of stimuli in terms of words which are consciously perceived as labels for a classification of some common characteristics. Learning is indicated by flexibility in thinking, the ability to recognize that different labels may be assigned to the same phenomena, and facility in formulating connotative concepts. Dysfunction in this area is indicated by difficulty in recognizing phenomena when there is contextual change, conscious thought which moves from particular to particular, the belief that concepts are unique to a given phenomena, and the inability to form connotative concepts.

    Learning of this component appears to be implemented through demand for, practice in, and reinforcement of connotative representation. In teaching this component it is suggested that the therapist provide problems which point out the limitations of the other types of representation but in particular denotative representation. Guidance in solving these problems and specification of the thinking process involved assists the individual in perceiving words as labels. Study of different theoretical systems which deal with the same phenomena is also useful.

   b. Use formal logic

    Formal logic is here arbitrarily defined as "the ability to maintain one premise during a reasoning sequence, to reflect back upon a reasoning sequence, and to base conscious thought and action on deterministic causality." The premise which is taken as the point of departure may vary from culture to culture, but it must be compatible with at least some of the ideas of one's cultural group. Learning is indicated by the behavior listed above. Lack of learning is indicated by an inability to return to the original point of departure in a reasoning sequence, contradictions during the sequence, selecting an original premise which is not accepted by one's cultural group, inability to perceive or correct contradictions in logic, and continued use of phenomenalistic causality.

    This component appears to be learned through interaction in an environment in which the use of formal logic is followed by a positive reinforcer.

    In translating this postulate into a treatment process, it is suggested that the therapist provide opportunity for practice in keeping one premise during a reasoning sequence. Debate is particularly helpful in this area. Demand for reflections back upon a reasoning sequence, corrections of

---

[17]Piaget states that this subskill is usually acquired between the ages of 10 and 12. Although the potential for development may be present at this age, our educational methods seem to impede its development. From limited personal experience, it is rare that one sees an undergraduate or graduate student who has acquired this subskill in an integrated manner.

error in the sequence (given the initial premise), and practice in going through the sequence again are also suggested as treatment techniques. Finally, differential reinforcement of various premises which are considered acceptable by the patient's cultural group, is also a useful device for teaching.

c. Work in the realm of the hypothetical
'Hypothetical' here refers to that which is future, unknown, conjecturable, or open to speculation. Learning of this component is indicated by the ability to engage in thinking which goes beyond the immediate here and now of current object interaction; to imagine "what might be"; perceive both the obvious and the subtle; deal with chance or probability; and solve problems by isolating all of the possible variables and relationships and, through experimentation and logical analysis, determine which of these possibilities is validated by the present data.

This component appears to be learned through an opportunity to deal with the hypothetical and reinforcement of the behaviors which are indicative of component learning.

The case study method of teaching is one example of how the postulate has been translated into a learning technique.[18]

DRIVE-OBJECT SKILL

The concepts of *need, drive,* and *object* were used in Chapter Three to identify common phenomena relative to man. Postulates stating the various relationships between these concepts described one aspect of man's behavior in relation to his human and nonhuman environment. (It is suggested that the reader review this section and the references before proceeding.) The ability to select appropriate and substitute objects and to enter into mature object relationships is here considered to be a learned human capacity. It has been labeled *drive-object skill.* Full maturation of drive-object skill is defined as "the ability to control drives and select objects in such a manner as to insure adequate need satisfaction."

Development of this adaptive skill is considered to be stage specific except for one aspect. That component of the skill which appears to be non-stage specific is the ability to delay need satisfaction, which seems to be quantitative rather than qualitative. The individual's capacity to accept a time lapse between the experiencing of a need and gratification of that need is minimal in infancy and slowly increases throughout the entire period of drive-object skill development.

The therapist evaluates for the learning of this component in conjunction with the assessment of drive-object subskill learning. Inadequate development is indicated by impulsive behavior, demands for immediate need satisfaction, maladaptive behavior in the presence of any degree of need deprivation, minimal attempt to solve problems, and disregard for the rights of others when

---

[18]Kenneth Anderson, *The Case Method of Teaching Human Relation and Administration* (Cambridge: Harvard University Press, 1956).

the individual experiences an unmet need. Adequate development is indicated by the absence of such behavior.

The ability to delay need satisfaction is acquired through consistent, and relatively immediate, need satisfaction followed by reinforcement of time lapse between the experienced need and its gratification. The time lapse must be increased in small increments for adequate learning to occur.

Various ways in which the therapist provides consistent and relatively immediate need satisfaction will be discussed in the teaching process relative to the first two drive-object subskills. Increasing the time between experienced need and gratification should not be initiated until after the first two subskills have been learned, for so doing interferes with the learning of these subskills. This process is usually initiated when the therapist begins to teach the third drive-object subskill and may continue in conjunction with the teaching of all the other subskills.

EVALUATION

There are no specific techniques available for assessing learning relative to drive-object skill. Although some indications of learning and lack of learning will be evident in his nonverbal behavior, discussion with the patient is also very useful. Such discussion should focus on the patient's needs and the manner in which he goes about satisfying these needs. Symbols produced by an individual appear to give much more specific information about learning of the various drive-object subskills than was the case with perceptual-motor or cognitive skill.[19] Symbols which reflect subskill learning and lack of learning will be identified in the following section whenever this is possible.

THE SUBSKILLS[20]

1. *The ability to form a discontinuous libidinal object relationship (4m-6m)*

[19] This is most likely true because we have learned to interpret symbols relative to this and the other adaptive skills which will be discussed later. Symbols probably refer specifically to perceptual-motor and cognitive development. This relationship may become evident when we acquire greater knowledge regarding symbols and these two adaptive skills.

[20] Major references for this subsection include: H. and F. Azima, "Outline of a Dynamic Theory of Occupational Therapy"; George Engel, *Psychological Development in Health and Disease* (Philadelphia: W. B. Saunders Company, 1962); Erik Erikson, *Childhood and Society* (New York: Norton, 1950); G. and J. Fidler, *Occupational Therapy: A Communication Process in Psychiatry*; W. Ronald W. Fairbain, *Psychoanalytic Studies of the Personality* (London: Tavistock Publications, Ltd., 1952); Anna Freud, *Normality and Pathology in Childhood* (New York: International Universities Press, 1965) and *The Ego and the Mechanisms of Defense* (New York: International Universities Press, 1966); Sigmund Freud, *The Basic Writings of Sigmund Freud*, A. Brill, ed. (New York: Random House, 1938) and *An Outline of Psychoanalysis* (New York: W. W. Norton, 1949); Peter Knapp, *Expressions of the Emotions in Man* (New York: International Universities Press, Inc., 1963); J. Pearce and S. Newton, *The Conditions of Human Growth*; Marguerite Sechehaye, *Symbolic Realization* (New York: International Universities Press, 1951); and Rene Spitz, *The First Year of Life* (New York: International Universities Press, 1965).

A discontinuous object relation is one in which the individual invests libidinal energy in an object only when the object is in the process of gratifying a need. The energy is withdrawn when the need is satiated. Prior to learning this subskill, all libidinal energy is invested in the self. Such an investment, often referred to as *primary narcissism*, is inherent and not a learned subskill. Although there is a shift in libidinal investment to other objects as the individual acquires drive-object subskills, some libidinal energy remains invested in the self. Learning of this component is indicated by recognition of and pleasant response to human objects which offer need satisfaction, perception of others as basically need satisfying, and the ability to distinguish one need from another (but in a relatively gross manner). In addition to the absence of the behaviors listed above, lack of learning is indicated by primary narcissism; preoccupation with physiological and safety needs; and the predominant use of symbols which refer to birth, womb, vegetative functions, that which nurtures and protects, preoccupation with self, unmet physiological and safety needs, seeking of need satisfaction, and complexes related to the oral period.

This subskill is learned through experiencing a nurturing relationship. A nurturing relationship is here defined as "an extensive interaction between two persons in which one individual receives consistent and relatively immediate need satisfaction, is not required to give any reciprocal satisfaction, and is free to engage in any behavior which is not destructive to self or others." The individual who gives nurturance must be accepting, permissive, delight in giving nurture and experience strong positive feelings toward the individual who is receiving nurturance. Absence of any of the above factors is considered to constitute a nonnurturing relationship.

In treatment interactions based upon this postulate, the therapist attempts in every way possible to meet whatever needs are presently being experienced by the individual. These may be needs which are verbalized by the patient or ones which are carefully deduced from the patient's behavior. An experienced need is a need which, when satisfied, gives rise to a pleasant response from the individual. Individuals who have not learned those subskills which are acquired through interaction in a nurturing relationship often experience the need to be fed and physically held. If this is the case and the patient is able to accept direct gratification of these needs, the therapist responds directly to these needs.[21] At times a patient experiences these needs but is unable to accept direct gratification. In this situation, the patient is often able to accept symbolic gratification. The need to be fed may be satisfied symbolically by such things as offering cigarettes, candy, chewing gum, soda, and coffee;

---

[21]The taboo regarding touching patients is not accepted in recapitulation. If the patient wants to be held or engage in any other type of nonsexual physical contact, the patient's experienced need is met. It is my belief that the issue of sexuality will never arise or be immediately resolved if the therapist is very clear about the difference between a sexual response and a nurturing response. If he is not clear regarding this difference, he should not attempt to teach any subskill which is learned through interaction in a nurturing relationship.

preparing a meal or snack together (the patient participating only to the extent that he wishes); and activities which make use of the mouth (blowing, sucking, singing, talking, etc.). The need to be held may be satisfied symbolically by such things as touching the patient's hand or shoulder, allowing the patient to sleep, assisting the patient with self-care activities, and involvement in activities which allow for some physical contact within the context of the activity.

There are some patients who have not learned subskills which are acquired through interaction in a nurturing relationship, who do not experience the need to be fed and physically held; it should never be assumed, therefore, that these needs are being experienced. With this type of patient the therapist is essentially concerned with gratifying any need (except sexual) that the patient is experiencing. For example, the patient may want to engage in some activity that is familiar to him, learn a new activity, go to a movie or out for a walk, complain, talk about his problems, play cards, etc. If at all possible, given the ingenuity of the therapist, the patient is assisted in doing whatever he wants to do. A commitment to engage in the activity for any period of time is never required. As a general rule of thumb the therapist never asks the patient to clean up, finish a task, be neat, do something for himself, work without assistance, do anything he doesn't feel like doing, thank the therapist, or even respond in a pleasant manner.

Permissiveness was mentioned as one of the characteristics of a nurturing relationship. However, this is subordinate to the patient's needs; if the patient is not comfortable in a permissive environment, the environment is altered— many patients feel more secure in a structured environment. The therapist offers suggestions, makes decisions, provides directions, and limits hostile expression to the extent that the patient indicates need for these types of responses.

Providing a nurturing relationship is not an attempt to regress a patient to a more primitive stage of development The patient who needs a nurturing relationship is at a primitive stage of development, although he may not act in an infantile or regressed manner. During the treatment process the patient's behavior may become more infantile. This is permitted if it does occur, but it need not occur for treatment to be successful. There is no attempt to make the patient dependent. Patients who lack subskills which are learned through interaction in a nurturing relationship are dependent even though this may not be manifest in overt behavior. If the patient acts in a dependent manner, his dependency needs are met directly. If the patient indicates that he has a need to maintain an independent stance, however, this need is also met.

The question whether or not other staff members in the treatment setting must also enter into a nurturing relationship with the patient is often raised. This is not necessary for successful treatment. The patient is responded to in a manner which is similar to the way in which the staff responds to other patients. This is, of course, assuming that staff members respond to patients in a humane manner--with profound recognition of individual needs. Still, the patient is required to adhere to the rules of the treatment facility, engage in self care activities to the extent that he is able, and participate in assigned tasks and required activities.

Another question often raised is whether the patient will ever move beyond a nurturing relationship. Phrased a different way: "If most of the patient's needs are gratified, will he ever move in the direction of independence and self sufficiency?" The answer is "yes"—just as a child demands autonomy and begins to want to do things for himself, so will the patient. It is only those individuals who have not had complete gratification of physiological, security, and love and acceptance needs who continue to demand and require dependent, caring for relationships with others.

Entering into a nurturing relationship with a patient is no easy task; it is very demanding of the therapist, who is often required to give far more than is required in any other type of treatment interaction. The therapist must be in a position where the majority of his needs are being met through interactions outside of the treatment process and has considerable free libidinal energy to invest in the patient. In addition, the therapist must feel affection and liking for the patient and be comfortable in making no demands of the patient. It is my belief that a therapist should not attempt to treat a patient through a nurturing relationship if the above-listed factors are not present

2. The ability to form a continuous, part libidinal object relationship. (8m-9m)

A *continuous object relationship* is one in which the individual invests libidinal energy in a need-fulfilling object even when the object is not currently satisfying a particular need. A *part object relationship* is one in which the individual recognizes only some aspects of the object. For example, the child who has learned this subskill clearly perceives his mother as different from and preferred to any other person and responds to the mother in a positive manner even when she is not directly satisfying his needs. However, the child does not perceive the totality of mother, her assets and limitations, her needs, and her interactions with others; the child, rather, invests libidinal energy in the aspect of mother which means "that which loves and takes care of me." At the time of learning this subskill, the individual's object relationships are profoundly limited. The mother is essentially the only object which is seen as need-gratifying. It is for this reason and because this is the first object relationship which is formed with an object other than the self, that the learning of this subskill is often referred to as the *primary object relationship*. There are two facets to this subskill. One is the investment of libidinal energy in the mother or mother surrogate. The other is the ability to trust the mother.

Learning of this subskill is indicated by perception of other objects which demand the time and attention of the primary object as disturbing factors, an active reaching-out to the libidinal object, and basic trust of others Lack of learning is indicated by perception of others as threatening to the integrity of the self, disturbance in sleep or eating patterns ranging from excessive indulgence to avoidance, symbiotic relationship with the primary object, difficulty in distinguishing between various others, fears of any positive emotional involvement with others, avoidance of reality-oriented behavior and withdrawal from the object world, and interaction in homosexual and heterosexual relationships which are primarily concerned with reenactment of the mother-child relationship. Lack of learning is also indicated by predominant use of symbols which refer to that which nurtures and protects, unmet love and acceptance needs, complexes related to the oral period, oneness or unity, arrested growth, free floating and/or uncontrolled libidinal energy, seeking need satisfaction in fantasy, dependency, withdrawal, and experience of object loss.

This subskill is acquired through interaction in a nurturing relationship.

The reader is referred back to the first drive-object subskill for discussion of treatment techniques deduced from this postulate.

3. *The ability to invest aggressive drive in external objects. (9m-12m)*

Up until this point in the developmental process, aggressive energy has been primarily manifested in crying and has been expressed in a diffuse and undirected manner. With the learning of this subskill, aggressive drive is invested in specific objects. Object choice may not be accurate, however, and the individual's ability to manipulate aggressive objects successfully is very limited. A child who has acquired this skill is comfortable in directing his anger toward human and nonhuman objects. He expresses this anger through hitting out, throwing objects, stomping his feet, angry vocalization, occasional temper tantrums, and engaging in forbidden activities. The mother or mother surrogate, objects perceived as rivals for the mother's attention, and nonhuman objects which the child cannot successfully manipulate are the major objects which are perceived as need frustrating and it is these objects which are invested with aggressive energy.

Learning of this subskill is indicated by the ability to express anger, attempts to manipulate aggressive objects, and minimal anxiety or guilt regarding covert or overt manipulation of aggressive objects. Lack of learning is indicated by absence of the above behavior, perception of the self as the primary obstacle to need satisfaction, self hate, self-destructive behavior, denial or repression of aggressive drive, perception of aggressive drive as destructive to others, and preoccupation with aggressive objects (but making no attempt to eliminate the objects through overt action). Dysfunction in this area is also indicated by predominant use of symbols which refer to evil or the devil, animal aspect of man, uncontrolled drives, aggressive energy turned toward the self, free-floating aggressive energy, inadequate need satisfaction, and mode of dealing with aggressive objects.

This subskill is learned through interaction in an environment in which there is an opportunity for symbolic expression of aggressive drive, optimal need frustration, positive reinforcement of aggressive drive investment in external objects, some success in manipulation of aggressive objects, and assurance that excessive or harmful expression of aggressive drive will be controlled by external forces.

The exact nature and function of symbolic expression of aggressive drive is not well understood. It is evident in the normal developmental process, however, and appears to be related to the learning of this subskill. Prior to learning this subskill the child engages in such behaviors as biting, hitting, throwing, pounding, scratching, loud vocalization, kicking, tearing, etc. These actions occur in the absence of need frustration, are engaged in with great pleasure, and are primarily directed toward the nonhuman environment. It is suggested that these behaviors provide practice in, and minimize fear of, the investment of aggressive energy in specific objects and manipulation of aggressive objects—it is almost as if the action is learned and then used for aggressive drive expression. Treatment techniques based upon this postulate involve synthesizing activities which allow the patient to engage in behavior such as that discussed above; activities which require gross motion, the manipulation of resistive material, and destruction of nonhuman objects are particularly useful. Some patients experience fear relative to these types of activities. If this is the case, the therapists regulate the activity so that it is nonthreatening to the patient.

Optimal need frustration is a degree of frustration with which an individual is able to cope. It is a degree of frustration which is not perceived as overwhelming or dangerous to self-integrity. The therapist must be finely-tuned to the patient's needs and frustration tolerances to regulate the withholding of need satisfaction. The therapist allows, encourages and reinforces expression of aggressive drive which is not harmful to self or others. In order to do this effectively, the therapist must be truly comfortable with aggressive drive expression. He must be able to accept the role of an aggressive object without fear, withdrawal, or retaliation—and to accept the fact that the patient is not going to like him or what he is doing all of the time. With this capacity the therapist is able to indicate to the patient that he (the therapist) is able to control the situation so that the patient will not harm himself or others. The patient's expression of aggressive drive must lead to the elimination of obstacles which interfere with possession of libidinal objects. In this way the patient learns that it is not only acceptable to invest in and manipulate aggressive objects but that such activity leads to need satisfaction.

4. *The ability to transfer libidinal drive to objects other than the primary object. (14m-18m)*

Although considerable libidinal energy remains invested in the primary object, with the learning of this subskill, the individual transfers some libidinal energy to other objects. The father, siblings, and other persons in the home are seen as need gratifying and invested with libidinal energy. From this point on the parental pair usually provides the security base for the child. The child also invests libidinal energy in nonhuman objects- a favored doll, his shoes, father's camera, and cake. Investment is indicated by the child's particular delight in seeing libidinal objects and by his possessive behavior toward these objects. In the process of acquiring this subskill the child often forms a special and profound attachment to one nonhuman object. This is usually a nonhuman object which shares some common characteristics with the mother. Typical examples are a doll, blanket, or pillow. These are referred to as *transitional objects*, for they appear to help the child move toward an increasingly independent position relative to the mother. They seem to provide a sense of security as the child tests out investment in other objects. With the learning of this subskill the individual's object relationships are considered to be *semidiffused*. The individual is able to satisfy his needs through investment in a number of different objects. His object relationships are not totally diffuse, because the mother or parental pair continues to be predominant and most important libidinal object.

Learning of this subskill is indicated by evidence of libidinal investment in a variety of human and nonhuman objects, less intense but continued investment in the primary object and willing acceptance of temporary separation from the primary object. Lack of learning is indicated by a catastrophic reaction to loss of the primary object (lethargy, weight loss and profound withdrawal); exclusive investment of libidinal energy in the primary object or objects seen as similar to the primary object; continued use of transitional objects; and predominant use of symbols which refer to retarded growth, protection and shelter, limited psychic energy available for acting on the environment, lack of self assertion, regression to primitive levels of functioning, and inadequate need satisfaction.

This subskill is acquired through interaction in an environment in which need-fulfilling objects are available and investment in these objects is reinforced by the primary object. Transfer of libidinal energy to other human objects can occur only if these objects are libidinal objects for the primary object.

In order to engage in the teaching of this subskill, the therapist must establish an object relationship with the patient. This is accomplished in a manner identical with the techniques outlined for teaching the first drive-object subskill. After an object relationship has been established, the therapist uses the postulates given above as the basis for treatment planning. There is great variation in the nonhuman objects which an individual experiences as need-fulfilling; it is therefore necessary for the therapist to be finely tuned to the patient's needs. For the first time in the treatment of this adaptive skill, other patients may be introduced into the treatment situation. Prior to this time, others would have interfered with subskill learning. The therapist uses a parallel group for teaching this subskill (Parallel group is discussed in conjunction with the group interaction skill). In addition, the therapist may use other staff members to assist in teaching this subskill; for example, if the patient expressed interest in photography, the therapist may assign the patient to a photography group. The staff leader of the group, knowing the subskill which the patient is in the process of learning, would provide considerable support and need gratification. Regardless of whether patients or staff members assist in the teaching of this subskill, these persons must be libidinal objects for the therapist. The therapist's feelings that these persons are inferior, inadequate, or lacking in sophistication will interfere with the patient's learning. Reinforcement of the patient's movement toward investing libidinal energy in other objects will occur if the therapist honestly desires such movement; wanting to remain the most important object to the patient, for instance, impedes learning of this subskill. This is probably the major factor which interferes with acquisition of this subskill in the normal developmental process. A word regarding transitional objects: if the patient appears to develop a strong relationship to a particular nonhuman object, this should be accepted. The therapist does not attempt to disrupt this relationship in any way; it will be terminated in a spontaneous manner as the subskill is learned.

5. *The ability to invest libidinal energy in appropriate abstract objects and to control aggressive drive. (4y-5y)*

Although it may appear that this subskill is made up of two components, this is actually not so. It is through investment of libidinal energy in appropriate abstract objects that the individual learns to control his aggressive drives. In this stage of development the values and norms of the cultural group are invested with libidinal energy. On the basis of these internalized values and norms the individual makes judgment on acceptable methods for dealing with aggressive objects. Appropriate abstract objects are relative to one's cultural group; ideally, the norms and values of the cultural group permit accurate identification of aggressive objects, investment of aggressive energy in these objects, and prohibit destruction of or physical harm to human objects. With the learning of this subskill the individual has acquired the ability to identify aggressive objects—but only those objects accepted by the cultural group.

Learning is indicated by aggressive object manipulations which are compatible with cultural norms, experience of some guilt or anxiety when cultural norms are disregarded, and effective manipulation of aggressive objects. Lack of learning is indicated by sociopathic or psychopathic behavior, maltreatment of aggressive objects, investment of libidinal energy in abstract objects which prohibit any type of aggressive behavior, anxiety or guilt arising from the contemplation or actualization of an aggressive act, and diffuse and poorly directed aggressive drive. Symbolic expression of lack of learning is similar to those outlined for the third drive-object subskill.

This subskill is acquired through interaction with a primary object which reinforces conformity to cultural norms and values and an opportunity to practice locating and manipulating aggressive objects.

The first phase of teaching this subskill involves establishing a primary object relationship with the patient. Once this relationship is established, the therapist requires and reinforces conformity to cultural norms. Requirements for conformity are minimal initially and are slowly increased over time. Role-playing is one technique which is often used to practice manipulation of human aggressive objects.

6. *The ability to engage in total and diffuse libidinal object relationships. (14y-18y)*

a. Engage in total object relationships

With acquisition of this component, the individual perceives and invests in the whole object. Learning is indicated by the ability to perceive both the assets and limitations of libidinal objects, continued investment in libidinal objects even when limitations are recognized, and lack of hero worship. How this component is reflected in symbols is unknown.

This component is learned through interaction with libidinal objects which provide reinforcement for recognition of assets and limitations.

In order to teach this component the therapist must first of all know himself and be comfortable in engaging with the patient in activities which point up his (the therapist's) limitations. The all-knowing, all-powerful stance which insecure therapists sometimes take interferes with the teaching and learning of this component.

b. Diffuse object relationships

When an individual's object relationships are diffuse, needs are satisfied through libidinal investment in a number of different objects. Although some objects are seen as more important than others, many objects are seen as need-satisfying. In learning this component the individual finally resolves his primary object relationship; the mother or mother surrogate is no longer perceived as the most important source of need gratification. Acquisition of this component is indicated by only occasional contact with the mother or parental pair; and by indications of pleasure and need satisfaction through interaction with a number of objects. Absence of learning is indicated by continued yearning for the mother, the need for frequent contact with the mother, a small number of libidinal objects, and demand that one or a few objects gratify all needs. Lack of learning is also indicated by the frequent use of symbols which refer to nurturance and protection, lack of wholeness, unmet love and acceptance needs, lack of need satisfaction, and considerable free-floating libidinal energy.

This component is acquired through interaction in an environment where there are a variety of need-satisfying objects and practice in securing gratification from these objects.

In teaching this component the therapist helps the patient to seek out need-satisfying objects; these are preferably objects in the patient's usual environment rather than within the treatment facility. Trial interaction with these objects is encouraged and the therapist offers support, guidance and advice as needed by the patient.

DYADIC INTERACTION SKILL[22]

Dyadic interaction skill is the ability to engage in meaningful interactions with another individual; in its mature form it is the ability to participate in a variety of dyadic relationships. It focuses on those one-to-one relationships which are usually referred to as *friendship, intimacy, nurturing,* and *interaction with authority.* In developing this skill, the individual learns to perceive others as unique and different from the self. Unless there is strong evidence to the contrary, he learns to act on the assumption that other persons are worthy of respect, nonthreatening to self-integrity, and free of the negative affect toward the self.

EVALUATION

It is usually difficult for the therapist to directly observe behavior which is indicative of learning or lack of learning of the various subskills which make up dyadic interaction skill. An interview which focuses upon general feelings regarding others, the nature of the patient's superficial and more intimate friendships, interactions with the marital partner and children, any caretaking relationships the patient may have had, and typical patterns of behavior relative to persons in authority positions. Some information may also be acquired through interpretation of symbols produced by the patient.

THE SUBSKILLS

1. *The ability to enter into association relationships. (3y-5y)*
   An *association relationship* is a type of interaction between two persons which is relatively casual, easily disrupted, minimally concerned with need gratification, and usually involves engagement in a shared task. Learning of the subskill is indicated by the ability to form casual relationships to interact with a peer comfortably and for a sustained period, and to engage in simple competitive and cooperative interactions. Lack of learning is indicated by absence of these behaviors as well as withdrawal, and lack of self assertion, and a predominant use of symbols which refer to the environment as overwhelming.

   This subskill is learned through interaction in an environment where association relationships are available and reinforced. The individual needs for

---

[22]Complete discussions of the subject may be found in J. Pearce and S. Newton, *The Conditions of Human Growth*; H. S. Sullivan, *The Interpersonal Theory of Psychiatry* (New York: W. W. Norton and Company, 1953); Erik Erikson, *Childhood and Society* (New York: Norton, 1950); A Gesell and G. Amatruda, *Developmental Diagnosis: Normal and Abnormal Child Development* (New York: Harper and Row, Publishers, Inc., 1947); George Homans, *The Human Group* (New York: Harcourt, Brace and World, Inc., 1950); Talcott Parsons and R. Bales, *Family, Socialization and the Interaction Process* (New York: The Free Press of Glencoe, 1955); and Floyd Ruch, *Psychology and Life* (Chicago: Scott, Forsman and Company, 1963).

safety and love and acceptance must be met outside of association relationships.

In teaching this subskill, the therapist encourages the patient to share a task with another person; the task must, of course, be compatible with the individual's capacity and interest. The shaping process is often used in teaching this subskill. The patient should have an opportunity to engage in several association relationships if at all possible. It is not necessary for the therapist to be present during the patient's interactions with others unless there is need for immediate and continuous external reinforcement. The patient's safety and love needs are met by the therapist.

2. *The ability to interact in an authority relationship. (5y-7y)*

In learning this subskill, the individual begins to perceive authority figures as different from his parents. They are seen as relatively powerful—but not as powerful as the parents. Acceptance of direction from an authority figure in a positive and cooperative manner indicates learning of the subskill; lack of learning is indicated by overcompliance, refusal to accept direction, and marked fear of authority figures. Predominant use of symbols which refer to potency and self-inadequacy may also indicate lack of learning.

This subskill is acquired through interaction with a libidinal object who has made reasonable demands upon the individual, and reinforced acceptance of these demands. In addition, it is learned through interaction with non-familial authority figures who make reasonable demands and provide at least some reinforcement for meeting demands.

In teaching this subskill, the therapist must first establish a libidinal object relationship with the patient, although this need not be a primary relationship. It may be necessary to use shaping to establish that behavior which has been described as being indicative of skill learning. When the patient is able to meet the demands made by the therapist, the therapist provides situations in which the patient has an opportunity to interact with other authority figures. Appropriate behavior relative to the new authority figures is reinforced by the authority figures and the therapist for as long as necessary.

3. *The ability to interact in a chum relationship. (10y-14y)*

A *chum relationship* is one in which another person is experienced as being extremely important to the self and the needs of the other are felt as equal to the needs of the self. This is an emotionally charged relationship characterized by mutual trust, sharing of confidences, and minimal competitive interaction. A chum relationship is usually shared with only a few members of the same sex. Parental figures are excluded from these relationships and their approval is not actively sought or desired.

An individual has engaged in chum relationships when he is able to perceive and meet the needs of others, experience his own humanness, and feel compassion for and empathy with another person. Lack of learning is indicated by the absence of these behaviors and the frequent use of symbols which refer to distance from people and by experience of the self as nonhuman.

This component is learned through interaction with peers who are developmentally ready to engage in a chum relationship. The environment must allow for privacy and provide an opportunity for separateness.

The therapist is not directly involved in teaching this subskill. He has (hopefully) advanced beyond this stage of development and is not, therefore, a suitable object for this shared learning experience. The therapist facilitates learning by helping the patient to locate other individuals who are ready to engage in a chum relationship and by allowing that relationship to develop. Approval of the relationship is communicated to the patient. The therapist does not question the patient about the relationship unless the patient indicates a wish to discuss it. In this way, the therapist respects the privacy which is needed for development of this subskill. The intensity and secrecy of the chum relationship has a tendency to arouse anxiety in some therapists—this is particularly true when there is evidence of shared deviant behavior. If there is grossly deviant behavior, the therapist must help the pair to alter their behavior or in extreme cases interrupt the relationship; if the deviant behavior is mild, it is recommended that the therapist ignore it. In making a judgment in this matter, the therapist must weigh the harmful effect of the deviant behavior against the importance of learning this subskill. The significance of this subskill is frequently not given sufficient consideration. We often err on the side of interrupting chum relationships which could ultimately lead to the development of very important human abilities.

4. *The ability to enter into a peer authority relationship. (15y-17y)*

Peer authority refers to a superior-subordinate relationship in which the individual perceives the authority figure as similar to the self except for their relative positions in a given situation. Learning of this subskill is indicated by realistic perception of the authority figure's power relative to the self, comfortable interaction with authority figures, recognition that there is a distinction between adaptive behavior relative to an authority figure when he is acting as an authority figure, and adaptive behavior in all other interactions with the individual, and the ability to judge the competence of orders issued by the authority figure and to act upon the bases of that judgment. As in the case of the second dyadic interaction subskill, the predominant use of symbols which refer to potency and self inadequacy may be indicative of lack of learning.

This subskill is acquired through interaction in an environment where there is an opportunity to take superior and subordinate roles and to observe others taking those roles. Additional learning of this subskill takes place through interaction with authority figures who provide reinforcement of those behaviors which are indicative of acquisition of this subskill.

One of the common techniques developed from the first postulate is formation of a patient group concerned with publishing a newspaper or news-letter. The role of editor is rotated, giving each group member an oppor-tunity to take subordinate and superior roles. Involvement in one committee as a chairman and other committees as a member is also a useful device for teaching this subskill. In application of the second postulate, the authority figure (whoever this may be) must clearly delineate his power relative to the patient, avoid unreasonable demands and arbitrary behavior, interact with the patient outside of order-giving situations and specifically indicate the differ-ence in the behavior expected of the patient, and encourage questioning of his (the authority figure's) competence and directions. The authority figure must be comfortable in his authority position and be capable of seeing the patient as a peer.

5. *The ability to enter into an intimate relationship. (18y-25y)*

An *intimate relationship* is mutually need-satisfying and characterized by a firm commitment to one's partner which is maintained regardless of normal demands for sacrifice on the part of the self; with development of this sub-skill the individual has acquired the true capacity for love of another person. Intimate involvement over a sustained period of time is possible and pleasur-able, for there is a comfortable sharing of responsibility and both individuals are able to give and receive from the other. The intensity and preoccupation characteristic of the chum relationship is absent and the individuals in the dyad are able to sustain their relationship through extended periods of absence. Both individuals are free to enter into a variety of intimate relation-ships or dyads of other kinds. This ability is basic to establishing a successful marriage and mature, need-fulfilling, stable friendships.

Learning of this subskill is indicated by the ability to experience love, maintain sustained relationships, and a continued sense of autonomy when participating in intimate relationships. Lack of learning is indicated by absence of these behaviors, perception of ordinary demands by others as ex-cessive and grounds for severing a relationship, and dyadic interaction char-acterized by jealous possessiveness and preoccupation with the relationship.

This subskill is acquired through interaction in an environment where there are persons available who are capable of establishing intimate relation-ships and living with others in a situation in which one is required to share responsibilities for tasks and need satisfaction.

As was the case in the third dyadic interaction skill, the therapist does not teach this skill directly. Instead, he helps the patient locate appropriate per-sons and situations for learning—he provides support, advice if requested, and validation of the patient's capacity to engage in an intimate relationship. To teach this subskill, the therapist must experience delight in the patient's movement into intimate relationships which, in a very essential way, exclude the therapist. Communal living of one type or another often provides an excellent environment for learning this subskill; living with others outside of a familial situation initiates demands and provides reinforcements which facilitate learning.

6. *The ability to engage in nurturing relationships. (19y-30y)*

A *nurturing relationship* is a characterized by satisfaction of the needs of another person without a demand of reciprocal satisfaction. Learning is indicated by unselfish giving of one's time and energy to the other, the giving of an unconditional love which respects the rights of the other for growth and uniqueness, and the ability to withdraw libidinal energy when the other is able to function independently. Engagement in or the desire and ability to engage in a nurturing relationship is often indicated by predominant use of symbols which refer to the birth-death-rebirth cycle, perfect being, that which nurtures and protects, femininity, and oneness or unity. Lack of learning is indicated by the absence of the above-listed behaviors or symbols, avoidance of nurturing relationships, ambivalence toward persons in need of nurturance, no enjoyment of the growth of others, premature withdrawal of energy from the nurtured object (or a tenacious holding on), anxiety and excessive feelings of loss when the nurtured object moves out of the relationship, difficulty in investing libidinal energy in created objects or difficulty withdrawing energy once investment has occurred and anxiety and feelings of object loss when sharing created objects with another.

Preliminary development of this subskill arises from caretaking activities relative to plants and animals and from taking partial responsibility of young children. Full development is dependent upon interaction with another person who requires nurturing. The environment in which this relationship occurs must be understood as being safe by the nurturing partner so that adequate time and energy may be devoted to the other, for there must be an opportunity for sufficient and consistent need gratification. The ability to terminate the relationship is dependent upon environmental opportunity for reinvestment of energy in other objects and continued gratification of those self-actualization needs which are gratified in the nurturing process.

GROUP INTERACTION SKILL

A group is an aggregate of people who share a common purpose and who are interdependent in the achievement of that purpose.[23] A distinction is sometimes made between primary groups and secondary groups. "A primary group is a face-to-face organization of individuals who cooperate for certain common ends, who share many common ideas and patterns of behavior, who have confidence in and some degree of affection for each other, and who are aware of their similarities and bonds of association."[24] A secondary group is any large group which does not allow for face-to-face contact of all members. The group members do not have close or intimate ties, but they do share some common interest or similarity; within a secondary group there may be one or more primary groups. The individual frequently interacts in a secondary group through his membership in one of the primary groups which make up the secondary group. (The family is, for example, a primary group—any group which has the above-listed characteristics may be termed a primary group.)

Group interaction skill is the ability to be a productive member of a variety of primary groups. Through acquisition of the various group interaction subskills, the individual learns to take appropriate group membership roles, engage in decision making, communicate effectively, recognize group norms and interact in accordance with these norms, contribute to goal attainment, work toward group cohesiveness and assist in resolving group conflict.

EVALUATION

Perhaps the best way to assess the extent of group interaction subskill learning is to directly observe a patient interacting in a small group. This may be a

---

[23]Further discussions of group interaction skills can be found in Erik Erikson, *Childhood and Society* and "The Problems of Ego Identity," in M. Stein et al (eds.), *Identity and Anxiety* (New York: The Free Press of Glencoe, 1961); George Engel, *Psychological Development in Health and Disease*; Anna Freud, *Normality and Pathology in Childhood* and *The Ego and the Mechanisms of Defense*; A. Gesell and G. Amatruda, *Developmental Diagnosis: Normal and Abnormal Child Development*; Heinz Hartmann, *Ego Psychology and the Problems of Adaptation* (New York: International Universities Press, Inc., 1958); J. Pearce and S. Newton, *The Conditions of Human Growth*; and Floyd Ruch, *Psychology and Life* (Chicago: Scott, Foresman and Company, 1963). See also references relating to group dynamics: D. Cartwright and A. Zanders, *Group Dynamics: Research and Theory* (New York: Harper and Row Publishers, 1960); A. Hare, E. Borgatta, and R. Bales, *Small Groups: Studies in Interaction* (New York: Alfred A. Knopf, 1965); George Homans, *The Human Group* (New York: Harcourt, Brace and World, Inc., 1950); Walter Lifton, *Working with Groups* (New York: John Wiley and Sons, Inc., 1961); Theodore Mills, *The Sociology of Small Groups* (Englewood Cliffs, N. J., Prentice-Hall, Inc., 1963); National Training Laboratories, *Group Development*, Selected Readings Series I (Washington: National Education Association, 1961); and J. Thibaut and H. Kelley, *The Social Psychology of Groups* (New York: John Wiley and Sons, Inc., 1959).

[24]H. and A. English, *A Comprehensive Dictionary of Psychological and Psychoanalytic Terms.*

group which is specifically designed for evaluation or an ongoing group which is designed to fulfill some other purpose (i.e. ward meeting, patient orientation group, etc.). It is suggested that the group used in the assessment of group interaction skill be task-oriented (group members actively involved in accomplishing a definable task) and patient-dominated. The therapist should be more an observer than an active group participant. Additional useful information can also be gained by discussion with the patient—such a discussion is focused upon the nature and extent of the patient's interaction in primary groups outside of the treatment facility.

Our current understanding of symbols is not sufficient to allow us to identify specific group interaction skill learning and lack of learning. However, interpretation of symbols produced by the patient does provide some information about general learning in this area. Symbols which are useful for the purpose are those which refer to self preoccupation, experiencing the self as inadequate, distance from people, experiencing the self as being overwhelmed by the external environment, being overly dependent upon others for need satisfaction, adapatability, insecurity, self assertion, and fear of self revelation.

THE SUBSKILLS

1. *The ability to participate in a parallel group. (18m-2y)*[25]

A *parallel group* is perhaps more an aggregate of individuals than a group in the strict sense of the word; it is a group characterized by individuals working or playing in the presence of others, by minimal sharing of tasks, and by mutual stimulation. Examples of this latter characteristic are: behavior which stimulates laughter in others, imitation, tentative testing of the effect of one's behavior upon others, and casual conversation. Learning of this skill is indicated by the ability to work or play in the presence of others, awareness of others in the group, and some verbal or nonverbal interaction with fellow group members. Lack of learning is indicated by absence of these behaviors, in addition to discomfort in the presence of others and interaction with others as if they were nonhuman objects.

This subskill is acquired through interaction in an environment where there is opportunity to work or play in the presence of others who are nonthreatening to the self. Need satisfaction and reinforcement of behavior necessary for adequate parallel group interaction must be available from a

---

[25]The concept of parallel group and the other labels which are used to delineate group interaction subskills have collectively been referred to as "developmental groups". Those are believed to be the various types of nonfamilial groups usually encountered in the normal developmental process. These concepts have also been used to identify various types of treatment groups which are used in teaching group interaction skill. These treatment groups are essentially a simulation of developmental groups, a situation which I discussed more fully in "The Concept and Use of Developmental Groups," *AJOT*, Vol. XXIV, No. 4, 1970.

significant human object. The work or play tasks with which the individual is involved must be compatible with his current capacities.

A therapist who is engaged in a group designed on the basis of the above postulates is often tempted to demand a type of sharing which is beyond the capacity of anyone who is in the process of learning this subskill. This is detrimental to learning. There should be sufficient tools, materials, or toys for all group members; such behavior as deliberately taking from another without seeking permission, grossly derogatory remarks, disruptive behavior, and biting and kicking another individual are discouraged. The idea of taking turns is more compatible, however, with learning at the next stage of group interaction. The therapist is primarily concerned with providing task assistance, meeting the needs of each group member (in particular the needs for safety, love, and esteem) and giving reinforcement for behavior necessary for successful parallel group interaction.

2. *The ability to participate in a project group. (2y-4y)*

A *project group* is characterized by membership involvement in short term tasks which require some shared interaction, cooperation and competition; perception of the task as paramount; and miminal interaction outside of the task. An individual who has acquired this subskill is still preoccuped with exploring and testing others in order to determine whether or not they can be trusted. Learning is indicated by the ability to engage in short term shared tasks, seek assistance from other group members, give assistance willingly and adequately, and evidence that the individual understands that one must help others to receive help from others. Dysfunction in this area is indicated by absence of these behaviors, the tendency to work alone, avoidance of contact with others, and fear that others will interfere with task completion.

Learning of this subskill is acquired through interaction in an environment in which there are shareable short-term tasks which are interesting to the individual, as well as other persons who are compatible and willing to seek and give task assistance. Need satisfaction and reinforcement of behavior necessary for adequate project group interaction must be available from a significant human object.

In teaching this subskill the therapist continues to meet the needs of the various group members. He also provides or helps the group to select tasks which require interaction of two or more persons for completion. The treatment situation must be such that the patients feel free to engage in trial and error behavior. Abortive attempts at task completion should be accepted. Tasks which must be completed by a specific time or tasks which require creation of a perfect end product interfere with the learning of this subskill.

3. *The ability to participate in an egocentric-cooperative group. (5y-7y)*

Egocentric-cooperative groups are characterized by group members selecting, implementing and executing relatively long-term tasks through joint interaction and individual response based upon enlightened self interest. "Enlightened self interest" refers to behavior relative to the rights and needs of others. The individual recognizes that his right will be respected only through respect for the rights of others. Similarly he realizes that his needs (particularly esteem needs) will be met only through meeting the needs of others. The tasks of an egocentric cooperative group involve cooperation and competition. An individual who has learned this subskill is able to gratify his need for esteem through interaction in various groups. His need for safety and love, however, must continue to be met by other significant persons.

Acquisition of this subskill is indicated by the ability to identify group norms and goals, use of this knowledge as a guide for action, active experimentation with various group membership roles, perception of self as a group participant with a right to belong to groups, respect for the rights of others, the ability to meet the esteem needs of others and to gain satisfaction of esteem needs. Lack of learning is indicated by absence of the above behavior, avoidance of competition (or preoccupation with competition), hesitant movement from one group to another, and a feeling that one does not belong to any group and will never be accepted regardless of behavior.

This subskill is learned through interaction in an environment where there is an opportunity to practice planning and implementing shared, long-term tasks; cooperative and competitive behavior, various group membership roles; and seeking gratification of and gratifying esteem needs. Behavior which is indicative of adequate subskill learning must be reinforced by group members and a significant other. Security, love, and some esteem needs must be met by someone else significant to the individual.

The above postulates do not appear to require elaboration. The only further comment is that the group is encouraged to select, plan, and execute their tasks with minimal assistance from the therapist. The therapist serves primarily as a resource person.

4. *The ability to participate in a cooperative group. (9y-12y)*

A *cooperative group* is characterized by homogeneous membership and mutual need satisfaction. In the normal developmental process this type is usually made up of individuals of the same sex. The task is often considered to be secondary to need fulfillment. Learning of this subskill is indicated by the ability to express both positive and negative affect in a group, to perceive the needs of others, and to meet the needs of fellow group members.

This subskill is acquired through interaction in an environment where there are others who are compatible and similar to the individual as well as developmentally ready to engage in a cooperative group. If group members have these characteristics it is believed that they will provide all the reinforcement which is necessary to learn to accurately perceive and satisfy the needs of others; the presence of an authority figure is detrimental to the development of this subskill.

The therapist is not directly involved in teaching this subskill; instead, he assists the patient in finding persons with whom this subskill may be learned. These persons might be located in a setting outside of the treatment facility. The therapist offers the patient support and some need satisfaction until he is able to acquire this from the outside group. To facilitate learning of this subskill within the treatment facility, the therapist may form a group of compatible individuals and then may continue to interact with the group until the members become comfortable with each other and the group develops some sense of cohesiveness. The therapist then withdraws from the group and relates to them in the role of an advisor.

5. *The ability to participate in a mature group. (15y-18y)*

A *mature group* is characterized by heterogeneous membership, participant flexibility in taking a variety of membership roles, and a balance between task accomplishment and the satisfaction of group member's needs. No sharp distinction is made between leader and follower roles—leadership functions are shared by all group members. Membership roles are often divided into two categories: task roles and social-emotional roles.

Task roles are oriented to the selection, planning, and execution of the group task. The following roles are included in this category:

1. the initiator-contributor, who suggests new ideas
2. the information seeker, who asks for clarification of facts
3. the opinion seeker, who asks for clarification of opinions or values
4. the informative giver, who offers facts
5. the opinion giver, who states his beliefs or values
6. the elaborator, who spells out suggestions
7. the coordinator, who clarifies relationships
8. the orientator, who defines the position of the group with respect to its goals
9. the evaluator-critic, who compares the accomplishments of the group to some standard
10. the energizer, who prods the group to action
11. the procedural technician, who expedites group movement by performing routine tasks[26]

Social-emotional roles are oriented toward the function of the group as a group and the gratification of members' needs. The following roles are included in this category:

---

[26]Talcott Parsons and R. Bales, *Family, Socialization and the Interaction Process.*

1. The encourager, who praises, agrees with, and accepts the contributions of others
2. the harmonizer, who mediates differences between members
3. the compromiser, who changes his own behavior so as to maintain group harmony
4. the gatekeeper, who facilitates and regulates communication
5. the standard-setter, who expresses standards for the group to achieve
6. the group observer, who notes, interprets, and presents information about group process
7. the follower, who goes along with movement of the group[27]

In a mature group, participants take those task and social-emotional roles which are required for adequate group functioning at any particular time.

Learning of this subskill is indicated by comfort in heterogeneous groups and the ability to take a variety of membership roles. Lack of learning is indicated by preference for a same sex or other types of homogeneous groups and excessive preoccupation with task accomplishment or satisfaction of social-emotional needs.

This subskill is acquired through interaction in heterogeneous groups which maintain an adequate balance between task accomplishment and need satisfaction and which provide an opportunity for exploration, practice, and reinforcement of a variety of membership roles.

In teaching this component, the therapist interacts as a co-equal group member. He takes a minimal number of membership roles as a way of encouraging other group members to take these roles. Some suggested techniques for increasing learning of membership roles and role flexibility are: verbal exploration of the various membership roles and behavior necessary to fulfill these roles, periodic examination of the group by group members in regard to membership roles currently being played and the need for additional or different ones, role playing of membership roles, members acting as observers of the group so as to see roles and role requirements from a more uninvolved position.

SELF-IDENTITY SKILL

The *self* is here defined as "the individual's physical body, a given space surrounding his body, total mental content, capacities, abilities, limitations, and his past experiences." *Identity* is the individual's perception of self and includes

---

[27]Talcott Parsons and R. Bales, *Family, Socialization and the Interaction Process.*

knowledge and judgments about and affect toward the self.[28] Mature self-identity skill is the ability to perceive the self as an autonomous, holistic, and acceptable object which has permanence and continuity over time.

A portion of self identity is conscience. The individual is able to say who he is, what he is and how he feels about himself. There are, however, some aspects of identity which are unconscious and not recognized by the individual, resulting in conflict between conscious and unconscious self identity—the individual may verbalize one identity but act in a contradictory manner. In the healthy, mature individual, unconscious and conscious identity are compatible and complementary.

The attributes of continuity and permanence are characteristic of mature self-identity skill and refer to the individual perceiving the self as persisting through time and space without essential change. (The word "essential" is important.) The individual may indeed perceive marked changes in himself as he progresses through the developmental process. This change is experienced as alteration in an enduring organism: the individual perceives the self that exists at this time and place as the evolution of the self which existed in the past and the fundament of the self which will exist in the future.

EVALUATION

Ideally, assessment of self-identity subskill learning involves observation of the patient interacting with human and nonhuman objects, discussion regarding the patient's judgment and feelings about himself, and interpretations of symbols produced by the patient. This is an adaptive skill which is particularly difficult to assess when a patient first seeks treatment, for the stresses which have led to a request for help tend to cover or impede manifestation of learning in this area. Because of his inability to cope with stress, the individual often verbalizes highly negative judgments of and affect toward the self. This action reflects current aggressive energy invested in the self more than self-identity subskill learning. For this reason, observation of the patient and interpretation of the symbols which he has produced often provide more accurate information

---

[28]The self-identity skill is discussed fully in George Engel, *Psychological Development in Health and Disease*, Erik Erikson, *Childhood and Society* and "The Problems of Ego Identity," in M. Stein et al, *Identity and Anxiety*; Paul Federn, *Ego Psychology and Psychoses*; Anna Freud, *The Ego and the Mechanisms of Defense* and *Normality and Pathology in Childhood*; Kurk Goldstein, *The Organism*; Peter Knapp, *Expressions of the Emotions in Man*; Elizabeth Kübler-Ross, *On Death and Dying* (New York: Macmillan, 1969); Abraham Maslow, *Toward a Psychology of Being* (Princeton: D. VanNostrand Company, Inc., 1962); George Mead, *Mind, Self and Society* (Chicago: The University of Chicago Press, 1934); Jack Rubins, "Self-Awareness and Body Image, Self-Concept and Identity," in J. Masserman (ed.), *The Ego*; Floyd Ruch, *Psychology and Life*; Paul Schilder, *The Image and Appearance of the Human Body*; Rene Spitz, *A Genetic Field Theory of Ego Functions* (New York: International Universities Press, 1959), H. S. Sullivan, *The Interpersonal Theory of Psychiatry*; and Robert White, "Competence and the Growth of Personality," in J. Masserman (ed.), *The Ego*.

than discussion with the patient. In interpreting the patient's verbalized behavior, the therapist must remember that derogatory remarks regarding the self
and objects produced by the self may refer to the patient's relatively temporary
feelings. Many times they are not at all indicative of self-identity subskill learning.

THE SUBSKILLS

1. *The ability to perceive the self as a worthy object. (4m-9m)*

The word *"worthy"* may be defined as "perception of self as deserving of
need satisfaction." As the following postulate regarding change will indicate,
learning of the subskill in the normal developmental process is dependent
upon the mother's communication of the child's worthiness to him. Such a
communication can occur in the absence of a truly nurturing relationship, but
it cannot help but be communicated in a real nurturing relationship. An
individual may therefore acquire this subskill without having acquired the
more primitive drive-object subskills. What appears to happen in these situations is that the mother is able to communicate worthiness but is unable to
provide need gratification.

The individual who has learned this subskill will demand need gratification
as an inherent right. Lack of learning is indicated by total withdrawal, no
expectation of need gratification, extended periods of depersonalization of all
or parts of the self, self destructive behavior, and perception of the self as
harmful to others, evil, or dirty. Lack of learning is also indicated by the
predominant use of symbols which refer to the self as evil, the womb, unity
(in the sense of that which is desired), and the birth-death-rebirth cycle.

This subskill is learned through the individual's primary object investing
libidinal energy in the individual; it is acquired through experiencing a nurturing relationship.

2. *The ability to perceive the assets and limitations of the self. (9y-12y)*

In learning this subskill the individual comes to an understanding of what he
is able and not able to do. Limitations are accepted—with perhaps some desire
to alter these limitations and attempts to do so. The individual recognizes at
the same time that some limitations do not reflect total ineptness; he has a
dawning recognition that all men have deficits which must be accepted. Assessment of assets and limitations is relative to skill in using the body, in both
a gross and fine manner, attractiveness, intellectual achievements, social skills,
and interests.

Learning of this subskill is indicated by a realistic assessment of assets and
limitations, acceptance of limitations, and the ability to perceive one's body
as a positive object regardless of athletic skills or the presence of attributes
which are currently fashionable. The tone and affect of the patient's symbols

which refer to aspects of the self also give information about accurate assessment of his capacities and limitations.

This subskill is learned through interaction in an environment within which the individual has an opportunity to observe his assets and limitations, alter his limitations to the extent to which he is able, and receive feedback regarding his assets and limitations.

In order to learn this subskill, the patient must have an opportunity to engage in a wide variety of activities. Feedback should be accurate and free. The patient's sensitivities are taken into consideration, but this does not prohibit the therapist from giving an honest response regarding what the patient is and is not able to do. Activities which have clearly established standards, prescribed modes of action, and predictable results are also useful in providing accurate feedback to the patient.

3. *The ability to perceive the self as self-directed. (16y-20y)*

This subskill refers to the individual's recognition of himself as capable of and responsible for his own need satisfaction, establishing personal goals, and selecting a preferred life style. Learning is indicated by recognition that needs are satisfied only through the efforts of the self, a feeling of independence from the parental pair, the ability to articulate current and future personal goals and to experience these goals as established by the self, the individual living in a manner which is comfortable for himself and not necessarily one which is valued by the cultural group, and perception of the self as competent in dealing with ordinary life problems. Predominant use of symbols which refer to the unconscious, that which nurtures and protects, stunted growth, self inadequacy, experiencing the self as being overwhelmed by the external environment, overinvolvement in fantasy, insecurity, and experience of uncertainty indicate lack of learning in this area.

This subskill is acquired through practice in being self-directed, communication by significant others that one is capable of being independent and reinforcement of such behavior.

In applying this postulate, the therapist is primarily concerned with the patient's behavior outside of the treatment facility. Although initial attempts at being self-directed may occur in the treatment facility, the patient is encouraged to turn outward toward the external environment as soon as possible. This is suggested for two reasons: (1) the patient cannot learn this subskill until he has acted effectively in the external environment and (2) it is often very difficult to independently order one's behavior in a treatment facility. The therapist indicates to the patient that he is able to establish personal goals, determine his own life style, and deal with ordinary life problems (for example, find an apartment, make travel plans, buy clothes, etc.). This support for the patient helps to sustain his efforts if there should be an initial failure. The therapist's occasional temptation to offer more than support and advice is never actualized, for this would interfere with subskill learning; as far as possible, reinforcement should be the patient's pleasure in successfully engaging in self-determining behavior. This is most likely to occur if the patient is truly free to make his own choices.

4. *The ability to perceive the self as a productive, contributing member of a social system. (20y-30y)*

This subskill refers to the individual's awareness of being a part of a community or social system and an understanding of how the roles which he plays assist in maintaining or constructively altering that social system. The roles which the individual perceives as productive and of a contributing nature may be relative to the family, the church, the political system, the economic system, education, or the arts and sciences.

Learning is indicated by the ability to identify roles which are important to the self, the ability to articulate in a positive manner how these roles contribute to the social system, a sense of knowing "what I am," and recognition of one's place in a social system as well as a feeling of participation in that system. Lack of learning is indicated by absence of these behaviors, an egocentric concept of self which is totally divorced from a productive role in the community, continued preoccupation with "what I am," perception of one's roles as worthless or degrading to the self, a feeling that one's talents or abilities are not being utilized and lack of effort to seek utilization, and no evidence of productivity outside of the economic system. The tone and affect associated with symbols which refer to the individual roles in a social system also provide useful information in assessing learning in this area.

This subskill is acquired through interaction in an environment which provides an opportunity for exploring roles relative to the social system; training necessary for gaining the knowledge, skills and attitudes which are required for preferred roles; and through acknowledgment by the social system that these roles are significant.

In teaching this subskill the therapist provides opportunities for the patient to explore roles relative to the social system and supports him while the exploration is taking place. The patient's sex, age, cultural background, abilities and interests are utilized in helping him to select particular areas for exploration. An apprentice relationship with others who are engaged in roles which the patient finds meaningful is useful in teaching this subskill; in such an apprentice relationship the individual interacts as a participant-learner. The training necessary for selected roles may be offered by the therapist or some other person in the treatment facility; it may be possible for the patient to acquire such training wholly through an apprentice relationship—or formal training may be necessary. Whatever the situation, the therapist assists the patient in acquiring whatever type of training is necessary. Perhaps the most difficult part of the teaching process is helping the patient to locate others who will provide acknowledgment that the roles which he has selected are significant to a social system. Many social systems give such recognition only for roles which are rare and overtly contributory. The therapist must be highly resourceful, therefore, in locating and helping the patient relate to others who are able to provide this necessary acknowledgment or reinforcement.

5. *The ability to perceive the self. (30y-50y)*

This subskill consists of the development of a profound knowledge of self. It goes far beyond the second self-identity skill, which is concerned with perception of one's assets and limitations. It refers to the individual's recognition of his essential being and, by extension, a willingness to act on the basis of that knowledge. With acquisition of the ability to perceive the self, the individual is in a position where he can begin to meet his self-actualization needs.

Learning of this subskill is indicated by evidence that the individual has continued satisfaction of all needs subordinate to the self-actualization need; disregard for the norms of one's cultural group if necessary in order to accomplish something which is perceived as special, unique, and highly significant to the self;a profound and sympathetic understanding that it is only through the support of those willing others that one is able to do a very special something; knowledge that this is the only course of action one can take and continue to be; and a special feeling of self-fulfillment when the individual is engaged in actions which are consistent with who he is. The symbol which tells us most about the learning of this subskill is the *mandala.* When an individual produces this symbol without any sense of longing but with joy and the experience that "this is me," he is well on his way to develop the subskill.[29]

Unfortunately, we do not have a clear understanding of how this subskill is developed. We do know that all needs subordinate to the self-actualization need must be met, and it also appears that there must be some persons in the environment who are capable of recognizing one's potential for and appreciating the result of self-actualization. As this subskill is based upon self-knowledge, perhaps the most efficient way of enhancing learning in this area is to engage in the type of treatment process suggested in object relations analysis.

There is some question concerning whether or not this subskill is prerequisite to learning the most advanced subskills. Recognizing our limited knowledge in this area, it is suggested that the therapist ignore learning of this subskill when treating patients who appear to require acquisition of the final self-identity subskill.

6. *The ability to perceive the aging process of the self in a rational manner. (40y-60y)*

"Rational" here refers to gracious acceptance rather than a positive feeling about one's aging process; an individual may perceive the aging process as

---

[29]Carl Jung, *Man and His Symbols.*

enhancing his capacity to deal with self and others, but it is the rare person who perceives it as a joyful, anticipated experience. The aging process diminishes capacities, severs relationships with loved ones, and presents practical problems. Learning of this subskill is indicated by resigned acceptance of the aging process and death, perception of one's life as useful and productive, engagement in activities which are compatible with actual physical and psychological capacities, and continued perception of the self as a contributing member of the social system. Lack of learning is indicated by the absence of these behaviors; excessive preoccupation with physical enhancement, religion, or making provisions for distribution of accumulated objects; denial of chronological age; and feelings that one is rejected by others. The tone and affect of symbols which refer to death, the birth-death-rebirth cycle, need satisfaction, potency, life or the soul, oneness or unity, spiritual growth, historical view of the developing self, and old age also provide information regarding learning.

This subskill is learned through interaction in an environment in which the individual's capacities are recognized, there is an opportunity to continue to be a productive member of a social system, in which there are others available who are capable of giving and receiving love, in which the degenerative process and death are accepted by others as part of the life cycle, and in which the profoundly unknown aspect of death and the state of being after death are seen as legitimate concerns and acceptable topics of conversation.

In teaching this subskill the therapist attempts to locate or provides an environment which is suitable for learning.

SEXUAL IDENTITY SKILL

"Identity," as used in the label of this adaptive skill, refers to awareness of, feelings about, and judgments regarding one's sexual nature; and interactions with others as a sexual being.[30] *Mature sexual identity skill* is the ability to perceive one's sexual nature as good and to participate in a heterosexual relationship which is oriented to the mutual satisfaction of sexual needs.

An individual who has attained full maturation of sexual identity, experiences delight relative to the sexual aspects of his body and the body of others. He perceives the genitalia and secondary sexual characteristics as a source of pleasure for the self and a means of providing pleasure for others. He is aware of

---

[30]Further material on the sexual identity skill may be found in Erik Erikson, *Childhood and Society* and "The Problems of Ego Identity," in M. Stein (ed.), *Identity and Anxiety;* Anna Freud, *Normality and Pathology in Children* and *The Ego and Mechanisms of Defense;* Sigmund Freud, *The Basic Writings of Sigmund Freud* (A. Brill, ed.) and *An Outline of Psychoanalysis;* Heinz Hartmann, *Ego Psychology and the Problems of Adaptation;* J. Pearce and S. Newton, *The Conditions of Human Growth;* Floyd Ruch, *Psychology and Life;* H. S. Sullivan, *The Interpersonal Theory of Psychiatry* and *The Psychiatric Interview;* and Paul Schilder, *The Image and Appearance of the Human Body.*

his own periodic need for the release of sexual tensions and the needs of the other with whom he is sexually involved. The needs of both partners are taken into consideration and regulate the extent and nature of sexual interaction. Various techniques relative to seduction, sex play, and intercourse have been learned and are used differentially to bring about mutual satisfaction. Diminished need for release of sexual tension of self and other is accepted with minimal alteration in one's perception of the self and other as a sexual being. Further, the individual is able to recognize and accept his cultural group's norms relative to nongenital interactions with others. This does not, however, interfere with identifying and acting upon opposite-sex characteristics of the self. Behavior motivated by one's inherent opposite-sex characteristics is finely tuned to the other and continually gives validation to the other's sexual nature.

EVALUATION

There are many ways to assess sexual identity subskill learning; observation of the patient relative to same-sex and opposite sex interactions; discussion with the patient regarding past and current sexual relationships, his feelings regarding his own sexuality and whatever fantasies he may have regarding sexuality; and interpretation of symbols produced by the patient. All three areas provide valuable information.

THE SUBSKILLS

1. *The ability to accept and act upon the bases of one's pregenital sexual nature.* *(4y-5y)*

In learning this subskill the individual perceives his sexuality as good, acceptable to others, and a source of pleasure. He also perceives that direct genital behavior is unaccepted at this period of his life span and that overt expression must be held in abeyance until a more appropriate time.

Learning of this subskill is indicated by knowledge regarding the sex of self and others, comfort in interacting with same sex or opposite sex individuals, knowledge of and skill in engaging in pregenital sexual roles, and flexible definition of appropriate sexual roles. Lack of learning is indicated by the absence of these behaviors; perception of the self as an asexual being; promiscuous homosexual or heterosexual behavior which has a flavor of confused sexual identity or a search for sexual identity; denial of sexuality; avoidance of objects or interactions which are perceived as sexual in nature; perception of all aspects of sexuality as dirty, bad, or harmful to self and others, continued genital attachment to the parent or parental figure of the opposite sex; search for persons similar to the same sex parent and avoidance of persons similar to the opposite sex parent; and a tendency to act in a manner considered more appropriate for persons of the opposite sex. The manner in which the individual uses symbols which refer to sex, and the obvious absence of or predominant use of sexual symbols also provide useful information regarding the learning of this subskill.

This subskill is learned through interaction in an environment where there is recognition of the individual's sexual nature, individuals of both sexes who have a clear understanding of their masculinity or femininity and who act on the basis of this understanding, a suitable individual of the same sex who encourages emulation of appropriate sex-specific behavior, an opportunity to interact in a variety of traditional opposite sex roles without loss of masculinity or femininity, and appropriate sex education. Interaction in a same-sex peer group facilitates inhibition of genital sexuality and consolidates pregenital sex-specific role learning. Some interaction in heterosexual groups helps the individual to learn about relating to the opposite sex. Finally, learning of this subskill is enhanced through interaction with a variety of nonhuman objects which provide an opportunity for experimenting with sex specific modes of behavior, and symbolic expression of genital-sexuality. Denial of or negative reactions to sexually motivated behavior, the sexual aspects of the body, or autoerotic behavior are detrimental to the learning of this subskill.

2. *The ability to accept sexual maturation as a positive growth experience.
(12y-16y)*

Sexual maturation refers to the growth of secondary sexual characteristics, resurgence of sexual impulses, and cultural requirements regarding appropriate nongenital behavior for genitally mature individuals. Learning is indicated by perception of the self as a genitally mature individual, control of sexual impulses without excessive effort, experiencing the self as sexually desirable, a positive attitude toward one's secondary sexual characteristics and integration of these characteristics with the other aspects of one's body *schema*, and the ability to engage in what is currently accepted as appropriate nongenital behavior for genitally mature individuals. In addition, an individual who has learned this component is able to engage in courting behavior with a relative degree of discretion regarding sexual activity, dress in a manner similar to members of one's gender, and interact with members of the opposite sex with some recognition of the male prerogative for taking the more aggressive task-oriented role and the female prerogative for taking the more passive social-emotional role. Lack of learning is indicated by the absence of these behaviors, denial of sexual impulses, or perception of them as threatening to the integrity of the self, promiscuous sexual activity, perception of the self as only a sexual object with little recognition of other aspects of the self, preoccupation with secondary sexual characteristics and a feeling that they are inadequate or excessive, a pregenital attitude toward the opposite sex (women perceived as inferior, silly, or stupid; men perceived as mean, dirty, or ill mannered), rejection of the idea of sex-specific behavior, and interaction in only those roles which the culture defines as neutral or more appropriate for a member of the opposite sex. Lack of learning is also indicated by predominant use of symbols which refer to negative affect regarding the sexual aspects of the body, animal principle, being overwhelmed by unconscious complexes, uncontrolled drives, and symbols which refer to the opposite sex.

This subskill is learned through interaction in an environment in which there is reinforcement for attending to the body, interaction with same sex peers who provide validation of one's sexuality, opportunity for interacting with members of the opposite sex who are interested in engaging in courting behavior, flexible guidelines for sexual activity, and appropriate sex education. In addition, the environment must recognize differing opinions regarding acceptable sex-specific roles. The individual must have an opportunity to explore a variety of behavior patterns and be free to take those roles which he finds most compatible with his goals and life style.

In teaching this subskill the therapist must be comfortable in discussing all aspects of sex but in particular the sexual aspects of the body of both sexes, the functions and responses of the sex organs, and various norms which govern sexual behavior. One suggested technique for enhancing attention to the body is to engage the patient in drawing or sculpting the nude body of both sexes with concurrent comfortable discussion regarding the body. The therapist helps the patient to locate some sex peers who are capable of providing validation of the patient's sexuality and suitable persons of the opposite sex who are likely to want to engage in courting behavior with the patient. The therapist provides support, encouragement, and guidance to assist the patient in interacting comfortably with these individuals. Although the therapist may provide an opportunity for one-to-one discussion of norms which may be used to guide sexual activity and information regarding sex, it is suggested that this take place in a group. Ideally, the group is heterosexual and includes a male and female discussion leaders, for this type of group tends to emphasize that sex is an acceptable topic for consideration and will point up the similarities and differences between the sexes. The consequences of selecting various norms to guide one's sexual activities should be explored. Sex education should be comprehensive, detailed, and specific, and should cover the physiological, psychological, and sociological aspects of sexuality. If there is likely to be a lengthy period before the group members will be able to engage in genital sexual activity, discussion should also focus on various ways of dealing with sexual impulses.

3. *The ability to give and receive sexual gratification. (18y-25y)*

Learning of this subskill is indicated by the individual's awareness of his sexual needs, the quality and quantity of his sexual responses, and the stimuli which maximize his ability to respond. The sexual needs of others are recognized and there is appreciation of the variation in sexual responses. Technique for satisfying self and others are available to the individual and he is able to vary his responses according to the needs of the others, and there is an understanding of the place of foreplay in sexual interaction. Sexual intercourse is seen as a way of expressing affection and satisfying physiological needs. Lack of learning is indicated by the absence of these behaviors. The way in which the individual deals with symbols which refer to sexual intercourse also provides useful information in the assessment of this subskill.

This component is learned through interaction in an environment in which there is an opportunity to engage in autoerotic activities without guilt and an opportunity to participate in sex play and sexual intercourse with others (or another) who perceive such activity as good, beautiful, rewarding—and fun.

In most cultural groups in the United States, autoerotic activities and sex play prior to a marital relationship are considered acceptable. This is a marked change from the norm of twenty-five years ago and has come about in part through the increased awareness of the role of these activities in the development of this subskill. Sexual intercourse prior to marriage, however, is still not acceptable to many cultural groups. The advantage of such activity is the opportunity to explore the sexual responses of self and another without the additional complication of initial adjustment to marriage. It is necessary to remember that intercourse outside of the marital relationship which generates anxiety or guilt is not conducive to learning this subskill.

In helping a patient learn to give and receive gratification, the therapist assists the patient in locating suitable persons for such learning. The therapist provides support and advice, clarifies values, and offers encouragement as needed.

4. *The ability to enter into a sustained heterosexual relationship characterized by the mutual satisfaction of sexual needs. (19y-30y)*

Acquisition of this skill does not necessarily occur at the time of marriage or within the confines of a marital contract, nor does occasional and transient sexual activity outside of a sustained relationship necessarily indicate the absence of this subskill. Learning is indicated by conscious awareness of one's commitment to a sustained heterosexual relationship, knowledge of the implications of such a commitment, and an intimate relationship with one's sexual partner. Typical relationships with the opposite sex are nongenital in nature, but appreciation of the sexuality of the other remains an important part of the relationship. Lack of learning is indicated by the absence of these behaviors, a relatively rapid sequential change in sex partners, or a number of simultaneous partners, perception of one's self or sexual partner as sexually inadequate, primary concern with the sexual satisfaction of the self or one's partner, avoidance of marriage or perception of marriage as a limitation of one's freedom, and evidence that the responsibilities of child-rearing or maintenance of social status is the only cohesive factor in a marriage. There do not seem to be any specific symbols which provide information relative to learning in this area.

This subskill is acquired through interaction in an environment where there are suitable others who have the capacity to learn this subskill and a desire to do so, a general sense of security, and sufficient time to focus upon the sexual needs of the self and one's partner.

The therapist assists a patient in learning this subskill in a manner similar to the one outlined for teaching the third sexual-identity skill.

It is usually after learning this subskill that the individual is able to recognize, explore, and act upon the opposite-sex characteristics of the self. It appears that acquisition of this subskill provides affirmation of one's sexual nature and eliminates any lingering doubts regarding potency or fertility to such an extent that the individual is able to perceive another aspect of the self.

5. *The ability to accept physiological and psychological changes which occur at the time of the climacteric. (40y-60y)*

Learning of this subskill is indicated by acceptance of altered sexual responses if these are evident, an understanding of the climacteric in relationship to the total maturation process, continued enjoyment of genital sexual activities, and continued perception of the self as a sexual being. Lack of learning is indicated by prolonged mourning over the perceived loss of sexuality; feelings of worthlessness; no attempt to participate in genital sexual activities or interest in such activities; disregard for the appearance of the self, personal hygiene, appropriate clothes, or maintenance of normal weight; excessive preoccupation with appearance; extreme attempts to maintain a youthfulness that is incompatible with chronological age; involvement with a sexual partner several years younger than the self; grandiose ideas regarding sexual capacity; and the need for continued reassurance that one is a desirable sexual object. Lack of learning is also indicated by predominant use of symbols which refer to potency, fertility, life-death-rebirth cycle, unmet needs, and object loss.

This subskill is learned through interaction in an environment in which the individual's sexual nature is recognized, there is opportunity to participate in nongenital sexual roles which are particularly meaningful to the individual, and opportunity to find another sexual partner if there has been loss of the usual partner.

In teaching this subskill the therapist assists the patient in locating and using an environment with the above listed characteristics. The therapist provides support, encouragement, and guidance as needed; the patient's sexual nature and needs are taken into consideration by the therapist at all times.

Conclusion

"Man experiences, he acts; and then he takes distance from the experience, the action, and begins to reflect on it, to conceptualize. At the point where he conceptualizes, he begins to set up a system of ideas about what has been experienced... They are ways of making the experience knowable; communicable ways of being able to tell others about it... (but) theory is pretty much a fairy tale because there are very few real knowns."

K. Overly, *Exploring How a Think Feels**

After a somewhat cursory —or even thorough—study of the preceding chapters, the reader may ask, "But what frame of reference is best?" and "What frame of reference should I use for a particular patient?" These are legitimate questions to which, unfortunately, there are no definitive answers. I can speak only to the questions and in answer, express my personal opinion. In the following discussion, I will refer to the three frames of reference outlined in this text. However, you are asked to keep in mind that these are examples of three categories. What is said, therefore, applies as much to the categories as it does to the specific frame of reference.

Studies which have been conducted indicate that no frame of reference is more effective or efficient in treating psychosocial dysfunction than any other frame of reference.[1] Further, methods for studying this question are quite primitive and crude at the present time; until more refined techniques of measurement are developed, therefore, we are not in a position to say what frame of reference is best.

However, if the question is altered to, "What frame of reference is best for me?" a less vague and more satisfying answer is possible. Each therapist is very special and unique. After working with patients for some time, each therapist

---

*K. Overly, in J. Mazer, G. Fidler, L. Kovalenko, and K. Overly, *Exploring How a Think Feels*, p. 7 and p. 27.

[1] See discussions in D. Ford and H. Urban, *Systems of Psychotherapy;* the writings of the Group for the Advancement of Psychiatry, *Clinical Psychiatry* (New York: Science House, 1967); Gardner Lindzey, *Handbook of Social Psychology* (Cambridge: Addison-Wesley Publishing Company, 1954); and L. Ullman and L. Krasner, *Case Studies in Behavior Modification* (New York: Holt, Rinehart and Winston, Inc., 1965).

develops his own style of interaction. He becomes aware of what fits and is comfortable for him and what seems alien and ego-syntonic. Although a therapist continues to learn, grow, and change throughout his professional life, he usually maintains a core idea of "this is me" and "this is not me." With this self-understanding, the therapist is able to knowledgeably select or formulate a frame of reference which is suitable for himself. This is the best criteria for selection and, really, the only one which has validity now. A frame of reference must become part of the self if it is to be a useful guide for action. *It cannot become part of the self unless it is compatible with all of the other aspects of the self.*

The beginning therapist often has only a budding concept of his own particular style of interaction, a distinct advantage in that the student can often be more flexible and openminded about frames of reference. Therapists who have practiced for some time seem to avoid looking at other frames of reference. The theoretical system basic to their treatment process appears to take on a strong denotative quality and is dealt with as if it were reality. They hold on to this reality with a tenacity that is startling to behold—everything else, the seemingly scary unknown, is either rejected or explored in a highly subjective manner.

It is therefore suggested that the beginning therapist study and use a variety of frames of reference. It is imperative that the student develop a nonjudgmental attitude. Only in so doing is one able to study frames of reference in an objective and scientific manner. Frames of reference are to be understood, not liked or disliked. Detailed knowledge of a frame of reference can be acquired only through application; one must read as well as do in order for adequate learning to take place. If at all possible, the initial efforts to use a frame of reference should take place in conjunction with competent supervision. After this suggested program of exploration, a therapist is probably prepared to select or formulate a frame of reference which is congenial with his style of interaction. But please, never let it become reality.

"What frame of reference should I use for a particular patient?" With some reservations (because there are so many unknowns) the following comments are offered: participation in a treatment process based on object-relation analysis would appear to require complete development of cognition (as outlined in Chapter Seven). Adequate participation on the part of the patient can occur only if he has the ability to represent objects in a denotative and connotative manner, perceive the viewpoint of others, decenter, reflect upon a thought sequence, use formal logic, and work in the realm of the hypothetical. Helping a patient to develop these abilities is not a part of object-relation analysis. Action-consequence seems to be applicable to all patients—perhaps it is the frame of reference which is most compatible with community-oriented treatment facilities. It relates the individual in a very immediate way to his community interactions and provides a guide for action relative to an environment which is maintaining individual dysfunction. Recapitulation of ontogenesis also appears to have wide applicability, and seems particularly appropriate for treatment of the younger patient.

In regard to types of patients, those patients who are described as regressed, mentally retarded or psychotic can perhaps best be helped through the use of either action-consequence or recapitulation. Patients who appear to be alienated or experience life as meaningless may find participation in object-relation analysis particularly beneficial. The adjustment of the geriatric patient can certainly be enhanced by application of action-consequence. This type of patient may also derive benefit from learning the last self-identity subskill (the ability to perceive the aging process of the self in a rational manner) and the last sexual identity subskill (the ability to accept physiological and psychological changes which occur at the time of the climacteric). These would be taught as splinter skills. That is, no attention would be given to the absence of more primitive subskills.

I appreciate this opportunity to share with you; if it has seemed a monumental chore or bewildering experience, I apologize. Whatever value this book may have, I hope that it stimulates you to explore and think about frames of reference and to use them knowledgeably in our helping work as therapists.

A.C.M.

Bibliography

Abt, L. and Bellak, L., *Projective Psychology* (New York: Grove Press, Inc., 1950).

Alexander, Franz, *Psychoanalysis and Psychotherapy* (New York: W. W. Norton and Company, 1956).

Anderson, Kenneth (ed.), *The Case Method of Teaching Human Relations and Administration* (Cambridge: Harvard University Press, 1956).

Arieti, Silvano, *The Intrapsychic Self (New York: Basic Books, 1967).*

Ayres, A. Jean, "The Visual and Motor Function," *American Journal of Occupational Therapy,*Vol. XII, No. 3 (1958).

Ayres, A. Jean, "Development of Body Scheme in Children," *AJOT*, Vol. XV, No. 3 (1961).

Ayres, A. Jean, "The Development of Perceptual Motor Abilities," *AJOT*, Vol. XVII, No. 6 (1963).

Ayres, A. Jean, *Perceptual Motor Dysfunction in Children,* Ohio Occupational Therapy Association Conference, 1964.

Ayres, A. Jean, "Tactile Functions", *AJOT*, Vol. XVIII (1964).

Ayres, A. Jean, "Deficits in Sensory Integration in Educationally Handicapped Children," *Journal of Learning Disabilities,* 2:3 (March 1969) pp. 160–168.

Azima, H. and Azima, F., "Outline of a Dynamic Theory of Occupational Therapy," *AJOT,* Vol. XIII, No. 5 (1959).

Bandura, Albert, "Psychotherapy as a Learning Process," in L. Rabkin and J. Carr, (eds.), *Sourcebook in Abnormal Psychology,* (Boston: Houghton Mifflin Co., 1969).

Becker, Ernest, *The Revolution in Psychiatry* (New York: The Free Press of Glencoe, 1964).

Berger, Milton, "Nonverbal Communication in Group Psychotherapy," *The International Journal of Group Psychotherapy,* Vol. VIII, No. 2 (1958).

Berger, Milton, "Some Implications of Nonverbal Communication in Psychotherapy, Medical Practice, Family Relations and Life in General," *The International Journal of Social Psychiatry,* Congress Issue, 1964.

Bindman, A. and Spiegel, A., *Perspectives in Community Mental Health* (Chicago: Aldine Publishing Company, 1969).

Boss, M., *Daseursanalyse and Psychoanalysis* (New York: Basic Books, Inc. 1963).

Bradford, L., Gibb, J., and Benne, K., *T-Group Theory and Laboratory Method* (New York: John Wiley and Sons, Inc., 1964).

Brown, Ira, *Understanding Other Cultures* (Englewood Cliffs, N. J.: Prentice-Hall, Inc., 1963).

Bruner, Jerome, *Studies in Cognitive Growth* (New York: John Wiley and Sons, Inc., 1966).

Bruner, Jerome, *Towards a Theory of Instruction* (Cambridge: Harvard University Press, 1966).

Buber, Martin, *Between Man and Man* (New York: The Macmillan Company, 1965).

Burswanger, L., "Existential Analysis and Psychotherapy," in Fromm-Reichman and Moreno (eds.), *Progress in Psychotherapy* (New York: Grune and Stratton, 1956).

Burton, Arthur, *Encounter* (San Francisco: Jasey-Boss Inc., 1969).

Campbell, Joseph, *The Mask of God: Primitive Mythology* (New York: Viking Press, 1959).

Caplon, Gerald, *Principles of Preventive Psychiatry* (New York: Basic Books, Inc., 1964).

Cartwright, D., and Zanders, A., *Group Dynamics: Research and Theory* (New York: Harper and Row Publishers, 1960).

Clayton, Thomas, *Teaching and Learning* (Englewood Cliffs, N. J.: Prentice-Hall, Inc., 1965).

Comming, J., and Comming, E., *Ego and Milieu* (New York: Atherton Press, 1962).

Coser, L., and Rosenberg, B., *Sociological Theory* (New York: Macmillan Company, 1957).

Diasio, Karen, "Psychiatric Occupational Therapy: A Search for a Conceptual Framework in Light of Psychoanalytic, Ego Psychology, and Learning Theory," *AJOT,* Vol. XXII, No. 5 (1968).

Dollard, J., and Miller, N., *Personality and Psychotherapy* (New York: McGraw-Hill, 1950).

Dotson, Dan, "To Work Effectively as Agents of Change," *Social Action,* Feb. 1965.

Dunham, Warren, "Community Psychiatry: The Newest Therapeutic Bandwagon," (and Discussions) in *Current Issues in Psychiatry,* Vol. 1, Selections from the *International Journal of Psychiatry* (New York: Science House, 1967).

Edelson, Marshall, *Ego Psychology, Group Dynamics and the Therapeutic Community* (New York: Grune and Stratton, 1964).

Ekstein, R., and Wallerstein, R., *The Teaching and Learning of Psychotherapy* (New York: Basic Books, Inc., 1958).

Engel, George, *Psychological Development in Health and Disease* (Philadelphia: W. B. Saunders Company, 1962).

English, H., and English, A., *A Comprehensive Dictionary of Psychological and Psychoanalytic Terms* (New York: David McKay Company, Inc., 1958).

Erikson, Erik, *Childhood and Society* (New York: Norton, 1950).

Erikson, Erik, "The Problems of Ego Identity," in M. Stein et al (eds.), *Identity and Anxiety* (New York: The Free Press, 1961).

Evans, Richard, *Dialogue with Erik Erikson* (New York: Harper and Row, 1967).

Eysenck, H., *Behavioral Therapy and the Neuroses* (New York: Pergamon, 1960).

Fairbain, W. Ronald, *Psychoanalytic Studies of the Personality* (London: Tavistock Publications Limited, 1952).

Farber, Leslie, *The Ways of the Will* (New York: Basic Books, Inc., 1966).

Federn, Paul, *Ego Psychology and Psychoses* (New York: Basic Books, 1952).

Ferster, C., and Perrott, M., *Behavior Principles* (New York: Appleton-Century-Crofts, 1968).

Fidler, G., and Fidler, J., *Occupational Therapy: A Communication Process in Psychiatry* (New York: The Macmillan Company, 1963).

Fidler, Gail, "The Task Oriented Group as a Context for Treatment," *AJOT*, Vol. XXIII, No. 1 (1969).

Flavell, John, *The Development Psychology of Jean Piaget*, New York (D. Van Nostrand Company, Inc., 1963).

Florey, Linda, "Intrinsic Motivation: The Dynamics of Occupational Therapy," *AJOT*, Vol. XXIII, No. 4 (1969).

Ford, D. and Urban, H., *Systems of Psychotherapy* (New York: John Wiley and Sons, Inc., 1963).

Frank, Jerome, "The Therapeutic Use of Self," *Proceedings, 1957 Institute-Conference* (New York: American Occupational Therapy Association, 1959).

Freud, Anna, *Normality and Pathology in Childhood*, (New York: International Universities Press, Inc., 1965).

Freud, Anna, *The Ego and the Mechanisms of Defense*, (New York: International Universities Press, Inc., 1966).

Freud, Sigmund, (A. Brill, ed.) *The Basic Writings of Sigmund Freud* (New York: Random House, 1938).

Freud, Sigmund, *An Outline of Psychoanalysis* (New York: Norton, 1949).

Gesell, A. and Amatruda, G., *Developmental Diagnosis: Normal and Abnormal Child Development* (New York: Harper and Row, 1947).

Glasser, W., *Reality Therapy* (New York: Harper and Row, 1965).

Goffman, Irving, *Asylum* (New York: Doubleday and Company, Inc., 1961).

Goldstein, Kurk, *The Organism* (New York: American Book Company, 1939).

Greenson, Ralph, "The Problem of Working Through," in M. Schur (ed.), *Drives, Affect, Behavior* (New York: International Universities Press, Inc., 1965).

Group for the Advancement of Psychiatry, *Clinical Psychiatry* (New York: Science House, 1967).

Guilford, J. P., *The Nature of Human Intelligence* (New York: McGraw-Hill Book Company, Inc., 1967).

Hall, C. and Lindzey, G., *Theories of Personality* (New York: John Wiley and Sons, 1956).

Hammer, Emanuel, *The Clinical Application of Projective Drawings* (Chicago: Charles C. Thomas, 1958).

Hammer, Emanuel, *Use of Interpretations in Treatment* (New York: Grune and Stratton, 1968).

Hare, A., Borgatta, E., and Bales, R., *Small Groups: Studies in Interaction* (New York: Alfred A. Knopf, 1965).

Harriman, Philip L., *An Outline of Modern Psychology* (Littlefield, Adams and Company, Inc., 1963).

Hartmann, Heinz, *Ego Psychology and the Problems of Adaptation* (New York: International Universities Press, Inc., 1958).

Head, Henry, *Studies in Neurology*, *Vol. II* (London: Oxford University Press, 1920).

Hebb, D. O., *Organization of Behavior* (New York: John Wiley and Sons, Inc., 1949).

Hilgard, E. and Bower, G., *Theories of Learning* (New York: Appleton-Century-Crofts, 1966).

Hollingshead, A. and Redlich, F., *Social Class and Mental Illness* (New York: John Wiley and Sons, 1958).

Homans, George, *The Human Group* (New York: Harcourt, Brace and World, Inc., 1950).

Hyde, Robert et al, *Milieu Rehabilitation* (Providence: Butler Health Center, 1967).

Jahoda, M., Deutsch, M., and Cook, S., *Research Methods in Social Relations* (New York: Dryden Press, 1951).

Jung, Carl, *Modern Man in Search of a Soul* (New York, Harcourt, Brace and World, Inc., 1933).

Jung, Carl, *Man and His Symbols* (New York, Doubleday and Company, Inc., 1964).

Jung, Carl, *Alchemical Studies* (Princeton: Princeton University Press, 1967).

Kasin, Edwin, "Interpretations as Active Nurture: An Interpersonal Perspective," in E. Hammer, (ed.), *Use of Interpretations in Treatment*, (New York: Grune and Stratton, 1968).

Kerlinger, Fred, *Foundations of Behavioral Research* (New York: Holt, Rinehart and Winston, Inc., 1964).

Kimble, Gregory, *Hilgard and Margis' Conditioning and Learning* (New York: Appleton-Century-Crofts, Inc., 1961).

Knapp, Peter, *Expressions of the Emotions in Man* (New York: International Universities Press, Inc., 1963).

Knickerbocker, Barbara, "Guide to Understanding the Perceptual-Motor Training Program," unpublished paper.

Koch, Sigmund, *Psychology: A Study of Science*, *Vol. II* (New York: McGraw-Hill Book Company, Inc., 1959).

Kramer, Bernard, *Day Hospital* (New York: Grune and Stratton, 1962).

Kris, E., *Psychoanalytic Exploration in Art* (New York: International Universities Press, 1952).

Kübler-Ross, Elizabeth, *On Death and Dying* (New York: Macmillan, 1969).

Lewin, Kurt, *Principles of Topological Psychology* (New York: McGraw-Hill, 1936).

Lewin, Kurt, *Field Theory in Social Science* (New York: Harper & Bros., 1951).

Lifton, Walter, *Working with Groups* (New York: John Wiley and Sons, Inc., 1961).

Lindzey, Gardner, *Handbook of Social Psychology* (Cambridge: Addison-Wesley Publishing Co., 1954).

Llorens, L., and Beck, G., "Training Methods for Cognitive-Perceptual-Motor Dysfunction," *Normal Growth and Development with Deviation in the Perceptual-Motor and Emotional Areas*, Proceeding of the Occupational Therapy Seminar, St. Louis, Missouri, March, 1966.

Llorens, L. and Rubin, E., *Developing Ego Functions in Disturbed Children* (Detroit: Wayne State University Press, 1967).

Lorenz, Konrad, *On Aggression* (New York: Harcourt, Brace and World, Inc., 1963).

Mager, Robert, *Preparing Instructional Objectives* (Palo Alto: Fearon Publishers, 1962).

Marx, M., and Hillix, W., *Systems and Theories in Psychology* (New York: McGraw-Hill Book Co., 1963).

Maslow, Abraham, *Toward a Psychology of Being* (Princeton: D. Van Nostrand Company, Inc., 1962).

Matsutsuyn, Janice, "The Interest Check List," *AJOT,* Vol. XXIII, No. 4 (1969).

May, Rollo, "Historical and Philosophical Presuppositions for Understanding Therapy," in O. Mowrer (ed.), *Psychotherapy: Theory and Practice* (New York: Ronald Press Co., 1953).

May, Rollo, *Existential Psychology* (New York: Random House, 1961).

Mazer, J., Fidler, G., Kovalenko, L., and Overly, K., *Exploring How a Think Feels* (New York: American Occupational Therapy Association, 1969).

Mead, George, *Mind, Self and Society* (Chicago: The University of Chicago Press, 1934).

Meerloo, Joost, *Creativity and Externalization*, (New York: Humanities Press, 1968).

Messing, Eleanor, S., "Auditory Perception: What Is It?" Proceedings of the Association for Learning Disabilities, *Academic Quarterly*, 1967.

Mills, Theodore, *The Sociology of Small Groups* (Englewood Cliffs, N. J.: Prentice-Hall, Inc., 1963).

Moorhead, Linda, "The Occupational History," *AJOT*, Vol. XXIII, No. 4 (1969).

Mosey, Anne C., *Occupational Therapy: Theory and Practice* (Boston: Pothier Brothers, Printers, Inc., 1968).

Mosey, Anne, "Recapitulation of Ontogenesis: A Theory for Practice of Occupational Therapy," *AJOT*, Vol. XXII, No. 5 (1968).

Mosey, Anne, "Treatment of Pathological Distortion of Body Image," *AJOT, Vol. XXIII, No. 5 (1969).*

Mosey, Anne, "The Concept and Use of Developmental Groups," *AJOT*, Vol. XXIV, No. 4 (1970).

Nagel, Ernest, *The Structure of Science* (New York: Harcourt, Brace and World, Inc., 1961).

National Training Laboratories, *Group Development*, Selected Readings Series I (Washington: National Education Association, 1961).

Naumburg, Margaret, *Schizophrenic Art: Its Meaning in Psychotherapy* (New York: Grune and Stratton Inc., 1950).

Naumburg, Margaret, *Psychoneurotic Art: Its Function in Psychotherapy* (New York: Grune and Stratton, Inc., 1953).

Newsweek, "The Group: Joy on Thursday," May 12, 1969.

Noback, Charles, *The Human Nervous System* (New York: McGraw-Hill Book Company, 1967).

Nosow, S. and Form, W., *Man, Work and Society* (New York: Basic Books, Inc., 1962).

O'Kane, Catherine, *The Development of a Projective Technique for Use in Psychiatric Occupational Therapy* (Buffalo: State University of New York at Buffalo, 1968).

Overly, Kenneth, "Developmental Theory and Occupational Therapy - Considerations for Research," Paper presented at the AOTA Convention, Portland, 1968.

Parad, Howard (ed), *Crisis Intervention* (New York: Family Service Association of America, 1965).

Parsons, Talcott, *The Social System* (New York: The Free Press of Glencoe, 1951).

Parsons, Talcott, and Bales, R., *Family, Socialization and the Interaction Process* (New York: The Free Press of Glencoe, 1955).

Pearce, J. and Newton, S., *The Conditions of Human Growth* (New York: Citadel Press, 1963).

Perceptual Motor Workshop, Princeton New Jersey, 1969. Major contributors: A. Jean Ayres, Barbara Knickerbocker, Eleanor Messing, and Patricia Wilbarger.

Piaget, Jean, *The Origins of Intelligence in Children* (New York: International Universities Press, 1952).

Piaget, Jean, *The Construction of Reality in the Child* (New York: Basic Books, 1954).

Piaget, Jean, *Logic and Psychology* (New York: Basic Books, 1957).

Pines, Maya, "Why Some 3-Year Olds Get A's—and Some Get C's," *New York Times Magazine*, July 6, 1969.

Pratt, Carroll, *The Logic of Modern Psychology* (New York; The Macmillan Company, 1948).

Read, Herbert, *Icon and Idea* (New York: Schocker Books, 1965).

Reese, Ellen, *The Analysis of Human Operant Behaviors* (Dubuque: Wm. C. Brown Company, Publishers, 1966).

Reilly, M., "Occupational Therapy Can Be One of the Greatest Ideas of 20th Century Medicine," *AJOT*, Vol. XVI, No. 1 (1962).

Reilly, M., "The Educational Process", *AJOT*, Vol. XXIII, No. 4 (1969).

Riessman, F., Cohen, J., and Pearl, A., *Mental Health and the Poor* (New York: The Free Press of Glencoe, 1964).

Rogers, Carl, *On Becoming a Person: A Therapist's View of Psychotherapy* (Boston: Houghton Mifflin, 1961).

Rubins, Jack, "Self-Awareness and Body Image, Self-Concept and Identity," in J. Masserman (ed.), *The Ego* (New York: Grune and Stratton, 1967).

Ruch, Floyd, *Psychology and Life* (Chicago: Scott, Foresman and Company, 1963).

Ruesch, Jurgen, and Kees, W., *Nonverbal Communication* (Berkeley: University of California Press, 1956).

Ruesch, Jurgen, *Disturbed Communication* (New York: W. W. Norton Company, Inc., 1961).

Scheidlinger, Saul, *Psychoanalysis and Group Behavior* (New York: W. W. Norton and Company, 1952).

Schein, E., and Bennis, W., *Personal and Organizational Change Through Group Methods* (New York: John Wiley and Sons, Inc., 1965).

Schilder, Paul, *The Image and Appearance of the Human Body* (New York: John Wiley and Sons, Inc., 1950).

Schur, Max, *The Id and the Regulatory Principles of Mental Functions* (New York: International Universities Press, Inc., 1966).

Searles, Harold, *The Nonhuman Environment* (New York: International Universities Press, 1960).

Sechehaye, Marguerite, *Symbolic Realization* (New York: International Universities Press, 1951).

Sechehaye, Marguerite, *A New Psychotherapy in Schizophrenia* (New York: Grune and Stratton, 1956).

Skinner, B. E., *Science and Human Behavior* (New York: The Macmillan Co., 1953).

Smith, A. and Tempone, V., "Psychiatric Occupational Therapy Within A Learning Theory Context," *AJOT*, Vol. XXII No. 5, 1968.

Spence, Kenneth, *Behavior Theory and Conditioning* (New Haven: Yale University Press, 1956).

Spitz, Rene, *A Genetic Field Theory of Ego Functions* (New York: International Universities Press, Inc., 1959).

Spitz, Rene, *The First Year of Life* (New York: International Universities Press, Inc., 1965).

Stanton, A. and Schwartz, M. *The Mental Hospital* (New York: Basic Books, Inc., 1954).

Sullivan, H. S., *The Interpersonal Theory of Psychiatry* (New York: W. W. Norton and Company, 1953).

Sullivan, H. S., *The Psychiatric Interview* (New York: W. W. Norton, 1954).

Thibaut, J. and Kelley, H., *The Social Psychology of Groups* (New York: John Wiley and Sons, 1959).

Time, "Psychiatry's New Approach: Crisis Intervention," May 9, 1969.

Thompson, Clare, *Psychoanalysis: Evolution and Development* (New York: Grove Press, 1957).

Thomson, Robert, *The Psychology of Thinking* (Baltimore: Penguin Books, 1959).

Towle, Charlotte, *The Learner in Education for the Professions* (Chicago: University of Chicago Press, 1954).

Ullman, L., and Krasner L., *Case Studies in Behavior Modification* (New York: Holt, Rinehart and Winston, Inc., 1965).

Vygotsky, Len S., *Thought and Language* (Cambridge: The M.I.T. Press, 1962).

Watanabe, Sandra, "Four Concepts Basic to the Occupational Therapy Process", *AJOT*, Vol. XXII, No. 5 (1968).

Weller, Jack, *Yesterday's People* (Lexington: University of Kentucky Press, 1966).

White, Robert, "Competence and the Growth of Personality," in J. Masserman (ed.), *The Ego* (New York: Grune and Stratton, 1967).

White, Robert, "Motivation Reconsidered: The Concept of Competence," in L. Rabkin and J. Carr (eds.), *Sourcebook in Abnormal Psychology* (Boston: Houghton Mifflin Co., 1967).

Wolpe, Joseph, *Psychotherapy by Reciprocal Inhibition* (Stanford University Press, 1958).

Wooldridge, Dean E., *The Machinery of the Brain* (New York: McGraw-Hill Book Company, Inc., 1963).

Glossary

Activities of daily living: Those activities which involve caring for the self, communication, and travel.

Acquisition frames of reference: Frames of reference which view inappropriate learning or lack of learning of relatively independent, quantitative, non-stage specific skills as the dysfunction of concern to the therapist. It is assumed that corrective learning experiences will lead to acquisition of required skills and thus allow the individual to continue the process of self-actualization.

Adaptation: Creative interaction in the environment so as to satisfy the needs of self and otners. It implies conformity only in the sense that the individual knowledgeably selects those environmental demands he wishes to meet.

Adaptive skills: A somewhat arbitrary delineation of seven capacities or abilities which are believed to be necessary for satisfactory interaction in the environment.

Adaptive subskills: A delineation of the developmental stages of the various adaptive skills.

Affect: The feeling tone or emotions which an individual experiences relative to objects.

Analytic frames of reference: Frames of reference which view unconscious content as the dysfunction of concern to the therapist. It is assumed that an individual will be able to continue toward self-actualization when symptom-producing unconscious content is integrated with conscious content.

Anima: The feminine part of man.

Animus: The masculine part of woman.

Archetypic patterns: Symbolic representation of archaic memory traces.

Archetypic symbolic content: The universal questions, experiences, and suffering of mankind.

Archetypic symbolic forms: Specific forms which have existed, with the same meaning, in numerous cultural groups that have been distant in time and space.

Archaic memory traces: Memory traces which are common to all mankind and acquired through phylogenetic heredity. They are concerned with the questions, experiences, anxieties and suffering of mankind.

Aversive stimulus: A stimulus which signals reduction of positive reinforcement or precedes other aversive stimuli. It increases the frequency of behavior which removes the aversive stimulus.

Avocational pursuits: All those activities which do not result in monetary reward. They may be purely recreational in nature or involve engagement in the public sector.

Avoidance: The process of emitting behavior in order to postpone the appearance of an aversive stimulus.

Chains of performance: A sequence of individual performances, each maintained by the stimulus it produces.

Cognition: The process of perceiving, representing, and organizing stimuli.

Cognitive organization: The process of associating, combining, or manipulating representations. When this process is conscious it is commonly referred to as *thinking.*

Cognitive representation: Refers to the manner in which stimuli are stored or remembered. Stimuli may be represented as exocepts, images, endocepts, or concepts.

Cognitive skill: The ability to perceive, represent, and organize objects, events, and their relationships in a manner which is considered appropriate by one's cultural group.

Collective unconscious content: Archaic memory traces or archetypes.

Complex: A gestalt of repressed affect, energy, and mental content which is associated with a conflict.

Component: One aspect of an adaptive subskill.

Concept: A word or phrase which labels some similarity between seemingly varied phenomena; a system of classification.

Concept representation: Memory of stimuli in terms of words or some other notational system.

Concept symbols: Symbols which are expressed through words.

Concrete object symbols: People or things which take on or are invested with symbolic meaning.

Conditioned reinforcer: A reinforcer which has been paired with a primary reinforcer or aversive stimulus. It is the actual reinforcer which maintains the frequency of a given behavior.

Conflict: Incompatibility between an individual's wishes, desires, needs, or actions and his abstract libidinal objects.

Connotative concepts: Words which stand for a classification of phenomena which have some common characteristics. Words are seen as a way of talking about objects and events.

Conscious content: Internal and external stimuli and memory traces of immediate concern to the individual.

Continuous reinforcement schedule: A one-to-one fixed-ratio schedule.

Cultural group: An aggregate of persons who share common norms and values.

Cultural symbolic content: The values, norms, preoccupations, and concerns of a particular cultural group.

Cultural symbolic forms: Nonhuman objects, gestures, words, and specific people which have been invested with symbolic meaning by the individuals of a cultured group.

Denotative concepts: Words which stand for or name objects. The word is perceived as part of the object or equivalent to it.

Developmental frames of reference: Frames of reference which view inappropriate learning or lack of learning of interdependent, qualitative, stage specific skills as the dysfunction of concern to the therapist. It is assumed that participation in situations which simulate those interactions stated as being responsible for the sequential development of a skill in the normal developmental, will facilitate skill learning.

Differential reinforcement: The process of providing a reinforcing stimulus for one type of behavior and withholding a reinforcing stimulus for another type of behavior.

Discrimination: A process of determining that a different frequency or form of behavior is necessary for response to one stimulus (as opposed to another stimulus).

Drive-object skill: The ability to control drives and select objects in such a manner as to insure adequate need satisfaction.

Drives: A concept utilized to describe an individual's available energy for dealing with need satisfaction. This energy facilitates need gratification and in and of itself generates a need state.

Dyadic interaction skill: The ability to participate in a variety of dyadic relationships.

Dysfunction: Phenomena which is subjected to alteration in the treatment process. It is used as a synonym for disordered condition, pathology, or the patient's primary problem.

Endocept representation: Memory of stimuli in terms of a felt experience.

Endocept symbols: Symbols which are expressed through bodily or physical sensations.

Environmental elements: Specific human, nonhuman, and abstract objects which are believed to contribute to the learning of adaptive subskills in the normal developmental process.

Escape: The process of emitting behavior which terminates aversive stimuli.

Evaluation: One aspect of a frame of reference which describes how the therapist determines whether or not a patient is in a state of function or dysfunction in the various areas of concern. As a process, it involves data collection, interpretation, and validation.

Exocept representation: Memory of stimuli in terms of the action response to the stimuli or action directed toward the stimuli.

Exocept symbols: Symbols which are expressed through the actions of the symbol producer.

Expected environment: A term used to identify the anticipated living conditions of a patient after termination of treatment.

Extinction: The process whereby a performance decreases in frequency because a reinforcing stimulus no longer follows the performance.

Feeling function: Apprehension and adjustment through evaluation of pleasant-unpleasant, like-dislike, accept-reject, etc.

Fine-grain repertoire: Performances which change in response to small variations in environmental stimuli.

Fixed-interval schedule of reinforcement: There is a constant time interval between reinforcements.

Fixed-ratio schedule of reinforcement: The same number of performances are required for each reinforcement.

Frame of reference: A set of interrelated, internally consistent concepts, definitions, and postulates that provide a systematic description of and prescription for a practitioner's interaction within his domain of concern.

Frequency: The number of times a given performance is emitted by an individual.

Function-dysfunction continuums: One aspect of a frame of reference which describes the nature of the dysfunctions which are to be treated by application of the frame of reference.

Generalized conditioned reinforcers: A reinforcer which is not dependent upon a specific deprivational state. Common generalized reinforcers are money, attention, and approval.

Group interaction skill: The ability to be a productive member of a variety of primary groups.

Growth-facilitating environment: An environment which provides appropriate environmental elements and learning interactions for the acquisition of adaptive subskills.

Idiosyncratic symbolic content: An individual's unique life experiences, world view, concept of self, object relations, and mental content.

Idiosyncratic symbolic forms: Forms which are unique to the individual and markedly different from archetypic and cultural forms.

Image representation: Memory of stimuli in terms of an internal, pictorial, quasi-reproduction of the stimuli.

Image symbols: Symbols which are expressed through a visual, pictorial reproduction.

Independent manipulation of the nonhuman environment: Using, handling, altering, or caring for nonhuman objects without interacting with others.

Individuation: The process of freeing oneself from the domination of consciousness.

Initiating methods: Techniques used to increase the probability of an individual's emission of behavior so that it is available for reinforcement.

Integrative learning: Complete acquisition of an adaptive subskill to the point that the individual need not attend to the subskill in order to use it in meeting personal needs and the demands of the environment.

Intermittent reinforcement schedules: See *variable-ratio* and *variable-interval.*

Interpretations in treatment: Articulation of the relationship between an individual's response in the treatment situation and his past, current, and future life situation.

Intuitive function: Apprehension and adjustment through identification of the possibilities or inherent potential of objects and events.

Learning: A process by which an activity originates or is changed through reaction to an encounter situation providing that the characteristics of the change in activity cannot be explained on the basis of native response tendencies, maturation, or temporary states of the organism (e.g. fatigues, drugs, etc.) (Hilgard).

Learning interactions: Need-gratifying environmental responses which contribute to the learning of adaptive subskills.

Limited conditioned reinforcer: A reinforcer that is effective only when the individual is experiencing a specific deprivational state.

Needs: Inherent predispositions which provide motivation for survival, maturation, development, and contribution to the continued existence and growth of man and his supporting environment.

Negative reinforcing stimulus: See *aversive stimulus.*

Nonhuman environment: A concept which refers to all aspects of the environment which are not human.

Nurturing relationship: An extensive interaction between two persons in which one individual receives consistent and relatively immediate need satisfaction, is not required to give any reciprocal satisfaction and is free to engage in any behavior which is not destructive to self or other.

Object relationship: The end result of a process of investing psychic energy in objects which satisfy needs (libidinal object relationship) or interfere with need satisfaction (aggressive object relationship).

Objects: Any human being, nonhuman thing or abstract idea which has the potential for satisfying needs (libidinal objects) or interfering with need satisfaction (aggressive objects).

Ontogenesis: The course of development of a species. Used in this text to refer to the developmental process of man.

Operant conditioning: A theory of learning which states that behavior is acquired through action directed toward the environment.

Pathology: See *dysfunction.*

Perception: The process of taking in stimuli. (See page 49 for a somewhat different definition.)

Perceptual-motor skill: The ability to receive, integrate, and organize sensory stimuli in a manner which allows for the planning of purposeful movement.

Personal unconscious content: Internal and external stimuli and memory traces related to the individual's own experiences which are not readily available to the individual.

Postulate: A statement regarding the relationship between two or more concepts.

Postulates regarding change: That aspect of a frame of reference which delineates the interaction between man and environment that is believed to alter dysfunction. These relational statements are deduced from the theoretical base and serve as a guide for planning and implementing treatment.

Preconscious content: Internal and external stimuli and memory traces which can be called up or focused upon by the individual without undue effort.

Primary object relationship: An intense relationship in which the other is seen as the source of all need satisfaction.

Primary process: Cognitive organization which is characterized by disregard for formal logic, confusion of spatial and temporal relationships, fusion of representations (condensation), association of affect with one representation which is usually associated with another and/or representation of an object or event by another object or event (displacement), confusion regarding what is external or internal relative to the self, perception of all events as determined by the will of man or anthropomorphized forces (teleologic causality), and inability to reflect upon a thought process once it has occurred.

Primary reinforcer: That which satisfies inherent, universal human needs.

Psychological functions: Various ways in which man apprehends and adjusts to the world. The four different functions which have been identified are *thinking, feeling, sensation,* and *intuition.*

Punishment A process whereby a given performance is followed by an aversive stimulus. It usually suppresses the emission of behavior but does not extinguish it.

Recapitulation: To repeat a process.

Repression: The process of active forgetting or pushing out of consciousness that which was previously conscious.

Reinforcement: A term used to identify the process whereby the frequency of a performance has increased because of a reinforcing stimulus.

Reinforcer: See *reinforcing stimulus.*

Reinforcing stimulus: Any event which increases the frequency of the performance it immediately follows.

Reinforcing successive approximations: See *shaping.*

Repertoire of behavior: The supply of performances available to an individual.

Rote learning: Superficial acquisition of a behavior pattern. Considerable attention and effort is required to utilize a pattern learned by rote.

Schedules of reinforcement: Patterns or ways in which reinforcement may occur.

Secondary process: Cognitive organization which is characterized by adherence to the rules of formal logic, attention to temporal and spatial relationships, lack of condensation and displacement, knowledge regarding what is internal and external relative to the self, reflectivity, and a search for the antecedent physical cause of an effect (deterministic causality.)

Self-control: An individual's ability to alter the frequency of some performance in his repertoire.

Self-identity skill: The ability to perceive the self as autonomous, holistic, and an acceptable object which has permanence and continuity over time.

Sensation function: Apprehension and adjustment through conscious sensory processes.

Sexual identity skill: The ability to perceive one's sexual nature as good and to participate in a heterosexual relationship which is oriented to the mutual satisfaction of sexual needs.

Shadow side: All of those human responses and affects which the individual judges as base or unworthy of himself.

Shaping: A process of developing a performance through providing differential reinforcements of approximations of the desired performance.

Shared manipulation of the nonhuman environment: Interpersonal relations which surround and are a part of manipulation of the nonhuman environment.

Sign: An action, object, image, or word which stands for another action, object, image, or word. It can be easily explained and understood because it has no hidden or unknowable aspects.

Stimulus control: See *discrimination*.

Strain: A term used to identify a period of time in which no relevant behavior is emitted because the behavior required for reception of reinforcing stimuli is seen as excessive by the individual.

Symbol: An action, object, image, or word which has special complexities of meanings in addition to its conventional and obvious meaning. It implies something vague or hidden and has an unknown aspect which can never be fully defined or explained.

Symbolic content: The referent (or referents) of a symbol. Content may be archetypic, cultural or idiosyncratic.

Symbolic form: The manifest structure of symbolic representation. The form may be archetypic, cultural or idiosyncratic.

Symbolic representation: Refers to the way in which a symbol is experienced or produced. Symbols may be represented as exocepts, images, endocepts, concepts or concrete objects.

Symptoms: Behaviors which point to or indicate dysfunction. Whether a given behavior is considered to be dysfunction or a symptom depends only upon the frame of reference which is being utilized.

Tertiary process: Cognitive organization which involves subjecting mental content to primary process organization for the purpose of restructuring the content. The newly organized content is then subjected to validation by secondary process organization.

Theoretical base: One aspect of a frame of reference which delineates the assumptions, concepts, and postulates which are necessary for an adequate description of man-in-environment. It specifies the nature of man and environment and their relationship relative to normal and deviant development.

Theory: An abstract description of a circumscribed set of observable events.

Therapy: A planned, collaborative interaction between therapist-patient(s)-nonhuman environment directed toward eliminating or minimizing dysfunction.

Thinking function: Apprehension and adjustment through logical, conscious, cognitive processes directed toward reaching a specific conclusion.

Transference: A response to objects in a manner similar to the way in which the individual responded to a complex related object in the past.

Treatment: See *therapy.*

Variable-interval schedule of reinforcement: Different time intervals between reinforcements.

Variable-ratio schedule of reinforcement: The number of performances required for each reinforcement varies from one time to the next.

Will: A concept used to identify man's capacity to select a specific course of action.

Work: An individual's primary occupation, which may or may not result in monetary reward.

Index